ENCYCLOPEDIA OF
FAMILY HEALTH

Marshall Cavendish Corporation

99 White Plains Road

Tarrytown, New York 10591-9001

© Marshall Cavendish Corporation, 1998

© Marshall Cavendish Limited 1998, 1991, 1988, 1986, 1983, 1982, 1971

Update by Brown Partworks

The material in this set was first published in the English language by

Marshall Cavendish Limited of 119 Wardour Street, London W1V 3TD, England.

Printed and bound in Italy

Library of Congress Cataloging-in-Publication Data

Encyclopedia of family health
17v. cm.
Includes index
1. Medicine, Popular-Encyclopedias. 2. Health–Encyclopedias. I. Marshall Cavendish Corporation.
RC81.A2M336 1998   96–49537
610'. 3–dc21   CIP
ISBN 0-7614-0625-5 (set)
ISBN 0-7614-0629-8 (v.4)

This encyclopedia is not intended for use as a
substitute for advice, consultation, or treatment by a
licensed medical practitioner. The reader is advised
that no action of a medical nature should be taken
without consultation with a licensed medical
practitioner, including action that may seem to be
indicated by the contents of this work, as individual
circumstances vary and medical standards,
knowledge, and practices change with time. The
publishers, authors, and medical consultants disclaim
all liability and cannot be held responsible for any
problems that may arise from its use.

ENCYCLOPEDIA OF

FAMILY HEALTH

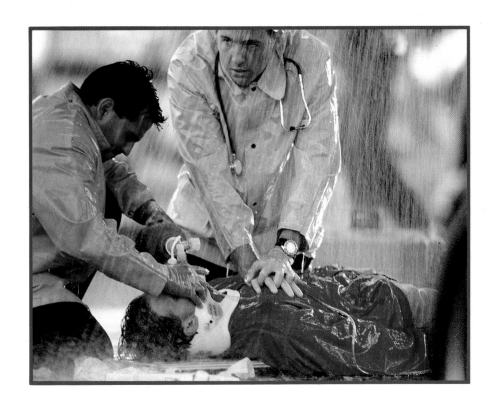

CONSULTANT
DAVID B. JACOBY, MD
JOHNS HOPKINS SCHOOL OF MEDICINE

VOLUME
4

DIAPER RASH—FLEAS

MARSHALL CAVENDISH
NEW YORK · LONDON · TORONTO · SYDNEY

INTRODUCTION

We Americans live under a constant bombardment of information (and misinformation) about the latest supposed threats to our health. We are taught to believe that disease is the result of not taking care of ourselves. Death becomes optional. Preventive medicine becomes a moral crusade, illness the punishment for the foolish excesses of the American lifestyle. It is not the intent of the authors of this encyclopedia to contribute to this atmosphere. While it is undoubtedly true that Americans could improve their health by smoking less, exercising more, and controlling their weight, this is already widely understood.

As Mencken put it, "It is not the aim of medicine to make men virtuous. The physician should not preach salvation, he should offer absolution." The aims of this encyclopedia are to present a summary of human biology, anatomy, and physiology, to outline the more common diseases, and to discuss, in a general way, the diagnosis and treatment of these diseases. This is not a do-it-yourself book. It will not be possible to treat most conditions based on the information presented here. But it will be possible to understand most diseases and their treatments. Informed in this way, you will be able to discuss your condition and its treatment with your physician. It is also hoped that this will alleviate some of the fears associated with diseases, doctors, and hospitals.

The authors of this encyclopedia have also attempted to present, in an open-minded way, alternative therapies. There is undoubtedly value to some of these. However, when dealing with serious diseases, they should not be viewed as a substitute for conventional treatment. The reason that conventional treatment is accepted is that it has been systematically tested, and because scientific evidence backs it up. It would be a tragedy to miss the opportunity for effective treatment while pursuing an ineffective alternative therapy.

Finally, it should be remembered that the word *doctor* is originally from the Latin word for "teacher." Applied to medicine, this should remind us that the doctor's duty is not only to diagnose and treat disease, but to help the patient to understand. If this encyclopedia can aid in this process, its authors will be gratified.

DAVID B. JACOBY, MD
JOHNS HOPKINS SCHOOL OF MEDICINE

Contents

Diaper rash

Diaper rash is a common and often persistent problem. Although it cannot always be prevented, prompt treatment will keep soreness to a minimum and prevent a lot of discomfort for the baby.

Q If my baby scratches the areas affected by diaper rash, will this make it worse?

A Scratching aggravates inflamed skin and is likely to make the condition even worse. There is also the danger that the skin may become broken and possibly infected. Try putting cotton mittens on your baby's hands and keeping the rash soothed with protective cream.

Q Will diaper rash occur less frequently as my baby brother grows older?

A All babies vary. However, the worst times for diaper rash are generally the first three months of life and from between six and eight months. During the second half of his first year, your brother's skin will become slightly tougher. On the other hand, he will probably be sleeping through the night, as well as producing a greater volume of urine, so his skin will be in contact with urine for longer periods of time. By the end of the second year, toilet training should solve diaper rash.

Q Does the elastic in disposable diapers cause diaper rash or could this be an allergic reaction?

A It is very unlikely that soreness would be due to an allergic reaction. Tight elastic that cuts into the legs will make the skin sore and more prone to inflammation. Also elastic around the legs will tend to keep moisture in and prevent it from evaporating. This will aggravate any soreness that is already present.

Q Does it matter what type of detergent is used to wash a baby's diapers? I have heard some can aggravate diaper rash.

A Detergents can be harsh, and unless diapers are rinsed thoroughly, traces of soap left behind may irritate a baby's skin, leading to diaper rash. You should never use biological detergents to wash a baby's diapers.

Most babies, however well cared for, will suffer from diaper rash from time to time. The irritation of their soft, sensitive skin is hard to avoid when diapers are constantly becoming wet and soiled. But by knowing how diaper rash occurs and what can aggravate this common condition, measures can be taken to insure that it never becomes a serious problem.

Causes

The most common form of diaper rash is called ammoniacal dermatitis, and is a direct result of the chemical breakdown of urine by bacteria in the feces. The (alkaline) ammonia produced by this process has a burning effect on a baby's soft skin.

Babies fed on formula milk may be more prone to ammoniacal dermatitis, as their stools are more alkaline than those of breast-fed babies, and the bacteria in the feces thrive in an alkaline medium. However, the main contributory factors of this particular type of diaper rash will apply to all babies. Ammoniacal dermatitis most commonly occurs if soiled diapers are not removed immediately, or if urine-soaked diapers are left on too long. It may also arise if cloth diapers are not washed and sterilized thoroughly, so that bacteria are still present.

Rough, hard diapers that rub against the skin, making it sore and less resilient to the harsh effects of ammonia, can often trigger a bout of diaper rash. The condition can also be aggravated by plastic pants, which prevent moisture from evaporating, keeping the wetness next to the baby's skin.

Another common cause of diaper rash is from the fungus infection *Candida albicans*. A baby contracts a yeast infection in the mouth, either at birth from a mother who has a vaginal yeast infection,

A baby will enjoy the freedom of crawling around without a diaper, and it will help keep diaper rash at bay, too.

Roger Payling

Q Can diaper rash actually be caused by a baby having strong urine?

A Mothers often complain to doctors that their baby's urine is strong; this is a common misconception. The pungent smell that is given off is not from the urine itself, but is the result of a chemical reaction that occurs when urine comes into contact with bacteria in the feces and causes ammonia to be produced. Ammonia has a stinging effect on the baby's skin, and this can set off a diaper rash; the longer a dirty diaper is left on a baby, the harsher this effect will be.

Contrary to popular belief, giving extra water to a baby to dilute the urine will not prevent diaper rash. However, changing diapers frequently, keeping the baby's bottom clean at all times, and applying a cream when needed will be a great help.

Q When I go back to work, I will have to leave my young baby with my mother. It would be more convenient if my baby wore disposable diapers, but I have heard that they can cause diaper rash. Is this true?

A As long as your mother insures that your baby is changed regularly, and that his or her bottom is kept clean, the chances of diaper rash occurring should be minimal. Used correctly, disposable diapers are convenient and very efficient.

Q My sister told me that putting plastic pants over diapers gives babies diaper rash. Is this really true?

A Although plastic pants do not actually cause diaper rash, they will aggravate any soreness present by preventing the evaporation of moisture, keeping wetness next to the baby's skin. If you do want to use plastic pants on your baby, and most mothers do find them convenient because they keep clothing and bedding dry, then try the tie-on variety, that allow more air to be circulated; tie them at the front and back for smaller babies, and at the sides for larger babies.

Useful tips

- Change diapers regularly
- Between changes, thoroughly clean the baby's bottom with soap and water, and dry well; if the skin seems sensitive, clean with baby lotion or baby oil
- Insure that diapers are properly washed, rinsed, and sterilized
- Apply zinc and castor oil cream or a barrier cream at any sign of soreness
- Whenever possible, leave off diapers and plastic pants

or when feeding from an unsterilized nipple. The bacteria of the yeast fungus travel down from the mouth and out of the anus in the baby's feces.

Occasionally cradle cap (seborrheic dermatitis) can cause diaper rash. Dandruff falling from the scalp spreads the condition to other parts of the body, including the diaper area.

Symptoms

Ammoniacal dermatitis starts in the form of moist red patches around the genitals. It can also be identified by the smell of ammonia that is given off. Unchecked it can spread over the whole diaper area, and beyond. Within a matter of hours, the rash can develop an extremely red and angry-looking appearance. During the stages that follow, the skin becomes thicker-looking and more wrinkled. It develops a paper texture and may peel. Eventually the skin becomes raw and ulcers may form.

When diaper rash is caused by a yeast infection, it starts around the anus, and as it progresses, may spread across the

baby's buttocks. The yeast fungus can also be seen inside the mouth as white patches, similar in appearance to milk curd, on the tongue, palate, and inside the cheeks.

The rash caused by seborrheic dermatitis is a brownish-red color. It is likely to be found on other parts of the body besides the diaper area.

Home treatment

Always clean a baby's bottom thoroughly using soap and water, or baby lotion or oil if it seems sore. Zinc and castor oil cream or a silicone-based barrier cream should also be applied before putting on a clean diaper.

Leave off diapers and plastic pants whenever possible, as this will help the evaporation of moisture and aid healing. If diapers have to be worn during the day, make sure they are changed as often as possible. Today's disposable diapers are more absorbent than washable ones, but should not be left on for too long. Some of them are made to absorb wetness where it is most needed—thicker at the front for boys and at the back for girls.

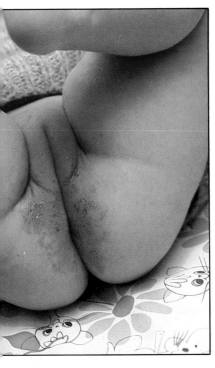

Washable diapers can be folded to give extra thickness where it is needed. Diaper liners are also useful, as the urine goes straight through keeping the baby's bottom drier.

Wash, rinse, and sterilize all diapers thoroughly. Avoid harsh detergents and make sure that all traces of the washing powder have been removed. A final rinse in an acidic solution will discourage the breakdown of urea. This solution can be bought or made at home, simply by adding about 1 fl oz (30 ml) of vinegar to 10 pt (4.7 l) of water.

Medical treatment

If a rash persists and does not seem to be getting any better, consult a doctor, as more specific treatment may be required. Left untreated, the rash could become

If left untreated, diaper rash (left) will soon become red and sore. To prevent this from happening, change diapers frequently and insure that the baby's bottom is properly cleaned and protected with cream.

Sally & Richard Greenhill

infected, and this in turn could lead to other infections in the genital area.

If a baby's rash is caused by the effect of ammonia on the skin, the doctor will prescribe an ointment to soothe the burning. Some creams may clear up the rash much more effectively than others. Therefore once a cream has been found that works for a baby, it should be noted, in case the rash returns.

If the rash is being caused by a yeast infection, the treatment usually involves applying a fungicide. Alternatively, antibiotics may be given in droplet form. A rash caused by seborrheic dermatitis can be cleared by a prescribed ointment. Special creams should help to get rid of the cradle cap.

Outlook

Diaper rash can be extremely persistent, but provided steps are taken to deal with the problem, it should not get any worse. Given the right treatment to fit the specific cause, it is likely that diaper rash will disappear completely.

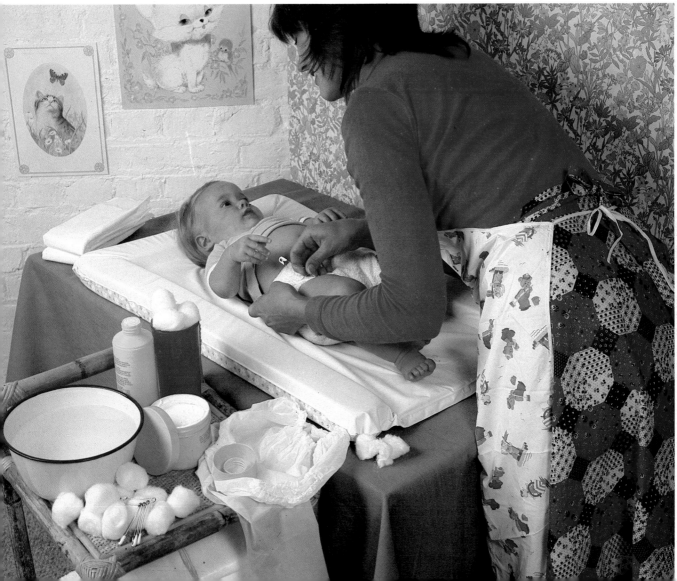

Diaphragm

Q Why do hiccups happen? My little sister asked me where they came from.

A Why hiccups should occur remains a total mystery, but we do known that they start when the diaphragm contracts, causing a sharp breath in. At the same time, the larynx (voice box) suddenly closes, causing the hiccup and stopping air from going into the chest. It is this breathing in with the diaphragm, while the upper part of the windpipe is closed that makes hiccups so uncomfortable.

Q Why are singers taught to breathe from the diaphragm?

A The diaphragm controls breathing rate and depth. Voice teachers help students to develop their abdominal muscles to control their diaphragm so that they can hold long notes and create vibrato.

Q The doctor has told my father that his indigestion is due to a hole in his diaphragm. Can you tell me what this means?

A Your father's doctor was referring to a condition called hiatus (diaphragmatic) hernia. This condition occurs when the top of the stomach slips up through the hole for the esophagus (gullet) and into the chest. Acid from the stomach then spreads up into the esophagus and causes pain. Hiatus hernia is treated with antacids (normally prescribed for indigestion). In severe cases the doctor may advise an operation.

Q I have just had an abdominal operation and now my diaphragm really aches. Why is this?

A This is because very often in the course of an operation other bodily organs may have to be handled for the surgeon to get to the cause of the trouble. This may cause some residual tenderness afterward, but you can rest assured that it will soon pass.

Although it is only a thin layer, the diaphragm is an important part of the anatomy, helping a person to breathe.

When a breath is taken, most of the work is done by the diaphragm, a sheet of muscle and fibrous tissue that forms a complete wall between the chest and the abdomen. The ribs provide the upper part of the cage that encloses the heart and lungs; the diaphragm forms the bottom. If it were possible to look at the diaphragm from above, a large central fibrous portion, connected by muscle fibers to the inside of the lower six ribs, could be seen. This resembles a sun, with rays spreading out toward the rib cage to anchor it. From the front, the diaphragm appears as a dome, attached by muscular strings to the inside of the ribs.

How breathing works

The muscular fibers of the diaphragm contract and flatten the dome of the diaphragm when a breath is taken in, drawing the highest central part down into the abdomen. This increases the volume of the lungs and draws air into the chest through the trachea (windpipe). Breathing out happens by simply relaxing the muscles, driving out the air in the same way as releasing a balloon into the air.

Like any other muscle, the diaphragm receives its instructions to contract or relax from the nervous system. The nerves which supply the diaphragm are called the left and right phrenic nerves. These nerves arise from high in the spinal cord, and they have to make a fairly long journey from the neck down to the bottom of the chest. The phrenic nerves can be damaged by injury or disease.

Although the diaphragm appears to be an essential piece of anatomical equipment, most people manage to breathe quite adequately if it stops working. Although most people are not aware of the diaphragm's movements, the whole activity of breathing can be consciously controlled during such activities as singing, playing a musical instrument, or swimming. A person cannot deliberately turn the activity of his or her diaphragm on and off, but he or she can learn to breathe either mainly from the abdomen or mainly from the chest.

The diaphragm separates the chest from the abdomen, and controls the volume of the lungs as air is inhaled and exhaled.

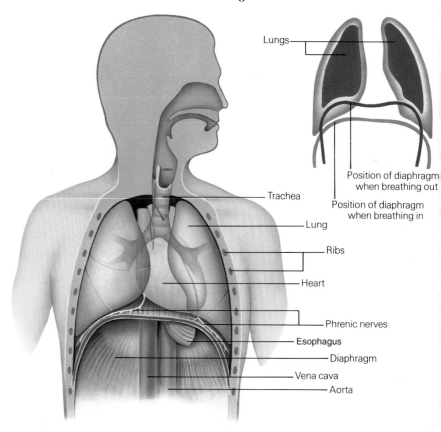

Lungs

Position of diaphragm when breathing out

Position of diaphragm when breathing in

Trachea

Lung

Ribs

Heart

Phrenic nerves

Esophagus

Diaphragm

Vena cava

Aorta

Diarrhea

Q **I am breast-feeding and I have been told not to eat grapes because they will give my baby diarrhea. Is this true?**

A Some foods can certainly affect a baby's intestines. These include fruit, onions, and spicy foods. The wise thing to do is to eat a rather bland diet when your baby is very tiny. Introduce foods you are fond of one by one, so if anything does upset your baby you can tell what it is.

Q **I am on the Pill. The clinic told me that I must take extra precautions if I get diarrhea. Why is this?**

A The Pill is taken every day and suppresses ovulation (egg production), so that you cannot get pregnant. If the hormones in the Pill are not absorbed, ovulation may occur. When you have diarrhea, food and pills move very quickly through the intestines where absorption normally takes place, so that the Pill may become ineffective.

Q **My grandmother started to get diarrhea, but when the doctor came, he said the problem was really constipation. How could this be?**

A This is a rather common symptom in the elderly, called spurious diarrhea. What happens is that the lower intestine gets clogged up with feces. However, some liquid matter manages to get past the blockage and leads to diarrhea, which may cause the older person to lose control of the bowels and become incontinent. It is very important to recognize this, as it can be easily treated.

Q **I find that whenever I eat cheese, I get diarrhea. Am I allergic to it?**

A You may be. Food allergies are more common than was previously realized. When you are allergic to certain foods you tend to get problems, such as rashes or wheezing, in other areas besides the intestines. If you suspect a specific food, try not to eat it and see if your symptoms disappear.

Every person is likely to have attacks of diarrhea at some time during his or her life. The cause may be trivial or more serious, but in most cases the correct treatment will alleviate the symptoms in a day or two.

Diarrhea is a symptom, not a disease. Usually it results from an infection in the intestines, though in some cases it may arise from a more serious problem. Diarrhea can be dangerous in children, particularly in babies, and therefore medical attention should be sought if there is an abnormal change in a baby's feces.

Causes

Diarrhea occurs when the lining of the intestine becomes irritated, due to an infection, the presence of a toxic (poisonous) substance, or some other cause. As a result, food and water pass through the length of the intestine much quicker than usual and fluid is not absorbed by the large intestine; this means that the feces remain very watery.

Not only may the walls of the intestine fail to absorb water, but they may also actually lose fluid as a result of inflammation, adding further to the body's water loss. In severe cases, serious dehydration may occur, which may be fatal.

Diarrhea may be due to a variety of causes. Spoiled food is one of the culprits.

In food poisoning, bacteria grow on fly-blown food, producing toxins, or poisons, that may lead to diarrhea and stomach upsets. This type of food poisoning is caused by the staphylococci toxins. Botulism is a fortunately rare example of such a disease. In other types of food poisoning, it might be the bacterium itself that causes the infection. One bacterium, known as salmonella, is responsible for causing diarrhea, in addition to intestinal pain and sometimes vomiting.

Diseases like typhoid and dysentery are spread by bacteria being eaten with food. Cholera is spread by drinking water that has been infected by feces. The difference between food poisoning and dysentery is that in food poisoning, diarrhea starts within a few hours of eating bad food. Dysentery may take up to 24 hours to produce diarrhea, and will also last longer.

The best remedy for diarrhea is a liquid diet. Fasting is recommended and once the diarrhea stops, solid food should be introduced gradually. A mixture of bacteria (inset) causes diarrhea.

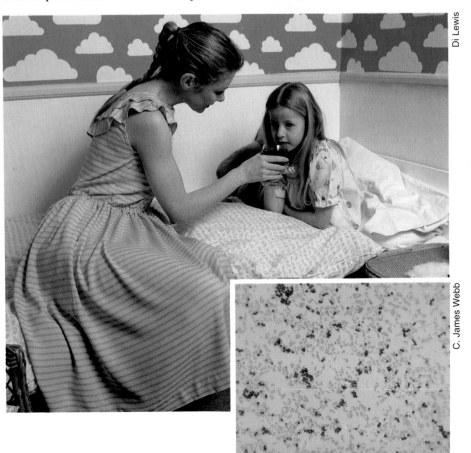

Di Lewis

C. James Webb

Much larger parasites can get into food and water and once ingested cause diarrhea. These include the ameba, a single-cell parasite, which can cause amebic dysentery. This disease is common in the tropics, and with its vague symptoms of malaise and diarrhea alternating with constipation, can go on for years.

Often diarrhea is not due to bacteria or larger organisms, but to the smallest of germs, the viruses. In gastroenteritis, a virus infection causes diarrhea, vomiting, and abdominal pains. It can go under a variety of names: gastric flu, summer diarrhea, and so on.

Travelers' diarrhea occurs when new strains of bacteria replace the usually beneficial bacteria that normally live in the large intestines. It is a rather common experience for people to have this form of diarrhea when they go abroad, and it is not caused by a change in the water as is commonly supposed.

Chronic problems

Chronic diarrhea is due not to infections, but to other medical problems. One of the most common is ulcerative colitis. The colon becomes inflamed and the bacteria invade the damaged mucous membranes. No one cause has been found to contribute to ulcerative colitis, and theories range from an allergic reaction to an emotional upset.

Diarrhea also occurs when other diseases of the intestinal wall prevent the proper absorption of foods. These malabsorption problems, which include celiac disease (in which the intestines cannot absorb gluten), not only cause diarrhea, but also leave patients undernourished.

Other causes

If there is sustained nervousness, fear, and anxiety, the intestine becomes overactive and diarrhea occurs. Highly spiced foods can upset the intestines if a person is unused to eating them. Large quantities of fruit and shellfish can also cause minor stomach upsets and loose feces.

In children, diarrhea can be caused by an infection that is completely unconnected with the intestines. Typically, this may happen in toddlers with ear and throat infections.

Gastroenteritis is a common affliction in babies, but loose feces should be distinguished from diarrhea. Newborn babies do not pass normal stools, but instead pass greenish-brown, sticky feces called meconium. Breast-fed babies often have very loose feces and they may pass several stools a day. Bottle-fed babies' stools are more like the consistency of adults', but the color may vary greatly. Despite the appearance of the stool, the baby who is breast-fed is less likely to

---

Controlling diarrhea

- Drink as much fluid as possible, but no alcohol. Fluid consumption should be particularly high for infants, because they become dehydrated very easily
- If possible, fast for a day. This will do you no harm. If you don't feel hungry, don't force yourself to eat. When the diarrhea begins to lessen, eat a very bland diet, with no spicy foods. Even if you feel ravenous, try not to overeat. Small meals at intervals are preferable
- To stop diarrhea, kaolin or a bismuth preparation may be taken
- Wash hands carefully after going to the lavatory and before eating or preparing food
- If a baby has diarrhea, give him or her half as much formula powder or liquid for the normal amount of water. If the baby is vomiting, see the doctor. He or she may suggest that you stop all milk feeding and only give clear fluids. A weak salt solution may be prescribed to correct salt lost
- To prevent travelers' diarrhea, drink only boiled or purified water, wine, or beer, and eat only well-cooked meats, peelable fruits, and breads

---

have gastroenteritis because the breast milk protects the baby's intestines from infections, and because unlike bottle-feeding, safe breast-feeding does not depend on sterilizing bottles or nipples.

Symptoms

Diarrhea is an uncomfortable symptom, particularly if it is accompanied by colicky pains in the abdomen. The stools are much more fluid and less well formed than usual. In severe diarrhea, the stool may be very watery and may be passed much more often than usual. In some cases, there may be a little vomiting.

Dangers

Diarrhea is not serious in adults or older children if it lasts only a day or two. However, in babies and young children, diarrhea can be dangerous, particularly if there is also vomiting, because very young children may not be able to take any fluid to replace the considerable amounts they are losing.

Persistent diarrhea can cause considerable loss of water and salt, which leads to dehydration. If untreated, this condition can be fatal. It takes much more to dehydrate an adult than a baby, but really serious infections, such as cholera, can

---

cause death by dehydration in a short period of time.

Treatment

In many instances, the treatment for diarrhea depends on finding out what is causing it, but basically the treatment is very simple.

The first, essential priority is to keep up the level of fluid intake by drinking plenty of liquids. Eating is not necessary, and if the patient does not feel like it food should not be forced, particularly if vomiting occurred initially.

Drugs may help by reducing the level of activity of the intestine and by slowing the passage of its contents. Kaolin and pectin are commonly used to add bulk to the feces and slow down the working of the intestines.

In some forms of food poisoning, especially those caused by bacteria, or in dysentery, sulfonamides (drugs containing bacteria-fighting sulfa) or an antibiotic may be needed to combat the infection. For cholera, sufficient fluids should be drunk to maintain those lost through diarrhea. Antibiotics are of secondary importance. The patient should not eat or drink infected foods or liquids, and should maintain scrupulous hygiene.

Colitis can only be treated by a change of diet to bland foods, or a course of antibiotics or sulfonamides to combat infection. If emotional disturbance is the cause, psychotherapy may be advised.

Diarrhea in babies is serious, particularly if the stools are abnormally loose and watery. Stop feeding the baby any solids immediately and give additional clear fluids and half-strength formula milk (half as much powder or liquid for the normal amount of water) when bottle-feeding. If the baby appears well otherwise and takes fluid, then keep a careful watch for the next 24 hours.

If the baby is ill, or is vomiting, or the feces are tinged with blood, the doctor should be called. When the doctor examines the baby, let him or her examine a soiled diaper.

The doctor may advise the parents to stop all milk feeding and to give the baby clear fluids; he or she may also prescribe a very weak salt solution to replace the salt lost in the diarrhea. It is very unusual to give medicine to dry up diarrhea in small babies; minor attacks usually get better quickly and seriously ill babies should be taken to the hospital.

Outlook

In the majority of cases diarrhea should clear up within a few days, with no serious aftereffects. If the diarrhea has been caused by an infection, swift treatment should alleviate the symptoms.

Diet

Q I have always given my daughter a proper diet, but suddenly she has become very thin—almost skeletal. I am afraid she is anorexic and is hiding her food. How could this have happened?

A Anorexia nervosa is commonly known as the dieter's disease, but it is much more complex than this implies. It almost always strikes young people between the ages of 11 and 30 (more girls than boys), and a dramatic loss of weight is the most obvious sign that something is wrong. There may be other indications, such as bouts of constipation that alternate with diarrhea, hypersensitivity about appearance, or sudden personality changes, such as withdrawal from friends. The anorexic may be secretly tortured by a basic lack of confidence, self-esteem, and a true idea of self. Under this lurks a fear of maturity, which makes thinness seem desirable: it is also possibly the result of an overly perfectionist approach to body image. If you suspect your daughter is anorexic, you must get her to see the doctor. The treatment depends on identifying and dealing with the underlying psychological causes.

Q My son often refuses to eat when he is sick. Should I insist that he eats?

A No. It is not necessary for him to eat solid foods when he is ill and may even be detrimental. Make sure he has plenty of fluids instead. Weak tea or milk with a little sugar will give him energy, and soups or broth will provide nourishment. When he feels better, he will ask for solid foods again.

Q I have suffered from eczema for five years. Is it true that allergies to certain foods can cause this?

A Yes. Research has shown that skin disorders may be caused by allergic reactions to some foods. Discovering the causes involves tests to isolate possible reactions. Some clinics offer this service, or your doctor may be able to provide a plan for you to test yourself.

The body is like an engine, and food is the fuel it needs to keep running. Just as gasoline comes in different octanes, so foods have different energy-producing levels. How efficiently the body works depends on what is consumed.

The food an individual eats is converted into energy and used by the body for its different functions. These include not just the obvious physical activities, such as walking or running, but also the equally important and constant process of growth and repair of the tissues in the body. Throughout life, body tissues are continuously broken down and replaced by new cells to keep the person whole and in good working order.

Everyone must eat just the right amount of food to supply energy for all of these needs. If more food is consumed than is required, the excess will be stored in the body and lead to that person becoming overweight.

Most foods have a chemical structure different from the body's, so they need to be changed into a form that the body can easily absorb. This absorption process is known as digestion.

Many of a child's favorite meals provide a large part of the dietary requirements for a full day, and will give him or her all the energy a rapidly growing body requires.

Types of food

Food can be divided into three main types: carbohydrates, proteins, and fats. Carbohydrates and fats are used to fuel all the body's processes and functions, while protein is used as building material for the body's tissues. This means that insufficient carbohydrate or fat in the diet will result in lack of energy and a general feeling of lethargy and fatigue, while a lack of protein will cause gradual wasting away of the tissues.

Carbohydrates

Carbohydrates are commonly found in starch and sugar. Starch is present in all cereals and root vegetables, and sugar is found in its natural form in fruits or honey, or in a refined state in table sugar. Carbohydrates are found in greatest quantities in potatoes, breads, bananas, peas, corn, beans and lentils, parsnips, rice, and yams. Sugar-rich foods include jams, cookies, chocolate, candy, and ice cream. These prepared products have

Di Lewis

417

Q My baby is fatter than my friend's baby, who is the same age. Is it just puppy fat or should I put her on a diet?

A Babies who are overfed will become obese and this is not normal. Ask your doctor if your baby is overweight. If the baby is, the doctor will probably suggest reducing the carbohydrate content of the diet and concentrating on protein foods. This means cutting out cereals, cakes, and sugar, reducing the amounts of potatoes and bread, and limiting milk intake to 1 pt (0.5 l) a day.

Q I want to become a vegetarian but my friends say I won't get enough protein if I don't eat meat. Is this true?

A It is perfectly possible to supply all the body's needs without eating meat, but to do so does mean making adjustments to the whole diet. For example, it is not recommended to replace meat with more eggs and cheese. Some of your protein will have to be provided by nuts, beans, and cereals. You may need to take extra vitamin B_{12}, as meat is by far the richest source of this.

Q My children will not eat any type of green vegetable. Is there any way I can insure they get enough of the right vitamins in their diet?

A Fortunately, children who develop these dislikes usually grow out of them if they are not made into a big issue. Also, your children will get much of what they need from other foods. But if you are worried, ask your doctor about giving them a multivitamin and mineral supplement.

Q I want to lose weight but I'm confused by all the different diets and their claims. What should I do?

A A reducing diet allows for about 1,000 calories a day. It should include a variety of foods low in fat, and plenty of cooked or raw vegetables, fresh fruits, meats, and grain products. Try to avoid using salt, sodium, and sugars. Drink alcohol in moderation.

high concentrations of refined sugar and so should be eaten in moderation.

Over half of an individual's dietary needs are met by carbohydrates, which are especially important for people doing heavy or strenuous physical work. Carbohydrates are converted to glucose (a form of sugar) in the body and this fuels the muscles and the brain. It is the sole form of energy for the brain, which uses more than half of the daily supply.

Sugar levels

The amount of glucose in the blood is kept at constant levels under normal conditions. If too much carbohydrate is eaten, the excess is stored as glycogen in the liver and the muscles. When these have taken as much as they can hold, the excess is stored in the fat of the body.

For a healthy diet, it is important to eat as wide a variety of food as possible, so that all the required nutrients, vitamins, and minerals are included. This will also help to maintain a healthy weight.

If the level of sugar in the body becomes too high, insulin (a chemical manufactured by the pancreas) is released to make the liver absorb the excess from the blood. And if the blood sugar level falls too low, the liver releases the stored glycogen and converts it back into glucose.

A diet that does not contain enough carbohydrate will lead to weakness and fatigue. To compensate for this, the body will instead convert fats into energy. However, the rapid burning of fats creates toxic by-products that make the blood too acidic. Carbohydrates are also important because they act to spare protein—that is, they are burned instead of protein, leaving the proteins to be used for body-building.

Protein

Proteins are chemicals that form an essential part of every living cell. Muscles, for instance, consist largely of protein and water. Proteins also go into the making of chromosomes (the gene

carriers), enzymes (substances that break down tissue), blood plasma (the liquid part of blood), and hemoglobin (the red-colored matter in blood).

In turn, proteins are made up of smaller units called amino acids. There are various types of protein, made of different arrangements of 20 or so amino acids. When protein is eaten, the digestive juices break it down into the amino acids. They are then carried in the bloodstream to various parts of the body and built up into new proteins as required.

Any surplus protein is burned as fuel for energy. The body uses 0.9-1.4 oz (25-40 g) a day and this is the minimum amount that must be replaced to maintain the health of the tissues. A good rule of thumb is to eat 0.3 oz (9.4 g) of protein for each 25 lb (11.3 kg) of body weight daily.

Children, however, need more protein than adults—a baby requires five times as much per unit of weight, young children two and a half times as much, and adolescents one and a half times as much.

Insufficient protein leads to stunted growth and weak body structure.

Sources of protein

Animal foods such as meat are very rich sources of protein, especially organs such as the liver, kidneys, and heart. Choose lean meat over fatty meat, remove the skin from poultry and broil, roast or boil these foods instead of frying them. Fish, eggs, cheese, and milk are also good sources, as are soybeans, nuts, and some pulses. Lentils and the seeds of pumpkin, squash, sunflower, and sesame are also rich in protein.

Complete and partial proteins

Complete proteins are those that have the same mixtures of amino acids as the body's proteins and can therefore be used whole. They are found mostly in meats, fish, eggs, and dairy products.

Partial proteins, typically found in vegetables and cereals, lack one or other amino acid and cannot be absorbed by the body without first being broken

down. This means that a vegetarian, for example, would have to eat more protein foods to make up the required daily amount of protein. Fortunately, different vegetable proteins have different missing amino acids and these can be combined to provide complete proteins.

In countries where animal foods are scarce or forbidden on religious grounds, many such food combinations have been developed. For instance, rice and beans are commonly eaten in Mexico. Also, a peanut butter sandwich or bread and grilled cheese are good combinations to make up complete proteins.

Fats

Fats provide more than twice as much energy as other foods, which means that considerably less of them is needed in the diet. In Western countries, people get about 40 percent of their overall energy from fats—a clear sign of prosperity. Fats may also add much taste and flavor to some foods, and make certain types of food easier to cook and process.

Brian Nash

Calories used in everyday activities

MC Library

Henry Grant

Colin Molyneux/Bruce Coleman

Sedentary occupations
office workers,
truck drivers,
doctors,
journalists

Calories needed over 24 hours
male 2,500–2,700
female 1,700–2,200

Moderately active occupations
cleaners,
mailmen,
plumbers,
light industry workers,
restaurant wait staff

Calories needed over 24 hours
male 2,700–3,200
female 2,000–2,400

Active occupations
coalminers,
construction workers,
laborers,
army recruits,
athletes

Calories needed over 24 hours
male 3,300–4,400
female 2,400–2,800

● These figures are an average guide; they will vary according to age and weight

In the body, fat provides a layer of insulation beneath the skin and helps to maintain an even temperature, especially in cold weather. It also serves as a cushion against minor injuries by absorbing the impact of blows or falls.

Types of fat
Fats are classified as saturated or unsaturated fatty acids, according to their chemical structure. Saturated fatty acids are found in the fat of animals, milk, butter, and some vegetable oils. Monounsaturated fatty acids are found in olive oil, peanut oil, and fish oils, while the polyunsaturated fatty acids used in margarine and cooking oils come from soybean, corn, sunflower, cotton seed, and safflower plants.

Certain of the polyunsaturated group are known as essential fatty acids, because the body cannot manufacture them and they must be provided in the diet. A lack of them can impair normal growth, making the skin dry and scaly. A diet high in polyunsaturated fatty acids may help to keep cholesterol levels low.

However, too high a proportion of saturated fats in the diet may damage the arteries and may lead to heart disease. Consequently, most nutritionists recommend using mainly unsaturated fatty

acids. This is achieved by eating only lean meat, cooking with vegetable oils instead of butter or animal lard, and by eating low-fat dairy products in moderation.

Vitamins
Apart from carbohydrates, proteins, and fats, the body must have vitamins and minerals. Vitamins are essential for normal growth and development, and because they cannot be manufactured in the body, they must be included in the diet, or in certain cases, they can be taken as supplements to the diet.

Vitamins are divided into fat-soluble and water-soluble types. The fat-soluble ones are vitamins A, D, E, F, and K, and the water-soluble ones are vitamins B and C. The body cannot store large amounts of water-soluble varieties. They circulate in the blood and any excess is eventually excreted in the urine.

In contrast, the fat-soluble vitamins are not excreted and any excess is stored in the liver. An excess of vitamin A and D, however, can be harmful, causing toxic symptoms in the system.

If there is a shortage of the water-soluble vitamins, the deficiency will become apparent within a matter of weeks. Reserves in the body are usually sufficient to prevent deficiency for weeks, or even

months, unless there is some other irregularity in the body. There is little cause for worry about vitamin deficiency in most developed countries—a good, mixed diet normally contains enough of them.

Minerals
Minerals are also essential for keeping the body healthy. They assist in many of the processes needed for normal nerve and muscle function and must be supplied frequently in the diet.

The minerals that the body requires are: calcium, phosphorus, iron, iodine, potassium, magnesium, fluorine, zinc, and copper. A balanced diet nearly always provides sufficient quantities of these, and as excess minerals may be harmful, it is not a good idea to take supplements except on a doctor's orders.

Roughage
Roughage, or dietary fiber, consists of the walls of plant cells that cannot be broken down by digestion, and therefore pass through the stomach and intestines in solid form. Their use is to stimulate the action of the intestine, so that food passes through the digestive system. They also provide the bulk to make feces solid. The best-known example of roughage is bran, which many people eat regularly as a natural method of

relieving constipation. Vegetables, nuts, and cereals also contain fiber. Some fibers carry increased quantities of bile acids down the colon and help reduce the level of potentially harmful fats in the body.

African tribespeople who eat a low-fat, high-fiber diet rarely have diseases of the intestines and colon, appendicitis, or hemorrhoids, reinforcing the belief that these are diseases of Western civilization. The advent of modern food processing techniques, some of which strip foods of many essential nutrients, while adding unnecessary fats, sugar, and salt, have been key factors in the rise of these problems. High-fat, low-fiber fast food is another culprit.

Energy

The food a person eats provides energy for the various activities of the body, from running fast to sitting and working in an office, or repairing body tissue. The amount of energy needed (and therefore, the amount of food) depends on how much is used.

The energy from food is traditionally measured in calories, which are also referred to as kilocalories. Carbohydrates and proteins yield about four calories per gram, while fats yield more than twice this amount—nine calories per gram.

The average person living in Western society gets about 15 percent of required energy from protein, 40 percent from fat, and 45 percent from carbohydrates. In Asia, where there is less animal food available, people get about 85 percent of their energy from carbohydrates, and less from proteins and fats.

Energy requirements

The amount of energy that a person needs varies not only according to the type of activities performed, but also with body size, sex, age, general health, and climate.

Figures are usually given for the needs of a person resting and this is known as the basal metabolic rate (BMR). It is lower for women than men, mostly because women have a better layer of insulation in the form of body fat (see Metabolism).

Special diets

There are times when the diet has to be changed. For example, a pregnant woman should increase her caloric intake by 300 per day, and ensure she eats more protein, but she should not increase her intake of fatty foods.

Patients suffering from kidney disease may be put on a temporary, protein-free diet, since the kidneys cannot remove waste products effectively and protein is harder to eliminate from the body. People suffering from liver or gallbladder disease will be put on a low-fat diet, since their ability to digest fats is impaired.

High blood pressure, heart disease, and liver disease all call for low-salt diets which will reduce the volume of fluids in the body and therefore take the strain off the affected organs .

Any drastic change in diet should only be undertaken on the advice of the family doctor, nutritionist, or a qualified health care practitioner. Too severe a change in both the type of food and the amount a person eats can be dangerous under certain circumstances. Dieting to lose a large amount of weight must be done gradually and under professional supervision.

A balanced diet

A balanced diet supplies all necessary

Calories used in everyday activities	
Activity	Calories used per hour
Sleeping	65
Standing still	110
Fast typewriting	140
Walking slowly	200
Carpentry and painting	250
Swimming	500
Walking upstairs	1,100

nutrients in quantities that suit the particular individual. The food guide pyramid (below) shows a range of servings for each food group. The number of servings a person requires depends on age, size, sex, and activity level.

What Is One Serving?

Dairy products (milk, cheese, yogurt, butter, or margarine): 1 cup of milk or yogurt; 1½ oz (40 g) of natural cheese; 2 oz (50 g) of processed cheese; 1 oz (25 g) butter, or margarine.

Meat, poultry, fish, dry beans, eggs, and nuts: 1 serving = 2-3 oz (50-75 g) of cooked lean meat, poultry or fish. One half cup of cooked dry beans, 1 egg, or 2 T of peanut butter count as 1 oz (25 g) of lean meat.

Vegetables: 1 serving = ½ cup. A dark green (spinach), or yellow vegetable (pumpkin or carrot) should be included at least every second day.

Fruit: 1 serving = 1 medium orange, apple, banana or other fresh fruit, or, ½ cup of chopped, cooked, or canned fruit, or, ¾ cup of fruit juice.

Bread, cereal, rice and pasta: 1 serving = 1 slice of bread, 1 oz (25 g) of ready-to-eat cereal, or ½ cup of cooked cereal, rice, or pasta.

How many servings do you need each day?

	Women, older adults	Children teen girls, active women, most men	teen boys, active men
Calorie level	about 1,600	about 2,200	about 4,000
Bread Group Servings	6	9	11
Fruit Group Servings	3	4	5
Milk Group Servings	2	3	4
Meat Group Servings	2–3**	2–3**	2–3**
	2, for a total of 5 oz	2, for a total of 6 oz	3, for a total of 7 oz

** Women who are pregnant or breastfeeding, teenagers, and young adults to age 24 need 3 servings

The food guide pyramid

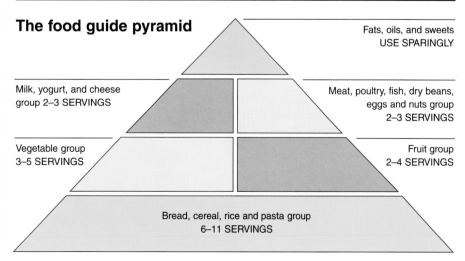

Fats, oils, and sweets USE SPARINGLY

Milk, yogurt, and cheese group 2–3 SERVINGS

Meat, poultry, fish, dry beans, eggs and nuts group 2–3 SERVINGS

Vegetable group 3–5 SERVINGS

Fruit group 2–4 SERVINGS

Bread, cereal, rice and pasta group 6–11 SERVINGS

Digestive system

Q I am trying to decide whether to breast-feed or bottle-feed the baby I am expecting. Is it true that babies cannot digest cow's milk?

A Compared with human breast milk, cow's milk contains large amounts of a protein called casein, and unlike the calves for which cow's milk is intended, babies do not have the equipment to digest this protein properly. The curds that can be seen in the motions of a baby fed on cow's milk are the result of the incomplete digestion of casein. The many powdered formula milks for babies are made from cow's milk, and therefore contain more casein than breast milk, but they are specially treated to make the casein more digestible. Thus, breast-feeding is better for your baby's digestive system, and better in other ways, too.

Q Why do some foods, like baked beans, give me very bad gas?

A Gases in the alimentary canal, known medically as flatus, are formed as a result of swallowing air during eating and by the action of intestinal bacteria on the undigested remains of food. Many of these gases are absorbed by the lining of the large intestine, but foods like baked beans are an ideal medium for the growth of bacteria. They tend to irritate the intestinal lining, causing food to be moved along quickly, so that there is less time for the gases to be absorbed. If gas is painful or a cause of embarrassment, it is best to avoid foods that cause it.

Q My three-year-old daughter loves very spicy foods. Won't they upset her stomach and her digestion?

A There is no reason why they should. By the age of three, a child's digestive system is able to cope with a very mixed diet and the degree of tolerance to spicy foods will vary, just as it does in adults. As long as these foods do not give her diarrhea or make her vomit, it is much better to give her foods that she likes, rather than having constant battles at mealtimes.

By understanding the process of digestion, a person can learn to recognize the signs of any potential problems.

Digestion is the process which breaks down food into substances that can be absorbed and used by the body for energy, growth, and repair.

How digestion works

The digestive system depends on the action of substances, called enzymes, on the foods eaten. These enzymes are produced by the organs attached to the alimentary canal and they are responsible for many of the chemical reactions involved in digestion.

The changes begin in the mouth. When food is chewed by the teeth, the salivary glands beneath the tongue increase their various secretions, one of which, the enzyme ptyalin, starts breaking down some of the carbohydrates into smaller molecules, known as maltose and glucose.

The food then travels down the esophagus and into the stomach, where a mixture of chemicals—including mucus, hydrochloric acid, and the enzyme pepsin—is poured onto it. Ptyalin stops working, but a new series of chemical reactions begins, triggered by a set of nerve impulses.

In the stomach

The quantity of juices in the stomach and intestine is governed by nerve impulses, the presence of food itself, and by the secretion of hormones. The hormone gastrin stimulates the stomach cells to release hydrochloric acid and pepsin once food is in the stomach, so that it can be broken down into substances called peptones. Mucus secretion prevents the stomach lining from becoming damaged by acid. When the acidity reaches a certain point, gastrin production ceases.

In the small intestine

The food leaving the stomach—a thickish, acidic liquid, called chyme—then enters the duodenum, the first part of the small intestine. The duodenum makes and releases large quantities of mucus which protects it from damage by the

How a cheese sandwich is digested

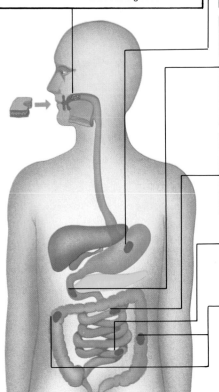

Saliva contains an enzyme called ptyalin, which breaks some carbohydrates into smaller molecules—maltose and glucose

In the stomach an enzyme called pepsin begins to break protein into smaller molecules —peptones.

The gall bladder releases bile into the duodenum. This breaks fat into small droplets so that an enzyme called lipase can break fat into smaller molecules—glycerol and fatty acids. Lipase is made in the pancreas, as are two other enzymes—trypsin and amylase. Trypsin breaks peptones into smaller molecules—peptides and amylase breaks carboghydrates into maltose

In the jejunum and ileum fat, carbohydrate and protein are broken into the smallest molecules; peptidases break peptides into amino acids, lipases reduce the remaining fats to glycerol and fatty acids, and other enzymes break down the remaining carbohydrate.

Now the molecules can begin to pass into the capillaries in the villi (small protrusions from the wall of the ileum).

The residual waste matter continues through the colon, where water is taken from it into the bloodstream. This makes the feces semi-solid when they are finally expelled from the body through the anus.

A cheese sandwich contains fat, protein, and carbohydrate, which must be broken down into very small molecules to be absorbed into the bloodstream and used by the body.

Digestive problems

Symptoms	Causes	Action
Dry mouth, furred tongue, possibly swelling and pain below ears and in neck	Lack of saliva, due to infection of salivary glands or blockage of the duct carrying saliva to the mouth	Take plenty of fluids. See a doctor, as drug treatment, and possibly surgery to remove blockage, may be needed
Pain in back or upper abdomen or chest (heartburn), up to two hours after a meal. Possibly vomiting and loss of appetite	Excessive secretion of acid, overactivity of stomach, destruction of mucus-secreting cells in stomach, often due to stress, smoking, or drinking liquor; eating highly spiced foods may lead to a gastric ulcer	Take antacids or milk for immediate relief. See a doctor if it persists. He or she will probably recommend a bland diet and no smoking. Barium meal and drug treatment may be needed
Burning or gnawing pain high in abdomen two to three hours after meal. Is relieved by eating. Vomiting and lack of appetite not unusual	Excessive secretion of acid in stomach, often due to stress or overwork; may lead to ulcer in duodenum	As above
Jaundice, pale feces, possibly pain high in abdomen on the right and in the right shoulder. Symptoms made worse by fatty foods. Possibly fever and vomiting	Lack of bile secretion due to blockage or inflammation of bile duct or gallbladder. Gallstones or liver disease may also be present	Take analgesics for immediate pain relief. See a doctor as soon as possible, as drug treatment and possibly surgery may be needed
Diarrhea, rapid pulse, possibly fever	Overproduction of mucus and water by large intestine, due to infection or disease; or lack of water absorption, due to food passing too quickly down intestine. Commonly due to gastroenteritis	Take fluids only for 24 hours. If symptoms do not improve in 48 hours, see a doctor in case there is something seriously wrong
Persistent indigestion, vomiting of blood or dark "coffee grounds" material	May indicate cancer of the stomach or ulcers	See a doctor, who will probably order further tests. Do not go on taking more and more indigestion medicine to relieve symptoms

acid in the chyme and other enzymes. The duodenum also receives digestive juices from the pancreas and large amounts of bile, made in the liver and stored in the gallbladder until needed.

Two hormones trigger the release of pancreatic juices. The first, secretin, stimulates the production of large quantities of alkaline juices, which neutralize the acidic, partially digested chyme. Pancreatic enzymes are produced in response to the release of a second hormone, pancreozymin. Bile is also released into the duodenum from the gallbladder, in order to break down fat globules.

Pancreatic enzymes help the digestion of carbohydrates and proteins, in addition to fats. These enzymes include trypsin, which breaks the peptones into smaller units known as peptides; lipase, which breaks fat down into smaller molecules of glycerol and fatty acids; and amylase, which breaks down carbohydrates into maltose. The digested food then enters the jejunum and ileum, further down in the small intestine, where the final stages of chemical change take place. Enzymes are released from cells in small indentations in the walls of the jejunum and ileum, known as the crypts of Leiberkuhn.

Most food absorption takes place in the ileum, which contains millions of minute projections called villi on its inner wall. Each villus contains a small blood vessel (capillary) and a tiny, blind-end branch of the lymphatic system known as a lacteal. When digested food comes into contact with the villi, the glycerol, fatty acids, and dissolved vitamins enter the lacteals. They are carried through into the lymphatic system and are then poured out into the bloodstream.

Amino acids from protein digestion and the sugars from carbohydrates (plus vitamins and important minerals, such as calcium, iron, and iodine) are absorbed directly into the capillaries in the villi. These capillaries lead into the hepatic portal vein, which transports food directly to the liver. This, in turn, filters out substances for its own use and storage; the remainder of the substances pass into the body's general circulation.

The surface of the ileum is covered with small, fingerlike projections called villi. These increase the surface area of the ileum, allowing food to be absorbed quickly into the capillaries (blood vessels).

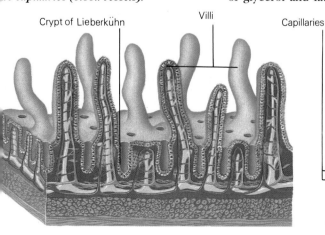

Crypt of Lieberkühn   Villi   Capillaries   Cilia   Lacteal

Dilatation and curettage

Q I have just had a D&C. Will my next period start at the normal time?

A It may, but if it doesn't, there is no cause to worry. After a D&C, there is a good chance that there may be a delay in the menstrual cycle beginning again, and more commonly, there may be an irregular vaginal blood loss for up to two months. But if these symptoms persist, do not hesitate to seek medical advice.

Q Should I stop taking the Pill before I have a D&C, and if so, when should I start taking it again? I do not want to get pregnant at the moment.

A You must ask your gynecologist whether you should stop taking the Pill, and if so, what would be the most suitable time to do so. The answer to this varies and will depend on the opinion of your doctor and also the length of time you will have to wait before the D&C is performed. If you wish to restart the Pill after the operation, you may take the first pill the following day. Take the pills as prescribed, even if you are bleeding irregularly, to insure that you do not become pregnant.

Q I have just had a miscarriage and a D&C. How long must I wait before trying to become pregnant again? I have received conflicting advice from friends and doctors.

A It is usually advisable to wait until you have had at least three normal periods, because this means that the lining of the uterus has returned to normal. It will also enable you to know the date of your last normal period when you do become pregnant, making it easier to figure out when the baby is due to arrive.

In the meantime, it is usually sensible to use condoms or the diaphragm for contraception. These will not affect the lining of the uterus or the production of eggs in any way, and therefore will help your menstrual cycle to resume its normal pace.

Many women need a D&C (dilatation and curettage) at some time during their lives.

Dilatation and curettage (D&C) is an operation of the uterus that may be performed for a variety of reasons (see Uterus). It used to be standard practice, during the teenage years, to use a D&C to cure painful periods. This treatment is seldom used now, as drug therapy is an adequate substitute.

During the reproductive years a D&C may be used to try and determine why a woman has not become pregnant. It can also be carried out to remove retained tissue following an early miscarriage (it is rare for the entire pregnancy to leave the uterus before 16 weeks). Similarly, a D&C can follow a normal birth, in cases where a small amount of placenta is left behind in the uterus.

A D&C is also performed when an intrauterine contraceptive device, or IUD, has become lodged in the uterus. Occasionally, an early pregnancy may be removed from the uterus in this way, so aborting the fetus.

D&Cs are also performed to cure some problems with menstrual periods. If a woman bleeds from the vagina between her periods it may be because of polyps, small overgrowths of the lining of the uterus. Very rarely, this bleeding may be due to cancer of the uterus.

Women who bleed from the vagina after sexual intercourse should also consult their doctor. Occasionally, a small polyp may be present in the neck of the uterus.

Heavy periods are another problem, especially as a woman approaches menopause. Excessively heavy periods may be treated not by a D&C, but by a synthetic form of progesterone, or the Pill. Bleeding

A curette can remove the lining of the uterus to diagnose or remedy medical problems.

from the vagina one year or more after menopause may be a result of the woman taking hormone pills for hot flashes, or more commonly because of atrophic vaginitis (the skin in the vagina becomes red, sore, and infected). In rare cases, the bleeding is due to cancer of the uterus.

How it is carried out
A D&C is usually performed under a general anesthetic. It is not necessary to make an incision or to use stitches.

A pair of forceps is passed through the vagina to grip the neck of the uterus. Except after a miscarriage, this is usually tightly closed, and so the canal from the vagina to the cavity of the uterus is stretched open by passing curved metal rods of wider and wider diameter into the cavity until the canal is almost half an inch (1 cm) in width.

Forceps can then be passed through the opening into the cavity in the uterus to grip and remove any polyp that may be present. An instrument called a curette is then used to remove the lining of the uterus and check that the cavity is of a regular shape and size. The entire operation takes approximately 15 minutes.

Outlook
Very often after a D&C, a woman will feel well enough to go home from the hospital on the same day that the operation is performed, though in some hospitals, the policy is to keep a woman in overnight. She should be able to go home and resume a normal life the next day.

If a D&C is performed after a miscarriage, a woman may feel depressed and tired. Under normal circumstances, she may need to have a few days' rest before she resumes her everyday life. Sexual activity will depend on how she feels.

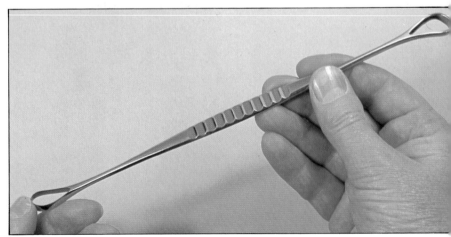

Diphtheria

Diphtheria is a disease which occurs mainly in children under the age of 10. Today it is relatively rare, due to the routine immunization of young children, usually in the first year of life.

Diphtheria is an acute infection of the throat and nose that may prove fatal if untreated or if treatment is delayed.

Causes

Diphtheria is caused by a bacillus (bacterium), the *Corynebacterium diphtheriae*. It produces powerful toxins, or poisons, that attack the mucous membranes of the throat and nose, and if no antitoxin is administered, the heart, nervous system, and kidneys. In the tropics, it has been known to affect the skin.

Diphtheria is usually contracted by contact with an infected person, who spreads the bacteria when coughing or sneezing. Diphtheria can also be transmitted by a carrier who has no symptoms of the disease, and sometimes by infected milk.

Symptoms

After a brief incubation period ranging from two days to a week, the patient develops a mild sore throat and fever, and feels weak and generally ill. A soft membrane, which gradually thickens from the consistency of raw egg white to a crust, forms over the affected tissues. The throat becomes painful, especially in swallowing and breathing, and the lymph glands at the side of the neck swell considerably, sometimes leading to a condition known as bull neck. The infection occasionally spreads further; in severe cases it can affect the larynx and bronchial tubes.

The growth of the membrane can impair breathing functions and a tracheotomy (an operation to open the airways) may be needed to allow the patient to breathe.

If the infection is not treated swiftly, it may begin to spread. The jaw becomes paralyzed, followed by the eyes, the pharynx, and finally, the limbs and trunk. A massive attack can kill within three days, but a slighter attack may take three weeks to cause heart failure.

Treatment

Hospital treatment in isolation is essential. Antibiotics are given to combat the bacterial infection in the throat and antitoxins to counteract the diphtheria toxins. Total bed rest is required, followed by a convalescent period and a very gradual return to normal routine. If treated in time, the patient should recover completely.

All infants must be immunized. This makes the body capable of producing antitoxins immediately after the infection occurs. An initial injection, followed by two more, and then a booster shot a year later, are usually sufficient, but a further booster can be given before the child enters school. The Schick test, where a small amount of toxin is injected into the skin, can determine whether a child is naturally immune before vaccination.

All children should be routinely immunized against diphtheria.

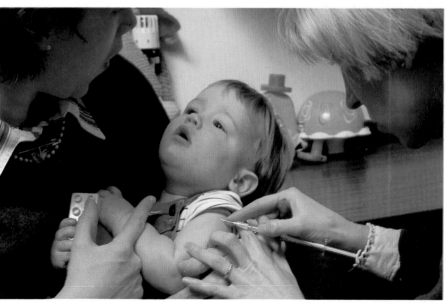

Camilla Jessel

Dislocation

Q I dislocated my thumb recently, trying to catch a ball. Is the joint likely to be loose now—and could it happen again?

A The thumb is one of the joints that can dislocate without causing too much damage to the surrounding soft tissue. All that is required is a splint, which should be worn for about three weeks; there should be no further trouble.

Q A few months ago, my neighbor slipped on ice and dislocated her shoulder. She had it put back in place, but has had a lot of aches and stiffness since then. Is there anything she can do about it?

A Pain and stiffness following a dislocation are fairly common. This is why it is important to have adequate physiotherapy following the injury to keep the joint mobile. Aspirin may help relieve the pain, but occasionally, an injection of a steroid drug into the tissue around the shoulder is required.

Q I dislocated my right shoulder several months ago when I was playing football. Now it dislocates very easily and I have had to give up playing. Is there anything I can do to strengthen the joint?

A It is possible to have an operation to increase the strength of the joint if a shoulder is repeatedly dislocating. Known as the Putti-Platt operation, it strengthens the front of the shoulder by building up the bone to make the socket deeper, so that it is more difficult for the bone to slip out. It takes about two months to heal completely.

Q I recently dislocated my hip. Is it likely that this may lead to arthritis when I am older?

A If the dislocation was a central one, fracturing the pelvis and damaging surrounding tissue, this could increase your susceptibility to osteoarthritis (the arthritis that comes through wear and tear) when you are older. Dislocation behind or in front of the pelvis, however, is unlikely to lead to arthritis.

Joints are the junction points between bones that allow the body to move, but they can become dislocated, often through accidents. However, this painful problem can usually be corrected very easily.

A dislocated joint looks misshapen and cannot work properly. Movement is difficult and there is considerable pain, especially if the bone presses on a nerve.

The joints in the limbs, spine, hands, and feet can all be dislocated. However, some joints dislocate more easily than others. It all depends on the joint's stability, which in turn depends on the strength of the surrounding muscle and tendons (the tough, fibrous tissue that joins muscle to bone). The shoulder and finger joints are less stable and dislocate more frequently than hip joints, which are very stable.

If dislocation is suspected, the patient should be taken to a doctor immediately, as the correction should be done as soon as possible. After 24 hours, the tendons begin to shorten and the dislocation is more difficult to correct. Do not attempt correction without medical help. The most common dislocations are in the shoulders, hips, neck, elbows, and fingers.

The shoulder
The shoulder joint is formed by the bone in the upper arm (humerus) and the shoulder blade (scapula). They form a ball-and-socket joint, with the head of the arm bone forming the ball, and the shoulder blade, forming the socket. The socket has to be shallow for the enormous range of movement that the shoulder makes, and this means that the joint is unstable. The bone may slip out of the socket in one of four directions—forward, backward, up, or down; these are known as anterior, posterior, superior, or inferior dislocations, respectively. About 90 percent of shoulder dislocations are anterior ones. The arm bone slips off the socket and lies in front of the acromium bone (the tip of the shoulder blade).

To get the joint back into place, the patient lies flat on his or her back on a bed. The doctor stands at the foot of the bed and places one foot in the patient's armpit, to gain leverage. The doctor then pulls down on the hand, twisting the arm inward while doing so. The joint slips back with a dull click, and immediately after this, the pain eases. Occasionally, the patient may be in so much discomfort that a general anesthetic is given before the procedure begins.

The hip
The hip is a ball-and-socket joint between the thigh bone (femur) and the socket in the pelvis (acetabulum). It is a stable joint and it takes considerable force to dislocate it. The majority of hip dislocations are the result of car accidents where the knee has hit the dashboard.

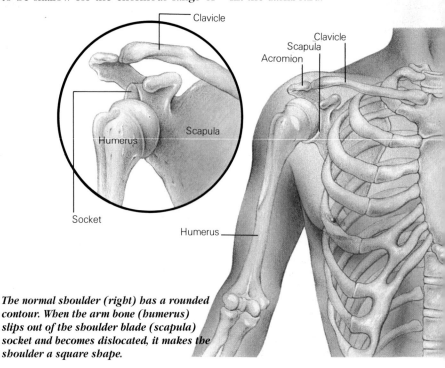

The normal shoulder (right) has a rounded contour. When the arm bone (humerus) slips out of the shoulder blade (scapula) socket and becomes dislocated, it makes the shoulder a square shape.

Treatment for a baby born with dislocated hips involves wearing splints. It needs to be started as soon as possible after birth to be successful (above).

Lines through the leg bones on the X ray indicate the head of the left thighbone is out of alignment in this baby girl's congenital hip dislocation (below).

Congenital hip dislocation

Occasionally, children are born with dislocated hips. This abnormality runs in families, affects girls more than boys, and is most common among the Czechs, Slovaks, Chinese, and Navajo Native Americans.

The deformity is easily corrected with splints if treatment is given within the first three months of life. The longer it is left, the more difficult it is to correct, and if the child reaches the age of five with the condition unrecognized, correction may be impossible. A midwife should check the hips, as a matter of routine at birth, by rolling the legs around in their sockets. If a new parent is in doubt, he or she should ask if it has been done; it could save the baby problems later in life.

The neck

The bones of the neck are prone to dislocation, because they have the least stable joints in the spinal column. A dislocation causes pressure on the spinal cord, which can result in paralysis of the arms and legs unless it is treated immediately. The majority of neck dislocations occur playing active, contact sports like football.

With neck dislocations, the patient is unable to get up and complains of numbness or paralysis in the legs or arms. This is a medical emergency and more damage can be done if the patient is not correctly handled. The golden rule is never to change the position of the head. Never allow the head to bend forward. Support the head, with a hand on each side of the face, while waiting for the ambulance and on the way to the hospital.

The elbow

Dislocation of the elbow is usually the result of a fall on an outstretched arm. The surrounding nerves and blood vessels may be damaged, and the injury is extremely painful. Correction under general anesthetic within 12 hours is essential. The patient can be made comfortable with a simple collar-and-cuff sling on the journey to the hospital.

The finger

If a finger is dislocated, it will look shorter than the others and it will swell up and become painful. The dislocation can be corrected by pulling the finger out in a straight line. A splint may be needed while the soft tissue is healing.

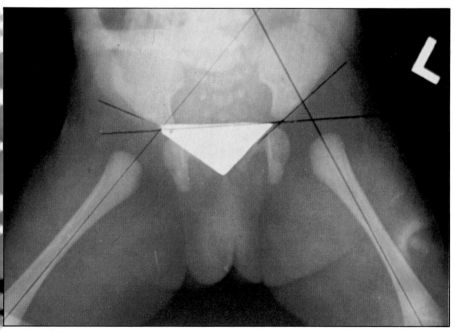

Dislocation may occur in one of three directions—in front of the pelvic socket (anterior), behind it (posterior), or the bone may have been driven through the socket, fracturing the pelvis at the same time (central dislocation). The posterior is the most common hip dislocation. In an anterior dislocation, the knee is turned outward, and in a posterior dislocation, the knee is slightly bent and turned inward across the opposite leg. It is very difficult to move the leg, unless the thighbone has been fractured, and this is one of the ways of diagnosing a dislocation. Hip dislocations are treated under a general anesthetic in the hospital.

Outlook

The soft tissues around a dislocated joint may have suffered damage, pain and stiffness may last for a few months. Physiotherapy may be given to restore full movement to the affected joint. Generally, the long-term outlook for dislocation injuries is excellent.

Diuretics

Continuous good health depends very much on an efficient fluid balance system. If this breaks down, or if fluid retention becomes a problem for any other reason, diuretics can help redress the balance.

Q A girlfriend of mine recently lost a lot of weight by using diuretics. Could anyone try to diet this way?

A This is not a good idea. It is fairly safe to predict that your friend has since put back on every ounce she took off. Diuretics cause the body to lose fluid, not body fat, and this is soon countered by a few cups of liquid. The only people who do sometimes benefit are jockeys who have to lose weight just before a race, but even this is regarded as unconventional. Any prolonged use of diuretics could be extremely hazardous to a person's health.

Q What is the best time of the day to take a diuretic?

A If you are taking a daily dose of a diuretic on your doctor's advice, always take it in the morning, unless your doctor specifically states otherwise. This is the time of the day when the drug is most effective, as the excretory system is at its most active. If you are taking a potassium supplement to replace what has been lost in the urine, try taking this at a different time, say at noon or in the evening, when the excretory system is less active. This allows the body to absorb it, rather than it being passed quickly out of the body.

Q I get a very swollen stomach just before my period. Is it true that a diuretic would relieve the pressure?

A Diuretics can be used for this purpose, but rarely are. Over the last five to seven days of the menstrual cycle, a woman suffering severe premenstrual fluid retention could be given a low-sodium diet and a diuretic, but symptoms are rarely sufficiently severe to justify this remedy.

Q Will a diuretic cure my high blood pressure?

A No. Diuretics are palliatives, meaning that they treat the symptoms of a condition, not the actual cause. Your doctor will be able to advise you on the best course of treatment.

If the body is unable to cope with an excess of salt, the salt is returned to the tissues. These tissues, in turn, retain fluid, causing swelling and bloating.

A diuretic is a natural or synthetic agent that, by encouraging the production of urine by the kidneys, works to rid the body of this accumulated fluid. It acts by breaking down the salt in the tissues, so that it can be released into the bloodstream and flushed out of the body by the urinary system. A corresponding amount of fluid is also released to assist in the removal of the salt in the urine.

Uses

Diuretics are used to treat the problem of fluid retention associated with disorders of the heart, liver, and kidneys. The resulting swelling, which used to be known as dropsy, is called edema.

The first places to be affected are the feet and ankles, and in cases where the patient is confined to bed, the lower back. The reasons for this are obvious: due to the effects of gravity, the fluid simply settles in the lowest parts of the body. Fluid may also collect in the abdomen, where it is known as ascites.

Diuretics are also used to counter salt and water retention produced by other drug treatments, and to assist in the

Mineral water is an excellent diuretic if drunk regularly.

Brian Nash

elimination of a drug from the body in the case of overdosing or poisoning.

Types

Water is nature's best diuretic, for the more a person drinks, the more he or she needs to urinate. Beer drinkers, who often seem to pass as much fluid as they imbibe, are taking two diuretics: the substances from which the beer is made and the volume of fluid in which these float.

The mechanism controlling this water balance is complex, involving receptors in the blood vessels adjacent to the brain that detect changes in the consistency of the blood. This complex mechanism can lead to a suppression of what is known as the antidiuretic hormone and the retention of fluid.

Other common natural substances that can be taken as diuretics are urea, sugar, common salt, sodium bicarbonate, and various other salts. Although it may seem contradictory to take something to alleviate symptoms caused by an excess of the very same substance, this gives a hint of the great complexity of the body chemistry involved. It is sufficient to say that the processes work by osmosis, whereby a weaker solution will pass across a membrane to dilute a stronger one.

For example, if a lot of salt passes into the urine, a similar amount of fluid is passed out at the same time.

Other natural diuretics, such as the caffeine in tea and coffee, work by directly affecting the kidneys; they increase the rate of blood filtration and reduce the kidney's ability to reabsorb salt.

Synthetic diuretics vary widely in their potency and their duration of action. A doctor will choose one suitable to both the individual's requirements and the disorder's severity. In kidney malfunction, an increased dosage may be necessary; in other cases, it may be vital that the dosage is not exceeded.

Because synthetic diuretics are stronger than those that are natural in origin, there may be side effects. Some cause a loss of potassium, which may have to be corrected with a supplement of the mineral. Occasionally there may be some muscle weakness or constipation, and in the case of gout and diabetic disorders, symptoms may appear that include hearing damage, nausea, skin rashes, and light sensitivity.

Diverticulitis

Q I have diverticulitis and I have been put on a diet that contains a lot of bran. Does this mean that I will eventually be cured of the condition?

A Unfortunately, no. The idea of giving you a high fiber-diet is that you will have less trouble from the intestinal diverticula than you currently have. You will also be less likely to develop more diverticula, but the ones you already have will probably remain with you.

Q I often get a queasy stomach with alternating bouts of diarrhea and constipation. My doctor has told me to eat more bran. I'm only 30; isn't that a bit young for diverticulitis?

A Yes. You probably have a condition called irritable bowel syndrome. Although this is not the same as diverticulitis, in both conditions the bowel has to work much harder than it should, thus causing pain. Bran works for irritable bowel syndrome in the same way as for diverticulitis. By softening the feces, it will alleviate the pressure on the colon, which has been caused by hard, immovable feces, and make defecation easier. Bran can be used both as a treatment and as a preventive measure.

Q My doctor suspects that I have diverticulitis and he is sending me to the hospital for tests. What are the tests, and will they be painful?

A The tests for diverticulitis are fairly simple. The doctor will first examine you rectally by inserting his finger to see if any mass or tumor is present. He will then look at your rectum through a sigmoidoscope, a rigid tube down which a light can be shone. You will then be given a barium enema. Barium, which shows up as white on an X ray, is put into the rectum and you will be positioned to allow the barium to flow backward around the colon to outline the walls. None of these tests is painful as the large intestine is not sensitive to pain. Only the nerve endings will respond to stretching, but this only causes minor discomfort.

Over half the population over the age of 80 has diverticula, that is, pouches on the large intestine. Usually they are no problem, but if they become inflamed, they cause the condition called diverticulitis.

Diverticulitis is a disease of the large intestine. As people age, they tend to develop pouches, called diverticula, at the weak points of the large intestine.

The high pressures generated by the muscular wall of the colon to move feces onward and to evacuate the intestine will cause diverticula to form. When these become obstructed with fecal matter, they cannot empty. Infection then builds up from the bacteria that are always present in the feces, causing the large intestine to become inflamed.

Dangers

Occasionally an inflamed diverticulum may burst and fecal matter may spill into the abdominal cavity. This causes peritonitis, which is a generalized inflammation of the abdominal area. If it is not treated immediately, it could be fatal.

Diverticulitis may cause bleeding from the large intestine. This may happen slowly over weeks or months or it may happen suddenly. Any bleeding from the intestine should be investigated immediately.

Infected diverticula may also form an abscess around the colon (the major part of the large intestine). The abcess has to be drained surgically, and the affected portion of the colon removed. An area of colon that is badly affected may narrow, eventually blocking the colon.

Symptoms

Inflamed diverticula can lead to abdominal pain, which can be quite severe, like that of appendicitis; this is why diverticulitis has been called left-sided appendicitis. In diverticulitis the abdominal area becomes tender and may be distended. There is nausea and sometimes vomiting.

In severe attacks, the patient will have chills, a fever, and feel generally unwell. A mass may be felt on the left side of the abdomen. If diverticulitis is chronic, diarrhea will alternate with constipation.

Treatment

The treatment for diverticulitis is rest in bed and a liquid diet for 24 hours, followed by a high-fiber diet. Antibiotics will clear up the inflammation. If there are frequent bowel movements, antispasmodic drugs may be prescribed. The patient should recover in a day or two. When attacks are recurrent or when there is bleeding, perforation, or blockage, surgery may be necessary.

In diverticulitis, bulges that have formed on the large intestine become inflamed.

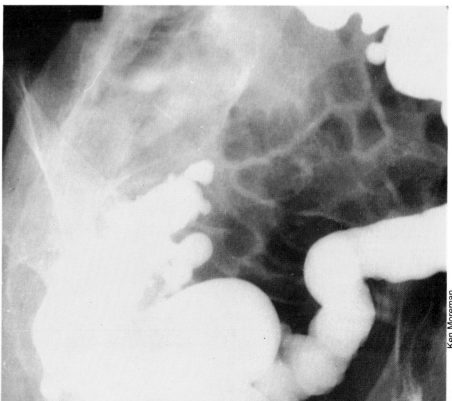

Ken Moreman

Dizziness

Q I don't really have a fear of heights, but on hiking vacations, I often feel dizzy looking over the edge of a cliff. Why does this happen?

A This type of dizziness is very common and can be caused by several factors. It may be what is known as altitude sickness, which is the result of the thin atmosphere at great heights supplying less oxygen to your brain, making you feel dizzy. Or it may be the natural anxiety you feel when looking down from a height. This anxiety causes the blood vessels in the brain to constrict, so less oxygen gets to the brain.

Also the unusual signals being sent to the brain by the eyes, which are closely involved in the body's system of balance, may cause the fluid in the balance organs, located within the inner ear, to make you feel giddy.

Q Why does putting my head between my knees seem to help me when I feel dizzy?

A There are two reasons for this. First the position of the body increases the flow of blood to the brain and provides it with extra oxygen. (It was lack of oxygen that caused you to feel dizzy in the first place.) Second balance problems are associated with the mechanisms of the inner ear, and feelings of giddiness can sometimes be overcome by deliberately fixing both the eyes and head rigidly in one position.

Q I read that pilots should not drink tonic water before flying. What harm could it do?

A Tonic water contains quinine, and quinine can sometimes affect the auditory nerve, which transmits messages to the brain. (Aspirin, antihistamines, some antidepressants, and various other drugs can also have this effect.) This may temporarily cause orientation problems, which is particularly dangerous for airplane pilots, because with no visual clues to act as a guide for them, it is very easy to begin to fly upside down, or even around in circles.

There are many normal, harmless reasons for dizziness, but it is a good idea to know how to recognize when these attacks might have a more serious cause.

Children relish the giddiness caused by playground rides such as this one.

In medical terms, dizziness means a disorientation and loss of balance. But in everyday language, the word is used to mean the sensation of light-headedness, falling, and losing touch that often precedes fainting. It is different from giddiness, which involves a loss of balance, and has a completely different cause.

Shortage of oxygen

Dizziness is the result of a temporary reduction in the amount of blood supplied to the brain; this means that for a short time, the brain gets less oxygen than it needs. This can happen to perfectly healthy people, for example, when they are hungry or suffering from emotional stress, or when they stand up too quickly. But it may also be a symptom of a more serious condition, such as anemia, heart disease, or a circulatory disorder.

The usual remedy for dizziness is to sit down and put the head between the knees to increase the flow of blood to the brain. Anyone who frequently feels dizzy for no obvious reason, however, should consult a doctor.

Giddiness

Giddiness usually occurs when, for some reason, there is a malfunction of the body's balancing mechanisms. Body equilibrium is controlled by a section of the brain called the cerebellum. It is supplied with information about the position of the body by the eyes, by feedback from the muscles and joints, and by the balance organs located in the inner ear. Here, two chambers, called the utricle and the saccule, detect the position of the head in relation to gravity; the three semicircular canals, filled with fluid, detect movements of the head.

Exaggerated body movements, especially in a rotary motion, set the fluid moving to such an extent that even when the head stops, the fluid continues to move for awhile. In response to this out-of-date information, the brain tells the body to compensate by moving in the opposite direction, causing a general loss of balance.

Controlling giddiness

Giddiness of this type can be controlled by fixing the eyes on something that is not moving. Pirouetting ballet dancers, for example, overcome giddiness by moving their heads in quick, 90° turns. Children, on the other hand, actually seem to enjoy the sensation of giddiness and often deliberately bring it on by rolling down hills or riding on playground merry-go-rounds.

Vertigo

Severe and recurrent attacks of giddiness, when the surroundings appear to spin around out of control, are known as vertigo. These attacks may be a sign of a disorder of the inner ear or the middle ear.

Donors

Q My brother had a serious automobile accident, and after a short time in the hospital, was taken off a life-support machine because his brain had ceased to function. As he carried a donor card, his kidneys were removed. How do doctors officially diagnose brain death in cases like my brother's?

A Doctors take every precaution to insure death has occurred. Here are the criteria that two independent doctors would use:

- they must know the cause of the brain damage, and that it is irreversible
- they would insure that the coma and lack of breathing were not caused by any of the following: depressant drugs, relaxant drugs, cold, and abnormalities in body chemistry and hormone function
- the reaction of the pupils of the eyes to light would be tested: they must neither contract nor dilate
- when the eyeball is touched, there must be no blink reflex
- the eyes should not move when the balancing system in the ears is stimulated
- there must be no gag reflex when the back of the throat is touched
- the cranial nerves to the head must not function (usually tested by the use of a painful stimuli)
- when the ventilator (breathing machine) is disconnected, there must be no signs of the patient trying to breathe

If the doctors are still unsure if brain death has occurred, the patient must be reassessed later.

Q Are body parts from animals ever transplanted into human beings?

A Animal organs have been transplanted into humans experimentally on numerous occasions. Unfortunately none has been successful long-term. The problem is not the function of the organ; both baboon hearts transplanted into humans and pig livers attached externally have worked adequately. However, the transplantation of animal organs into humans has been met with rejection by the immune system.

Transplant surgery represents one of the most skilled aspects of medicine today. But it would not be possible without donors, the people who donate parts of their bodies to be transplanted.

Modern medicine and surgery can cure many diseases. But when treatment is not possible, or fails, and the patient's life is threatened, one possibility is to replace the affected part with a new one, transplanted from a donor.

In medical terms, a donor is someone who gives part of his or her body to be transplanted into someone else who needs it. For tissues that the body readily replaces, such as blood and bone marrow, only live donors are used. But for organs that the body cannot replace, like the heart and liver, the donor must have recently died. The exception is the kidneys, where the donor may be alive or dead. A live donor may give one kidney and function successfully on the remaining organ. Live donorship of a kidney is usually done when the recipient is a relative, as the likelihood of the kidney being compatible is greater than if the donor were unrelated.

For some medical problems, the patient him- or herself can donate healthy tissue, such as skin and bone, to be transplanted to a new site in the body where diseased tissue has been removed. This is called an autograft, and usually

Packed in a brightly colored box, a donor heart is rushed to the hospital.

works well because the patient readily accepts tissue that has originated from his or her own body.

Who can be a donor?

Most people can be donors, provided that they can afford to lose the relevant organ or tissue, and provided that they themselves do not have any disease or previous injury affecting the donated part. For instance, someone with prolonged high blood pressure will probably have partially damaged their kidneys, and so would be an unsuitable kidney donor. Similarly, the heart of an elderly person may be too near the end of its natural lifetime to be suitable for a transplant. Since accidents are a common cause of death, accident victims are the commonest organ donors.

All living donors must give permission for the operation. A donor card states the donor's wishes and gives a relative's telephone number. If a dead potential donor was not carrying a donor card, for a doctor to remove their organs, the deceased must be known not to have expressed any objection to such an operation during his or her lifetime.

The donor's tissue type must be compatible with the patient's. This can be a major problem, in that if the patient's

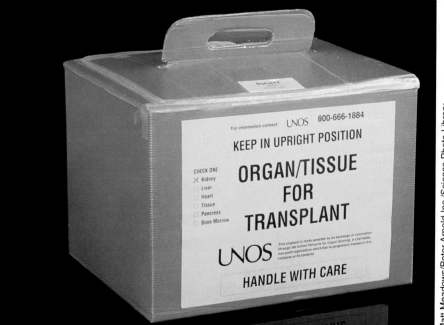

For information contact: UNOS   800-666-1884

KEEP IN UPRIGHT POSITION

CHECK ONE
☒ Kidney
☐ Liver
☐ Heart
☐ Tissue
☐ Pancreas
☐ Bone Marrow

ORGAN/TISSUE FOR TRANSPLANT

UNOS

HANDLE WITH CARE

Conditions that benefit from transplants

Cornea

Lung

Heart

Liver

Pancreas

Kidney

Blood

Bone marrow
(from the iliac crest)

Mike Courtney

Typical disease in recipient	State of donor	Organ removed	Technique for removal
Kidney failure; patient on dialysis	Alive, if related to recipient, or deceased	Kidney	Surgical incision in loin
Heart failure; cardiomyopathy and certain other heart diseases	Deceased	Heart	Surgical incision through breastbone
Aplastic anemia (destruction of bone marrow that produces blood cells)	Alive	Bone marrow	Withdrawn from pelvic bone by syringe
Anemia (lack of red blood cells)	Alive	Blood	Withdrawn from vein by syringe
Scarring of the cornea (lens at front of eye); may be due to accident. Results in blindness	Deceased	Cornea	Eye removed, but only the front is transplanted
Lung fibrosis (fibrous tissue in lungs caused by respiratory ailments)	Deceased	Lungs*	Surgical incision through breastbone
Liver failure (various causes)	Deceased	Liver*	Surgical incision in abdomen

body recognizes the transplant as foreign material, it will try to destroy it. To combat this, the tissue types of patients requiring a transplant are filed on a computer. Any potential donor's tissue type is fed into the computer, which decides which patient has the most compatible tissue type, and so will benefit most.

Donating the organ

Tissue starts to deteriorate immediately after a donor dies, or after removal of the organ in a live donor. This can be slowed by freezing, but speed is essential for transplants. Organs need to be removed from deceased donors within an hour of death, except in the case of eye donations, since the cornea can survive much longer.

As a result, ethical problems have arisen with accident victims who are kept alive by an artificial respirator (breathing machine) and tube feeding, when they are in fact dead. Brain death means that the brain has irreversibly ceased to function, usually due to a period of a few minutes without oxygen,

when breathing ceased at the time of the accident. However, modern resuscitation methods make it possible to restart the heartbeat and artificially ventilate the lungs, so that no other tissues suffer the irreversible changes that the highly sensitive brain cells have. The kidneys and other organs are therefore in good shape.

The difficulty comes in diagnosing that irreversible changes have occurred in the brain. The heart can still beat without any stimulus from the brain, but the lungs need nervous impulses from the brain stem for breathing to function. The diagnosis of brain death is therefore made by showing that there is a complete lack of brain activity controlling the muscles of the body, face, and eyes; and that when the ventilator is stopped, in spite of the usual stimulus to the brain from a buildup of carbon dioxide (the waste product of breathing) in the bloodstream, breathing does not spontaneously restart. All this is assessed by two doctors, who also check that the patient was not on drugs that could influence the findings. Every

possible step is taken to insure that the patient is actually dead.

If there are no objections from relatives, the brain-dead patient becomes a potential donor. A suitable recipient is found, and the relevant organs are then removed while the donor's body is still being oxygenated, so that the transplant tissue remains in the best condition. After this, the respirator is switched off.

There is little danger to live donors. With kidney donors, the remaining kidney enlarges to take the extra load. With blood and bone marrow donors, the body quickly makes up new cells. Sperm can also be donated to help in cases of male infertility; it is used to artificially inseminate a woman whose partner is infertile. Techniques are being developed for removing eggs from women. These are donated to women who are otherwise unable to conceive.

A person wishing to donate his or her organs should tell relatives. Many states will also provide a donor card, or will indicate this wish on a driver's license.

Double vision

Q I've noticed that after drinking alcohol, I sometimes have double vision. Why does this happen?

A Too much alcohol weakens normal vision, because it affects the coordination of muscles in the eyes and elsewhere. If you already have a tendency to squint, there will be a definite tendency for the condition to get worse when you've had a few drinks too many.

Q Can you explain why a distant object often appears double when I am looking at something close to me?

A This has to do with the way the eyes focus. When you focus your gaze on a near object, objects in the distance may appear double, and vice versa.

Q I often see an overlapping ghost image superimposed on an object I know to be single. Am I suffering from double vision and should I seek medical attention?

A This does sound like a form of double vision in its early stages. See if the ghost image disappears when you close one or the other eye. If so, it could be a sign of deteriorating control over both eyes, in which case, you should see an eye specialist as soon as possible. Catching it early could prevent it from getting worse. If the ghosting is still seen when you close one or the other eye, you have distortion, which can be corrected by wearing glasses. You should see an optometrist or ophthalmologist, who can attempt to remedy the problem.

Q I had double vision one day but the next day it was gone. Should I have seen my doctor about this?

A It may simply have been the temporary result of a hangover or fatigue, but see your doctor if it recurs, as he or she may want to test your eyes and nervous system, to insure that there is no serious underlying cause. In the majority of cases, double vision is not serious.

Seeing double can be frightening, but the causes are not often serious and can usually be treated easily.

Double vision, or diplopia, is the seeing of two objects where there is, in fact, only one. When it occurs because of a defect or weakness in the sight of both eyes, it is called binocular diplopia. Such a weakness causes an intermittent or constant deviation of one or the other eye, a squint.

A squint that develops in an adult may result in double vision. Children, however, rarely suffer from seeing double, because the brain develops its own suppression mechanism which shuts out the second image. But as children grow up, this mechanism lessens.

When one eye suffers from double vision, it is known as monocular diplopia. This is usually caused by an eye defect, e.g., an injury in the cornea (the transparent tissue covering the eyeball), or astigmatism (a defect in the eye that prevents light rays being focused correctly).

Causes
Eyes have six muscles (the extraocular muscles), each of which keep the eyes parallel in all directions of gaze. If any of them weaken, a squint and double vision may occur (see Eyes and eyesight).

Fatigue after an illness, emotional stress, shock, or an unusual amount of work can cause defects. A mild weakness from childhood can surface in later life. An injury to the eye or surrounding area, or a disease that affects the muscles, can cause partial or complete paralysis of the extraocular muscles. Alternatively, the muscles may be paralyzed if the nerve supply to one or more of them is damaged.

Symptoms and dangers
Double vision may occur without any general symptoms or specific eye (ocular) symptoms being evident. It may, however, be accompanied by tired strained eyes, eyeache, headache, or fuzzy vision. Since it may be the first symptom of a more serious disease, a doctor or optician should be consulted if symptoms persist. If necessary, he or she can send a patient to an eye specialist (ophthalmologist).

Treatment
The therapist treating the complaint may make the patient do eye exercises. An optometrist or ophthalmologist can prescribe prism glasses. In severe cases, a minor operation may be necessary.

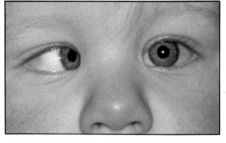

Institute of Ophthalmology

The extraocular muscles coordinate the eyes, so that the object of interest hits both foveas (the most sensitive part of the eye). Light rays from other objects hit different points and are not seen clearly. If the muscles do not work properly, the image hits the retinas at different points and is seen as double.

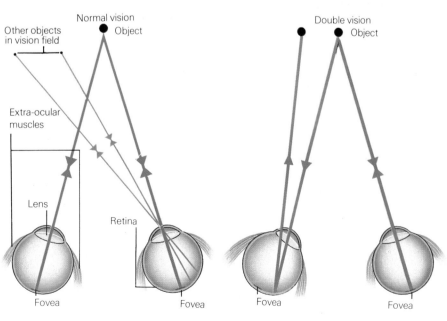

Down's syndrome

Q I am 36 and expecting a baby. What are the chances of my child having Down's syndrome?

A The chance is one in 150 births, or about 15 times more than if you were 20. When the mother is this age many doctors recommend an amniocentesis test to examine the fluid in the womb surrounding the baby. It is important that this is done at an early stage, so that the health of the baby can be assessed before pregnancy proceeds too far. The test is usually done at 16 weeks.

Q My mother has a Down's syndrome child. Is it likely that I could have one too?

A It would be wise to discuss this with your doctor, to rule out the possibility that your mother carries the familial type of Down's syndrome. This type is very rare.

Q Is there any danger that a mentally deficient person with Down's syndrome may become criminally violent?

A No. Down's syndrome children are usually easygoing and placid and they grow into adults of a similar disposition. Criminal tendencies or violent behavior are unusual. If any criminal act does occur, it is possible that the individual does not fully understand what his or her action means.

Q My friend has been told that she is carrying a Down's syndrome child. Is she within her rights to insist upon a termination of pregnancy?

A Under current laws in the US, yes. The diagnosis of congenital abnormality can now be made beyond reasonable doubt by examining the amniotic fluid. The discovery of a severe congenital abnormality such as Down's syndrome will persuade most doctors to perform a termination of pregnancy, if that is what your friend wants. Early diagnosis is important, so that the pregnancy can be terminated before the 28th week of gestation.

A chance genetic error can cause abnormalities to a fetus, resulting in a child born with Down's syndrome. Coping with a child thus affected is a great challenge, but it can also be a rewarding one.

Down's syndrome describes a collection of abnormalities that develop during the baby's time in the womb and result from an inherited irregularity of the chromosomes. Children affected by Down's syndrome have the characteristic feature of rather small, almond-shaped eyes that slant toward the nose. They are all mentally handicapped to a greater or lesser degree, but with care can develop into happy, loving adults. Many die before adulthood, especially in the first few years; but of those who do survive, some are able to hold down jobs.

Outward signs

The abnormalities may not be too obvious just after birth, but a very striking and characteristic feature of the baby at this early age is his or her floppiness. The limbs feel disturbingly boneless.

In the first few days of life, other features become more obvious. The eyes are rather small, almond-shaped, and slanting. The bridge of the nose is small too, giving

Children with Down's syndrome are mostly happy and loving. With care and attention, they can realize their full potential.

Ron Murdoch

The cause of Down's syndrome

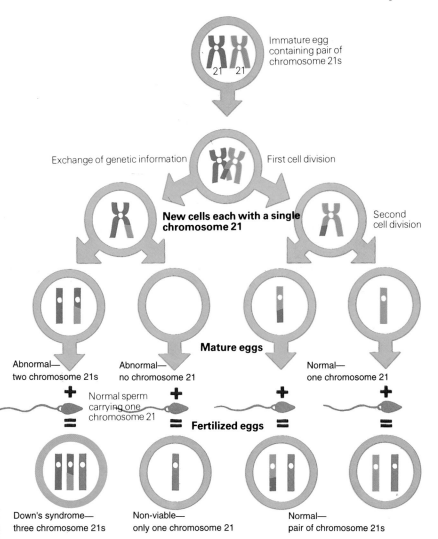

Immature egg containing pair of chromosome 21s

Exchange of genetic information — First cell division

New cells each with a single chromosome 21

Second cell division

Mature eggs

Abnormal— two chromosome 21s

Abnormal— no chromosome 21

Normal— one chromosome 21

Normal sperm carrying one chromosome 21

Fertilized eggs

Down's syndrome— three chromosome 21s

Non-viable— only one chromosome 21

Normal— pair of chromosome 21s

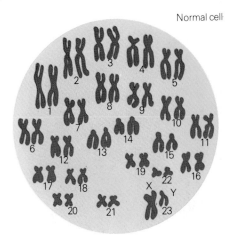

Normal cell

Down's syndrome cell

John Hutchinson

the nose an upward curve; these abnormalities of the nose cause the baby to sniffle. The mouth is also small, but the tongue is of a normal size and it therefore tends to protrude.

As the baby grows, abnormalities of the hands and feet begin to show. The hands are short and broad, with a short little finger that curves toward the thumb. The gap between the big toe and the other toes is unusually large and the feet tend to be rather square.

There are also internal problems that may need corrective surgery. As many as 25 percent of Down's syndrome children suffer heart defects. Hernias are common too, and some children can be badly constipated as a result of intestinal problems associated with the condition.

But apart from these physical problems, the most obvious feature is mental handicap. Generally the IQ ranges from 30 to 70, but it may go beyond 70 (the average for the general population is

100). However, with special care and teaching, the quotient can be raised by up to 20 points. Despite all these troubles, Down's syndrome children are usually easygoing, happy, and friendly, and like all people, they respond to love.

Cause

Down's syndrome is caused by an abnormality of the chromosomes—the parts of the cells that carry the hereditary elements that everyone gets from their parents. The syndrome occurs in one in every 660 births in the US and is the most common type of mental handicap.

Normally, people have a total of 46 chromosomes in matched pairs of 23, which are numbered from the largest (number 1) to the smallest (number 23). These pairs split for reproduction purposes and one of each pair appears in the female egg and male sperm, so that the offspring has half its 46 from the mother and half from the father.

With Down's syndrome, there are three chromosome 21s (circled above), instead of two, in each body cell. The sequence that produces this (shown left) starts with an immature egg (the same principle could apply with a sperm). The top circle shows that this contains a pair of chromosome 21s. In the first cell division, this starts to exchange genetic information. If this is normal (right side of diagram), each cell has one chromosome 21. When this is fertilized by a normal sperm with one chromosome 21, the resulting fertilized cell will carry a pair of chromosome 21s. With abnormal division (left side of diagram), one cell may carry two chromosome 21s and one may carry none. Although these are fertilized by normal sex cells, the result is either Down's syndrome or a nonviable cell, containing only one chromosome 21.

With Down's syndrome, there are 47 chromosomes instead of the usual 46. The abnormality always develops in the

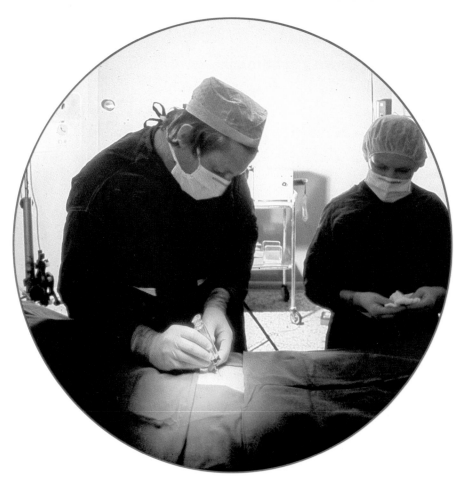

because his testicles will be underdeveloped and unable to function properly.

With mothers over the age of 35, it is now routine to perform a test known as amniocentesis (see Amniocentesis). A simple, quick, and painless process, it involves removing a small amount of the amniotic fluid from inside the womb to study the cells shed by the baby, who floats in this fluid. These cells are then studied under a microscope, where any genetic abnormality is easy to spot. It is then a matter for the parents and physician to decide whether or not the pregnancy should be terminated. The chances of losing a Down's syndrome fetus are high anyway; between 65 and 80 percent of these pregnancies end naturally. Another test for Down's syndrome is CVS (see Chorionic villus sampling), which is a procedure similar to amniocentesis but can be carried out earlier.

Action

It is essential that the parents are told as soon as possible of any abnormality, so that they can prepare themselves to deal with the problem in whatever way best

In the amniocentesis test for abnormality in unborn babies, a hollow needle painlessly extracts fluid from the womb.

same chromosome—number 21. There are three main types of abnormality in this chromosome, but 92 percent of Down's syndrome children suffer from what is called trisomy 21. The result of these abnormalities is that there are three number 21s, instead of the usual two.

Doctors do not know how this extra chromosome makes an appearance, but the most recent theory is that it happens either when the egg or sperm is preparing for reproduction just before conception or earlier. So far, medical research has revealed little more than this.

Incidence of Down's syndrome

The condition is very much related to the age of the mother, but there is also some evidence to show that the age of the father is marginally relevant. When the mother is 20, the chance is one in 2,300. This reduces to one in 290 at 30 years old and one in 80 over 45 years old. Once a woman has had a Down's syndrome baby, the chances of having a second are doubled. If a Down's syndrome woman has a baby (a rare occurrence), there is a or in two possibility that he or she will ve the syndrome. No man who has syndrome can father a child,

Coping with a Down's syndrome child

- Contact the local parents' group of the national group dealing with Down's syndrome as soon as possible. It can advise and counsel right from the start, when you need it most
- Your child needs just as much love and attention as any normal child—perhaps even more—so don't stint in that direction
- Stimulate the baby's senses from the earliest age; this will help in his or her long-term development and make the child aware of the surrounding environment
- Allow your child to develop at his or her own rate, with lots of encouragement. Be firm, however, otherwise he or she could become quite a tyrant and be difficult to manage
- Make sure your child mixes with other children, both normal and with similar handicaps. It will help mentally, physically, and socially
- Being made to feel clumsy and stupid can add to your child's problems, so try not to criticize

---

suits them. They may choose to have the abnormal fetus aborted if they feel they cannot face the prospect of giving birth to and caring for a mentally and physically handicapped child.

If they choose to continue the pregnancy and feel that they want help, they can contact an appropriate association or parents in a similar situation for help, advice, and support. In New York, the National Down's Syndrome Society can provide help and practical advice for parents and can send information booklets to parents in any part of the world. It also has connections with other groups in 30 other countries. Organizations like these provide information on the development of the child and also give help to parents who are adjusting to their own feelings. Guilt is a common reaction to having a handicapped child and it can last for months or even years, but discussion with other parents in the same situation can help new parents to overcome this.

Down's syndrome children need stimulating, creative play to develop as fully as possible within their capabilities.

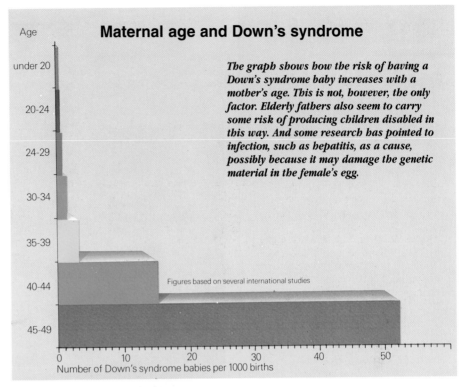

Maternal age and Down's syndrome

The graph shows how the risk of having a Down's syndrome baby increases with a mother's age. This is not, however, the only factor. Elderly fathers also seem to carry some risk of producing children disabled in this way. And some research has pointed to infection, such as hepatitis, as a cause, possibly because it may damage the genetic material in the female's egg.

Figures based on several international studies

Age: under 20, 20-24, 24-29, 30-34, 35-39, 40-44, 45-49

Number of Down's syndrome babies per 1000 births

Aziz Khan

Development

On the whole, Down's syndrome children grow up to be happy, contented people. If they are given sufficient care and attention, a few may develop well enough to earn their own living, although it is unlikely that they will ever be able to perform anything much more involved and demanding than a routine job. Those who have jobs are reported to be reliable, cheerful workers who rarely take days off for sickness.

The important factor in the development of Down's syndrome children is that they should be stimulated from the earliest possible age. Love and affection are, of course, very important from the very beginning of their lives. Also parents should try to stimulate all their senses, by moving the child's limbs, playing different sounds to stimulate hearing, placing the child in contact with different textures, and keeping the child visually interested. If this is not done, Down's syndrome children will not show a great deal of interest in anything and their condition will deteriorate.

Because of their low IQs, few Down's syndrome children learn to read or write very well. However, some experts claim that with proper teaching some Down's children can achieve up to a 20-point improvement in their IQ test results.

There is usually no difficulty in toilet training these children or teaching them to dress and feed themselves. Those with higher IQs may also be able to handle simple tasks like collecting the items on a

Q Why are more Down's syndrome children born to older women?

A The answer is not known for certain, but it seems possible that it is related to the age of the egg. Remember that by the time menstruation begins, all the eggs are formed and ready in the ovary. They are then produced at the rate of one every month, with each ovary taking it in turn to produce. It is possible, therefore, to have an egg resting in an ovary for a period of 30 or 40 years before it is used. The same is not true of men, who produce sperm at a constant rate. The long period of time that an egg lies around could make it more prone to genetic damage from such things as virus infections. But as it is extremely difficult to test the makeup of the female egg in the ovary, scientists are not absolutely sure of this theory.

Q Do Down's syndrome children live as long as other people?

A No. The risk of severe pneumonia is increased during childhood and the inherited abnormalities of the heart may result in an early death. However, if there is no cardiac abnormality and the child passes the early years without trouble, there is no reason why a Down's syndrome child should not have a normal lifespan.

Q Can there by any real improvement in mental ability in children with Down's syndrome?

A There is not much that can be done about improving intelligence as such. There has been some exciting research done, however, involving giving large doses of vitamins to Down's syndrome children, and great improvements have been reported.

On the other hand, this has not been proven yet and it would be wrong to take such reports as fact, however encouraging they are. It is also true to say that if Down's syndrome children are properly trained and taught as much as they can learn, then it can seem that their ability is improved; in fact, they are realizing their potential.

Anthea Sieveking/Vision International

shopping list, but even so they may have some difficulty with money calculations. Keeping up with normal children at school is rarely possible and Down's syndrome children are best cared for in schools specializing in the teaching of educationally subnormal children.

Adolescence can sometimes be difficult for the child's parents as well as for the child and it is sometimes possible to arrange vacations away from home with groups of other children who are similarly handicapped, through either a local welfare or church group.

The future
Some doctors believe that the mental ability of Down's syndrome children can be improved by feeding them large doses of vitamins, including vitamin E, and there have been some remarkable cases reported of children improving after only a few months of vitamin treatment. However, this has not yet been proven by

Bringing up a Down's syndrome child in the family is not all sacrifice and hard work. Caring for the less able can help normal brothers and sisters by making them more than usually responsible and unselfish.

scientific research. Some authorities are skeptical about the method, so it may be wise to wait and see what develops from this line of research rather than to have personal hopes dashed. It is important to remember that Down's syndrome children, like any others, vary enormously in personality. Each child should be treated in a way that matches his or her state of emotional and intellectual achievements—the same as with any child.

Finally, having a handicapped child can cause disruption in some families; all kinds of conflicts can arise between members of the family and sometimes a relationship can be badly affected. Others find that working together to help a handicapped child enriches their lives.

Dreaming

Q Why can't I always remember my dreams?

A Sometimes a dream has an emotional impact but the images are inadequately filed in our memory and thus cannot be remembered in detail. Alternatively there could be a normal recall problem, just as there is with some waking events. Often if something happens during our waking day to jog our memory, the whole dream may come flooding back.

Q I heard a program recently which talked of lucid dreams. What are they?

A Lucid dreams are those in which we realize that we are dreaming while actually asleep. Some people have reported that they can only remain asleep if they make no attempt to influence the course of the dream. Others have reported that they are sometimes able to manipulate events in the dream without awakening, or to wake themselves up if a dream becomes too alarming or frightening.

Q I have been dreaming the same dream for many years. Why is this?

A Dreams may result from naturally produced electricity. Recurrent dreams probably occur because some groups of cells are stimulated more than others, each time producing the same images. If, however, dreams are regarded as having a purpose and a meaning, the recurrent dream may be one in which the dreamer likes the dream and plays it over many times. Alternatively the dream may be trying to convey a lesson that needs learning.

Q Why does my son have recurring nightmares?

A Adults have nightmares about once in every 2,000 dreams. They are associated with periods when dreams are interrupted, such as recovering from a feverish illness. Children have a great need to dream, spend a greater proportion of their sleep dreaming, and are more prone to fevers, and so have more frequent nightmares.

Each person dreams several times a night, although not every dream will be remembered. So why does this happen, and do dreams have any purpose or meaning?

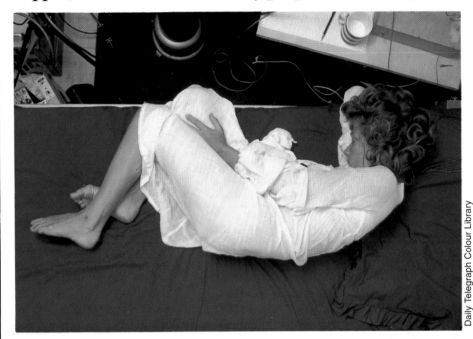

Daily Telegraph Colour Library

Brain activity can be measured during sleep in a dream laboratory, to detect when a person is dreaming.

Science has no clear idea why dreams occur, but apparently they help humans to maintain their mental stability. Studies show that a person who is prevented from dreaming for a few nights becomes irritable, restless, and unable to concentrate or perform routine tasks. If left to sleep undisturbed, the same person dreams much more, as if to catch up on lost dreaming time.

Why dreams occur

The simplest, though as yet unproven, theory as to why humans dream is that they do so by chance. If a person is woken up at the end of a dream period, which can be identified by rapid eye movements (REMs) in the sleeper, each dream recalled usually consists of a very simple image: a picture with one or two people, a few objects, and one or two actions. If a tiny electric current is passed across a small area of the brain, a similar sort of image or memory is conjured up: a scene, a sound, an action, or an event.

One theory states that while deeply asleep, some brain neurons (nerve cells) charge slowly with electricity by means of a spontaneous natural process, stimulating neighboring cells the same way as when a fleeting idea occurs when one is awake. This random firing of groups of cells alerts memories and displays them as action scenes; they are remembered upon waking and are called dreams.

Outside influences

Digestive activity in the body, or anything else that changes the level of arousal in the brain, may produce more active dreams. Alternatively this activity may enable a person to remember dreams more easily by waking during the night. This theory explains the popular belief that certain foods stimulate dreaming.

Other outside factors and influences reveal more about the brain than about dreams. If a fine spray of cold water is directed at the sleeper's face at different points in the dream period, the feeling of the spray is often incorporated into the dream. From a report of the experience, it is evident that the dream spans the same amount of time as it would if the event occurred in real life. Humans do not, as is commonly believed, dream dreams in a flash or in just a few seconds.

Other effects can be produced by outside stimuli. A moderately loud buzz will easily wake someone who is dreaming at the time. They are less likely to wake if they are not dreaming. If a dreamer's name is spoken, however, the person will be woken as easily during a nondreaming period as during a dream period. This shows that part of the brain is awake even when the dream sense is not operating.

The way we dream

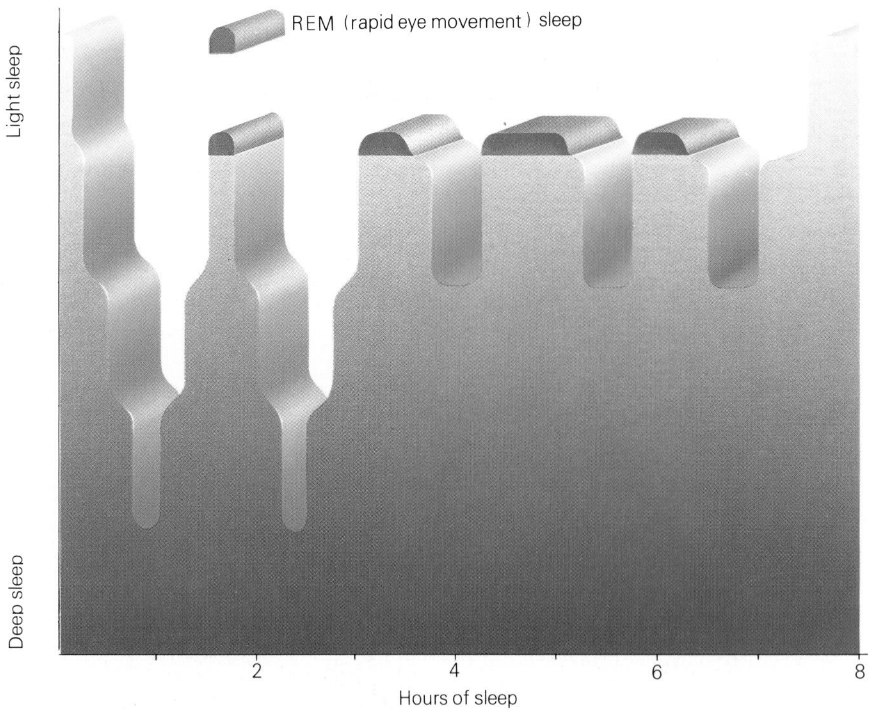
REM (rapid eye movement) sleep
Light sleep
Deep sleep
2
4
6
8
Hours of sleep

Aziz Khan

Humans have several dreams every night, lasting about 20 minutes each. The eyelids flicker continuously during the dream.

Unanswered questions

Many other questions about dreams still remain unanswered. It is known that some people always dream in color, while others dream only in black and white. It is also known that some people become experts at controlling their dreams and the events that take place in them, while others are never even aware that they are dreaming at the time. In particular, one recommended cure for repeated nightmares is for the patient to try to imagine themselves successfully resolving the situation while dreaming.

Moreover, it is known that some people have recurring dreams, sometimes for most of their lives, while other people experience a dream only once. And as everyone knows, some people are experienced at remembering their dreams while others can never remember them and so believe that they never dream.

Western science still has no clear idea as to why these differences exist and what significance dreams have. However, cultural traditions around the world are rich in methods of dream interpretation, with great importance being attached to their purpose and meaning.

The purpose of dreams

The idea of dreams having a meaning and purpose rather than being random occurrences is as old as history itself. People ranging from psychiatrists to fortunetellers have voiced theories on this point.

Freud, the famous psychiatrist, believed that dreams portrayed wish fulfillments that could not be expressed in daily life because they were frowned upon in the dreamer's society. Not all of these wish-fulfilling dreams were literal expressions; very often they appeared in disguised or symbolic form, which the dreamer would then have to interpret.

Later theories have centered on the idea of dreams being trial solutions to problems in the dreamer's daily life. In these kinds of dreams, the logic of the problem is not worked out, but instead the dreamer experiences the emotional consequences of the solution. Often the dreamer either rejects or fails to remember the dream upon awakening if it appears to have no relevance to his or her problem. Only dreams that actually have some bearing on the dreamer's life are remembered.

In the end, neither science nor psychiatry are really certain if dreams do have an emotional purpose or if they occur completely by chance. Some researchers have argued that dreaming cannot be a method of solving problems because dreams present totally irrelevant and pointless images; others have argued the opposite. The truth might lie in the combination of some of the various theories. It is possible that dreams may occur as the result of the random neuron firings in the brain, but they are remembered or forgotten according to their relevance and interest to a dreamer's way of life and the problems that are in it.

Interpreting dreams

Dream interpretation has been a part of almost every culture on Earth for thousands of years. Whether such interpretations are always useful is another matter, although it is possible that images presented to us in sleep can, if interpreted correctly, help us to solve present problems or prepare us for the arrival of future ones.

Unfortunately, dream interpretation does not simply amount to associating the meaning of a dream with a fixed symbol, such as a snake symbolizing a penis or a bluebird happiness, although for hundreds of years the traditional beliefs of various peoples have held this to be possible. In dreams there are no fixed meanings; a simple object can signify different things to the same person at different times. Dreams do not always reflect problems in any one particular way, nor do they always portray what will happen in a given set of circumstances.

With this in mind, can dream interpretation be of any use? It is likely that it can give a person insight into him- or herself, family, friends, and the environment, but only if the actions and feelings in the dream are related by the dreamer to his or her current life.

However, the following should be noted: not every dream has a meaning. Some dreams are simple wish fulfillments or play dreams, while others may only be a random set of images, remembered because of their bizarre associations.

Dreams should never be interpreted by anyone other than the dreamer, since the images may have meanings to the dreamer that are totally unknown to anyone else. Therefore, when someone asks, "What do you think my dream means?" the best answer is, "What does it mean to you?"

Sometimes the dreamer does not realize the meaning, if any, of a dream right away. By asking questions about the detail of the dream, such as, "What did the thing that chased you in the dream look like? What did it remind you of?" the dreamer will be helped to relate the dream image to the real-life problem that the dream has symbolized.

Finally, it is probably the emotions attached to a meaningful dream that are important to the dreamer. If, for example, a man dreams that his partner has left him, it means neither that she will leave, nor that he wishes she would, but it may enable him to assess his feelings about the relationship.

Dressings

Many scratches, cuts, burns, and abrasions can be treated in the home. It is therefore essential to be aware of the various kinds of dressings available.

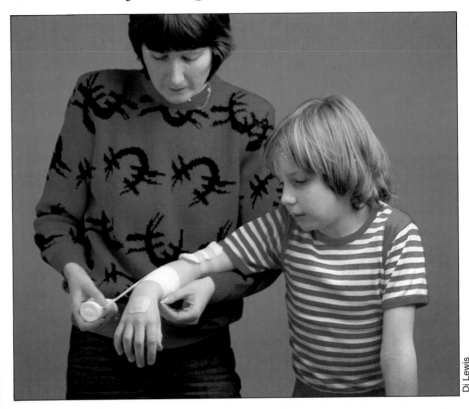

Di Lewis

A dressing is a protective covering that is applied to a wound. It has four main functions: to prevent infection entering the wound; to absorb blood or a discharge, such as pus; to control bleeding; and to protect the wound from further damage.

Dressings are made of various substances, including natural products like sphagnum moss. They must be nonirritating and the patient must not be allergic to the components. They must be clean and sterile to prevent infection being introduced into the broken skin. They must be large enough to cover the wound, and must also be porous to allow air to get in and sweat to get out.

Types

Dry dressings consist of dry materials, such as gauze, that have been put directly onto the wound without any creams or antiseptics. They are suitable for wounds (such as small cuts, burns, or abrasions) which are clean and healing normally.

Wet dressings (which are soaked with a saline solution) should be applied to infected or discharging wounds that have first been dabbed with a substance (such as an antiseptic or an antibiotic) that will fight any infection.

The nature of the wound or injury will dictate the type of dressing to use.

A nurse or doctor should always apply more complex dressings used for ulcers, discharging abscesses, or large wounds. Do not attempt to do these at home.

Dressings may be nonadhesive or adhesive; the choice of the appropriate one depends on the seriousness of the wound and whether it is discharging or not.

Adhesive dressings consist of a pad of absorbent gauze or cellulose on an adhesive backing, with perforations that allow sweat to evaporate. Adhesive dressings should be used on small wounds that are not discharging heavily.

Nonadhesive dressings consist of layers of gauze covered by a pad of cotton with a bandage to hold it in position. Because nonadhesive dressings minimize the risk of the healing tissue being removed when the dressing is taken off, they are morre suitable for wounds that may stick to the dressing.

Preparation

The hands should be washed thoroughly before the wound can be cleaned. Gently stroke or dab the wound from the center

Applying and removing dressings

Before applying a dressing, wash your hands and make sure that they never come into contact with the wound during the treatment.

If there are any foreign bodies in the damaged tissue that you cannot easily remove, call a doctor to deal with them.

No dressing should be too tight or too loose; it should cause the patient the minimum of pain, discomfort, and distress.

Gently clean and dry the wound, using sterile cotton soaked in a mild antiseptic solution diluted in water.

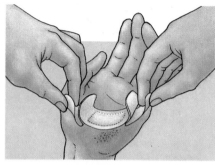

Peel off the protective strips on the back of an adhesive dressing and then lower it carefully onto the wound.

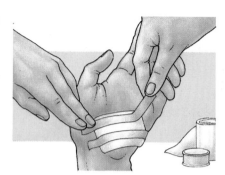

If the wound requires padding but does not warrant bandaging, use adhesive bandages to hold the dressing in place.

M Appleton

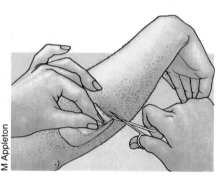

If hairs are stuck to the sticky part of an adhesive dressing, cut them with scissors as you peel back the dressing.

Cut off as much dressing as possible before soaking the wound in a warm antiseptic solution for at least 10 minutes.

Layers of the dressing should float off. Then the rest can be peeled back without pain or damage to the wound.

outward, using fresh cotton for each stroke. Insure that the wound looks pink and healthy and that any major bleeding has stopped.

Dry the wound gently with dabbing movements, taking care not to touch it with the fingers. Decide on the type of dressing to be used and whether medicated cream or ointment is needed.

Applying and changing

When applying an adhesive dressing, first insure that the skin around the wound is completely dry. Wipe off any excess ointment or the dressing will fail to stick securely. If necessary, shave off the surrounding hairs to prevent pain when the dressing is removed. Choose a dressing that has a padded area large enough to cover the wound.

Hold the dressing over the wound, then slowly peel back the strips while pressing the dressing onto the wound. Smooth down the edges to insure that the dressing is adhering to the skin.

When applying a nonadhesive dressing, lay the first layer of medicated gauze gently on the wound. Insure that it is large enough to cover the entire wound and overlap the edge by about 5/8 in (1.6 cm). Then apply layers of cotton or gauze; where a discharge from bleeding or pus is likely, or the area is tender, pad liberally. Finally, apply a bandage that is neither too tight nor too loose to hold the dressing in place. Alternatively, secure it with strips of adhesive bandage.

Dry dressings covering small wounds can be changed every three days, but if the dressing becomes dirty, uncomfortable, or wet, or if the wound is infected, the dressing should be changed as soon as possible. A dry dressing over a noninfected wound can be left as long as seven

to ten days, provided that the wound is healing. A wet dressing that is covering an infected or discharging wound will require daily replacement. If a dressing gets stained or wet, it should also be changed as soon as possible.

Removing

Great care should be taken when removing an adhesive dressing. It is best to remove an adhesive bandage quickly but firmly, folding it back on itself so that there is minimum pull and irritation to the skin. With elderly patients, however, dressings should be removed more gently to minimize the risk of tearing the skin.

A nonadhesive dressing consists of layers of gauze covered by a pad of cotton with a bandage to hold it in position. Because nonadhesive dressings minimize the risk of the healing tissue being removed when the dressing is taken off, hey are suitable for wounds that are likely to stick to a dressing.

Surgical dressings

Various kinds of dressings are used by specialists after surgery. Dressings used after minor surgery range from simple adhesive dressings to acrylic or other plastic coverage that is sprayed on from an aerosol can. Plastic dressings of this type are highly effective but may be difficult to remove, especially if sprayed over stitches. Special solutions may have to be used to soften and then dissolve the plastic spray-on material.

After major surgery through a long incision, it is common to apply a large, well-padded wool and gauze pack, which is fixed in place with strapping, attached clear of the surgical wound. This protects the tender area of the incision. Such a dressing is, however, by no means universal; many surgeons prefer to leave their sutured incisions exposed. In either case, it is usual to keep bedding off the incision by means of a light metal cradle.

A variety of medicated dressings is used in special cases. Various pastes and lotions may be applied as required. In many cases the medication is designed to clean, and draw water from, infected wounds. A strong paste of magnesium sulfate (Epsom salts) is sometimes used because of its excellent water-drawing (hydroscopic) properties.

Eye pads

It is no longer considered good surgical practice to bandage injured or infected eyes. Tight dressings of this kind cause a rise in temperature and encourage infection (see Infection and infectious diseases). At the same time, it is often very uncomfortable to have the affected eye left open, especially if the cornea is abraded and blinking causes pain. For these reasons, eye dressings are usually limited to oval pads consisting of a layer of wool sandwiched between two layers of gauze. The pad is applied diagonaly and is held in place by a single strip of tape applied from the center of the forehead diagonaly down and out to be secured to the cheek. Tape applied to the nose is uncomfortable and is avoided. The tape is fixed firmly enough to apply gentle pressure to the closed lids but not so tightly as to compress the eyeball. Plastic tape is preferable to adhesive cloth tape as it is less liable to cause allergic reactions in the skin.

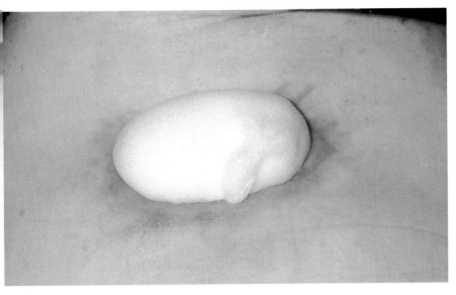

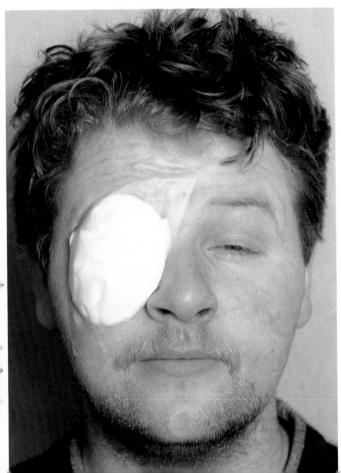

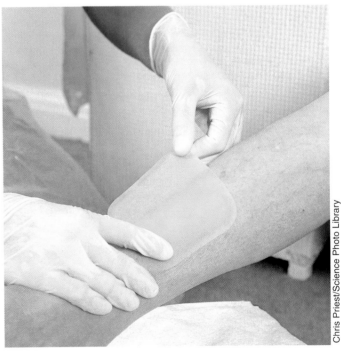

A foam plug is used in some wounds (top). A damaged eye is covered by an oval pad kept in place by Scotch tape (left).

A hydrocolloid flexible dressing (Granuflex) (above) keeps the wound surface moist and is useful in the treatment of ulcers.

Drowning

Drowning is an accident that should never happen. Unfortunately, thousands of people lose their lives this way every year, yet some basic precautions can prevent this tragedy and make for a safer swimming environment.

Q Is it true that someone who is drowning comes to the surface three times before sinking for good?

A No. This is an old wives' tale. Once the person takes a breath underwater, they are very unlikely to resurface. That is why you often hear eyewitnesses state that one moment they saw the victim and the next minute he or she had completely disappeared.

Q My young son recently wandered off to the deep end of the local swimming pool and jumped in. He went under the water for a minute and almost drowned. Now he is afraid to go anywhere near water. How can I get him to take swimming lessons, so that this can never happen again?

A It is best to introduce your son to the idea of swimming gradually. You may want to find a professional swimming teacher and explain to him or her what has happened. And because he has been through a traumatic experience, therapy may help your son to overcome his fear.

Q I read that if breathing and circulation stop for more than four minutes, resuscitation attempts are pointless because the patient is permanently damaged. Is this true?

A With victims who suffer from failure of the circulation due to a heart attack, this statement is generally true. However, there have been some remarkable escapes from drowning. The most amazing is the story of a Norwegian boy, who was saved after spending 40 minutes totally immersed beneath an icy river and managed a full recovery. Many first aid books say that blue-colored skin and dilated pupils signify death. This is not true of victims who almost drown. There are reports of people who have recovered after 15, 20, 30, and 40 minutes completely submerged in water. A victim must never be assumed to be dead even if he or she appears that way; resuscitation should be continued for at least half an hour.

Death by drowning results from lack of oxygen, or asphyxiation, in the same way as in death caused by strangulation or suffocation. The reason for drowning is usually that the victim panics and loses control of breathing. Water enters the victim's lungs in nine out of 10 cases and it makes no difference whether this water is fresh or salty.

Why it happens

Drowning claims thousands of lives in the US alone each year. This sad and unnecessary figure has remained the same for about 20 years. Overall, male victims outnumber females by three to one, with a peak age between 15 and 29 years. In almost a third of these incidents, alcohol is considered to be an important contributory factor.

About two-thirds of all drowning accidents in the USA, UK, Australia, Canada, and New Zealand occur in inland waters. It has therefore come to be assumed that immersion in fresh water is more dangerous than in salt water. However, the true reason for the large number of people drowning in fresh water is the lack of rescue services in those areas. Inland lakes and rivers are rarely adequately guarded, whereas most public beaches are protected by lifeguards employed by the local authority. So the opportunity to drown in inland waters is much greater than it is on the coast.

The rescuer keeps the victim's head above the water with an arm around his neck, and pulls him to safety. Resuscitation should be performed if a victim is not breathing.

Contrary to popular belief, most people who drown are able to swim and tragically, the majority die within 33 ft (10 m) of the shore. The victim is most likely to be someone who is unfamiliar with the particular stretch of water in which he or she is swimming. These points, plus alcohol intake, suggest that drowning in many cases may be due to carelessness or irresponsibility.

Signs of drowning

The swimmer who is in difficulty faces toward the shore and usually decides to swim breaststroke. This results in a vigorous bobbing of the head. As the swimmer gets more tired, his or her body becomes more upright in the water and when he or she stops swimming, the body is completely vertical.

At this point, the drowning sequence begins and is very rapid. The victim no longer faces toward the shore, but may turn in any direction. Nor is the victim able to raise the arms above the head to signal, because this causes him or her to sink immediately. The victim is usually too out-of-breath to shout for help. The important point to realize is that the person about to drown may give no indica-

Family safety

Keep your family safe from drowning by following these basic rules:

- Whenever you are near water, don't let young children out of your sight
- Never leave a baby in a bath alone; even a few inches of water could be fatal
- Teach your children to swim early in life; this can be as soon as they can walk and certainly before they go to school
- Don't let children play ducking games in the water—whether playing in swimming pools or at the beach

- Don't let children—or adults—try to rescue beach balls that are floating out to sea. It is not worth the risk involved
- Don't eat a big meal before swimming, as it can cause cramps. A light snack is fine
- Be sure to follow beach safety signs, for example, warning flags
- Teach children never to swim out of their depth until they are really strong swimmers, capable of swimming a good distance without stopping or panicking
- If children are going boating, make sure they wear life vests

- Don't use inner tubes or air mattresses in the sea. They may seem safe but can be swept away by strong undercurrents
- Explain to children that if they get cramps they should not panic but try a sidestroke or backstroke until the cramps have worn off; then they will be able to swim to safety
- Remember that even a backyard pool can be dangerous to small children
- Take special care in the countryside. Small ponds can be unexpectedly deep, riverbanks treacherously slippery, and trees overhanging water a hazard to enthusiastic tree climbers

---

on of his or her state, so it is up to the ould-be rescuer to watch for the patrns of swimming behavior.

irst aid

life can be saved by prompt, effective tificial respiration applied at the water's lge. As soon as the victim has been rought to shore, he or she should be irned on one side so that the mouth can e cleared of obstructions. If the victim is ot breathing, he or she should be rolled nto the back with the head tilted backard to prevent the tongue from bstructing the passage of air. Finally, the ictim should be given five rapid breaths f mouth-to-mouth resuscitation.

It is a good idea to stop at this point nd place a cheek against the victim's iouth to check whether he or she is reathing. If there is breathing, the victim iould be turned again to the side and ursed in that position. If the victim is ot breathing, mouth-to-mouth resuscitaon should be continued for up to half an our. Adults should be given between 2 and 15 breaths a minute and children bout 20 breaths a minute.

In the event of a cardiac arrest (when ie heart has stopped), firm pressure iust be applied to the chest at the same me as artificial respiration is given. This iakes resuscitation very complex and it best performed by someone who nows the technique.

In the hospital, the doctor will check ie oxygen level in the patient's blood; ie amount of water inhaled; temperaire and heartbeat. The oxygen level is ie most critical and is almost always ow. The doctor will give the patient a igh concentration of oxygen. Victims vho have inhaled water run the risk of eveloping a kind of pneumonia hours fter the accident. This is known as secndary drowning and in the past was sually fatal; but with modern hospital quipment and the improved understandng of the physiology of the lungs, secndary drowning rarely poses a problem.

Rescuing a drowning person

CAUTION: Do not try this without first consulting a doctor, unless you are properly trained.

Prompt action is essential to save a drowning person. If you see someone in trouble and you are not a strong swimmer, call for help. Only if you are an extremely strong swimmer should you swim out toward the person. When you reach him or her, concentrate on keeping the victim's head above water. Then follow the procedures described below.

To maintain a good hold on the victim, grasp him or her underneath the arms.
Swimming on your back, head for shore.

Place the victim on his or her side, and clear the mouth and nose of any obstruction that may be blocking the air passages.

Roll the victim onto his or her back and give mouth-to-mouth resuscitation, for up to half an hour if necessary.

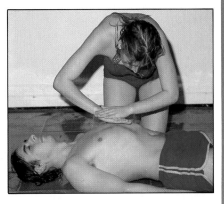

If there is heart failure, cardiac massage must be given at the same time as mouth-to-mouth resuscitation.

Brian Nash

Drowsiness

If a person suffers from drowsiness even when he or she has had an adequate amount of sleep, there is usually a simple explanation. Occasionally, however, drowsiness is a warning sign of an underlying health problem.

Q When I go out for dinner with friends, I always feel really drowsy after eating. Why does this happen?

A After a meal, additional blood is diverted to the stomach to help with digestion. This means the brain and other tissues are left to rest while food is digested, making you feel drowsy.

Q I have been prescribed sleeping pills, but I am worried that they will make me feel drowsy or lethargic the next day. Will they?

A This depends on how long-acting the type of sedative in the sleeping pill is. If it is very short-acting, you should experience no signs of hangover.

Q Is it safe to drink a lot of coffee when I feel drowsy?

A Coffee contains a stimulant called caffeine and it is possible to have too much of it. The symptoms of caffeine overdose are palpitations, tremors, sleeplessness, and anxiety. You may only develop these if you drink vast amounts of coffee, otherwise there is no danger. But keep in mind that some people are much more sensitive to the effects of caffeine and may develop these symptoms after drinking only a very small quantity of coffee.

You should also be aware that although caffeine does temporarily banish drowsiness, it is not a cure. You should look for the cause of your drowsiness and try to do something about that, rather than trying to keep yourself awake with any kind of stimulant.

Q My elderly aunt nods off to sleep when I am talking to her sometimes. Why is this?

A Most elderly people do not sleep a solid eight hours a night, but tend to catnap instead. A regular daily routine of getting up and returning to bed at set times can help to prevent this. Your aunt should consult her doctor if she is taking any prescribed medications that could cause her regular bouts of drowsiness.

Even the most alert person suffers from drowsiness at times. Concentration may be poor, it may be difficult to remember things, and facts must be repeated before they are grasped. Movements are slow and clumsy and there is a general lack of vitality. This occurs even if the person has had enough sleep, and is very different from weariness caused by a lack of sleep.

Common causes

The drowsy feeling sets in as a result of a lowering of brain activity and this may result from several different causes. Lack of fresh air is one. In a poorly ventilated room, there is a buildup of the level of carbon dioxide breathed out by the occupants. This makes the body's tissues, including the brain, work less efficiently. The warm, stale air also increases water evaporation from the eyes, which obliges a person to blink more and more and makes the eyelids feel heavy, adding to the sensation of drowsiness.

Daily Telegraph Colour Library

A repetitive job can cause drowsiness if the brain is not stimulated by receiving new information. Background music can help.

Cold

Many small animals hibernate through the winter; in humans, cold produces the same instinct to curl up in a ball and go to sleep. It is not surprising, therefore, that drowsiness is an important symptom of hypothermia (below-normal body temperature), which especially afflicts older people living in poorly heated places.

Boredom and drugs

Boredom can lead to drowsiness, because the brain goes to sleep unless it has the stimulus of information coming in and work to do. Drowsiness caused by drugs and alcohol are common problems, as those who take tranquilizers or drink at lunchtime know only too well.

More serious causes

Drowsiness is inevitable when someone has a major illness; the body is using all its reserves of energy to fight the disease. If it starts within 48 hours of a blow to the head, especially if accompanied by vomiting and/or visual problems, a doctor should be consulted.

Drowsiness can be a symptom of meningitis (inflammation of the outer casing of the brain). If besides the drowsiness the patient is feverish, has a headache and a stiff neck, and finds bright light uncomfortable, meningitis should be suspected.

It can also be a common symptom of diabetes. Anyone who becomes progressively more drowsy over a few days, seems increasingly thirsty, and is urinating frequently, should consult a doctor.

Cancer, anemia, malnutrition, and lack of the thyroid hormone can all cause drowsiness, so persistent drowsiness that cannot be put down to one of the obvious causes ought to receive medical attention. In the absence of other symptoms, it is unlikely to be serious.

Treatment

All too often the simple but overlooked cure for drowsiness is to open a window or drink less alcohol. Background music often helps to relieve boring situations by stimulating the general level of brain activity. But if drowsiness is a real and persistent problem with no identifiable or treatable underlying cause, drug treatment may occasionally be necessary, but only under a doctor's supervision.

Drug abuse

Q My son often appears dreamy, is losing weight, stays out late, and lies about where he has been. Could he be a heroin addict?

A It is impossible to diagnose whether your son is an addict without seeing him. However, the signs you should be looking out for are poor appetite, no interest in personal appearance, sudden and unexplained absences from home, long periods spent in his room, slow and halting speech, and disinterest in organized activities.

Check his clothing for blood spots and, if possible, his arms for tracks made by the syringe. Look over his room for fully burnt matches, teaspoons, small plastic or paper envelopes, and even a syringe. These items are all part of the paraphernalia of taking heroin, and if you find them, speak to your son and suggest to him that he seek professional help as soon as possible.

Q I heard that newborn babies whose mothers are drug addicts can suffer from withdrawal symptoms. Is this a fact?

A Unfortunately yes. Doctors are familiar with this problem, but as the baby has a metabolic system that is still developing, it is often a difficult condition to treat. The majority of addictions, however, normally start in the teenage years, peak in the second and third decades of life, and decline thereafter.

Q I am very overweight and my doctor has prescribed diet pills for me. Could I become addicted to them?

A Tolerance to diet pills that contain amphetamines is gradual, but you may become psychologically addicted to them. Not only will you get a high, but you will also have the incentive to keep taking them, because you will be losing weight. These pills should only be taken under your doctor's guidance. If you feel you are becoming addicted to them tell your doctor, who may or may not wish you to continue taking them.

The abuse of many types of drugs is becoming an increasingly common problem, particularly among young people. It is essential for parents to recognize the signs of drug-taking, along with its effects and dangers.

Brian Nash

Young people are especially likely to abuse drugs, because of frustration and a need for companionship that the private world of drug-taking fulfills.

A person is said to be addicted to a drug if he or she cannot stop taking it, either because of the need to experience its effects or because he or she feels terrible if the drug is not taken.

Only certain drugs, such as barbiturates and heroin, are truly addictive in the sense of both physical and mental dependency. With drugs such as LSD and crack, users may develop only a mental dependency, but may still find it difficult to give them up.

What happens in addiction

Addictive drugs affect the nervous system, particularly the brain. If used in too large quantities, they tend to become almost a part of the body's own chemistry. They often mimic a naturally occurring chemical in the body; for example, the opiates (the most powerfully addictive drugs) resemble endorphins, the brain's natural painkillers.

An addictive drug also has a potent effect on key points in the pathways of the nerves. Whichever is the case, the more a drug becomes built in to the body's processes, the stronger the addiction becomes.

Drug tolerance

Another feature of drug addiction is called tolerance and this simply means that the body becomes so used to the drug it is receiving that increasingly large doses are needed.

Who is at risk?

There is no simple way to predict what type of person may be at risk from drug abuse. Occasionally addiction starts because a seriously ill or badly injured person has been on painkilling drugs longer than they ought to have been; for example, after an accident at sea, when it has taken days to reach proper medical help. Sometimes addiction happens because of boredom and sometimes it happens because of pressure; some apparently successful, high-powered professional people may be secretly dependent on drugs.

Fashion plays a large part in drug addiction, for drug-taking is, and always was, done for pleasure, kicks, or thrills. Those who become addicts in this way may often be part of a group that believes in drug-taking as a technique that expands or improves the mind.

Equally, addiction can start by accident, or at least as far as the addict was concerned. Young people are increasingly being sold marijuana or other soft (that is, not physically addictive) drugs which, unknown to them, have had hard, addictive drugs such as heroin added. If the user becomes addicted (hooked), the supplier, or pusher, has a continuing sale.

Inadequacies

Doctors generally agree that most addicts have personality problems. Many resort to tension-relieving drugs in the first place because they cannot handle life's everyday troubles. Although a deprived or unsatisfactory home background is sometimes given as a reason for drug addiction, addicts may come from any social background and may be educated or not.

The dangers

Although some people may be quite heavily addicted to a drug as potent as heroin and live apparently normal lives, it is more usual for addiction to bring with it an increasing spiral of disasters.

Apart from deteriorating health, the addict suffers from a lack of direction and motivation, losing the urge to do anything except take the drug. In this state it is an easy step to losing one's job.

Without money it may be difficult to purchase the expensive black market supplies that are needed to satisfy the craving. From here the next step is often crime, especially drug trafficking, to pay for the all-important doses.

Opiates

The most notorious of the addictive drugs are the opiates, so-called because they are made from opium, or are chemically similar. Opium itself is extracted from the seeds of the opium poppy plant, grown mainly in Asia.

Morphine is the most widely used opium extract in medicine, and of the several synthetic opiates, the best-known is diamorphine, or heroin.

All the opiates are, to a greater or lesser extent, addictive, but heroin is the most commonly abused because it is the quickest-acting and most potent. It is also in relatively plentiful supply through black market or illegal channels.

The opiates are superb painkillers, with the essential and marvelous ability to make terrible injuries and the last stages of incurable illness bearable, possibly even comfortable. In carefully controlled quantities, given under medical supervision, there is a minimum danger of addiction and the relief from what may be excruciating pain undoubtedly justifies the risk.

Effects on the addict: The effects of the different opiates vary from person to person. In general the high achieved from a substantial dose of opiate goes through a number of phases, typically beginning

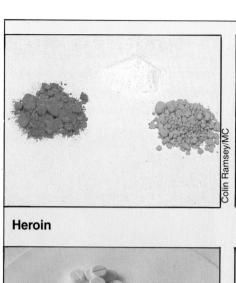

Colin Ramsey/MC

Heroin

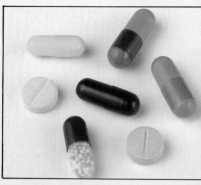

Barbiturates

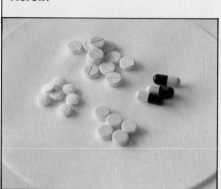

Amphetamines

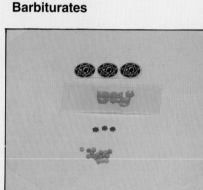

LSD

Dry-cleaning fluid

Alcohol

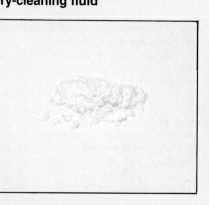

Cocaine

Marijuana

The most common dangerous drugs and their effects

Name of drug	Form of drug	Method of use	Effects	Dangers of abuse
Heroin (slang: H, horse, junk)	White powder when pure. Sold on the streets, it is often impure, ranging in color from white to brown	Injected or inhaled (snorted). Injecting into the skin not as dangerous as into a vein (mainlining)	Dramatic, pleasurable high, but also some nausea and drowsiness	Regular use ends in addiction. Withdrawal effects particularly unpleasant. Tolerance develops rapidly
Barbiturates (common types are Phenobarbital and Amobarbital)	Pills, capsules, and some may be injected	Taken by mouth or injected	Relaxation, sleep; if injected, elation	Regular use ends in addiction. Withdrawal causes anxiety, disturbed sleep, confusion, uncontrolled limb movements, seizures, and unconsciousness
Amphetamines (slang: speed, blues, pep-pills, purple hearts; common types are Methedrine, Benzedrine)	Capsules and tablets of different shapes and colors. Methedrine may be in liquid form	Taken by mouth or, in case of Methedrine, injected	Instant high, extra energy, elation at first then rapid unconsciousness	Loss of appetite, skin problems, aggression, delusions of persecution, depression, excessive exhaustion or fatigue, long-term emotional or psychological problems, suicide
LSD (slang: acid; proper name lysergic acid diethylamide)	Variety of colored tablets; sometimes liquid	Taken by mouth or, if liquid, on a sugar lump. Tiny doses	Dramatically altered mental state (a trip) with bizarre hallucinations, grossly altered vision, and delusions (false beliefs as to physical powers). Can last up to 18 hours	Not physically addictive, but the trip may be nightmarish. Impure LSD may be physically harmful. Disturbed behavior on a trip may cause physical harm to user; for example, trying to fly from upstairs windows
Glue or other products such as dry-cleaning fluid	Usually straight from the container, but user may try to concentrate dose by improvising a small tent from a plastic bag	Inhalation	Short-lived buzz or confused state of mind	Not physically addictive, but the young people who mostly try such activities for kicks suffer serious damage to the health including brain, liver, and heart damage
Alcohol	All the well-known forms, though liquor is, of course, more potent	Social or private drinking	In small doses, relaxation, slight anesthetic effect, loss of inhibition, talkativeness; in large doses, memory loss, aggression, slurred speech, and drowsiness	Alcoholism is the most common form of drug addiction in the West. General damage to the health and to work and family life. Dangerous to drive a car
Cocaine (slang: coke, snow) and crack	White crystalline powder or small white marbles	Fine powder is sniffed in (snorted) through the nose; crack is smoked in a water pipe or regular pipe	Strong feeling of exhilaration, extra energy, ability to concentrate, and impression that one is being brilliantly lucid in conversation and thought	Use can lead to mental dependence. Chance of circulatory problems and damage to membranes of nose and lungs. Use during pregnancy causes underweight, addicted babies
Marijuana (slang: dope, shit, pot, hash, grass). It is made from the Indian hemp plant	Two forms: dried, crumbled leaves or resin. The first is called grass, the second is called shit	Grass is smoked in pipes or as a cigarette; resin is sometimes mixed into regular cigarette tobacco; grass and resin are sometimes cooked in food and eaten	Mild intoxication (being stoned); extra sensitivity to music, pictures, touch, loss of recent memory, sedative effect after a few hours. Large doses may cause hallucinations	Much debated. Not physically addictive, but effect on lifestyle can be a marked lethargy and lack of motivation.

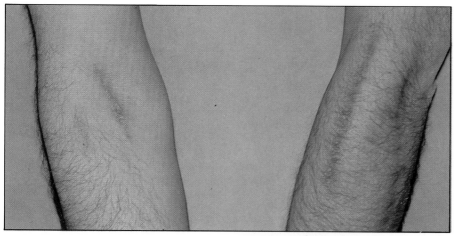

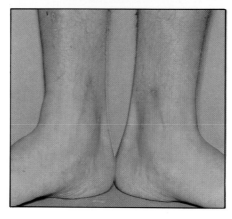

The most obvious sign of a heroin or amphetamine addict is tracks near arteries on arms or legs, caused by repeated insertion of the needle.

with a warm feeling of peace, then often progressing to, or being combined with, sensations of nausea, disorientation, and drowsiness.

Detecting an addict: The heroin addict has skin damage at the points where he or she repeatedly inserts the needle to give the dose (the fix) from a syringe. He or she is likely to suffer from loss of appetite, loss of weight, constipation, and loss of sex drive. The pupils of his or her eyes may be very tiny, about the size of pinpoints.

Withdrawal: The addict dreads withdrawal from the drug. It takes different addicts in different ways, but in general there is vomiting, abdominal pains, cramps in the limbs, general agitation, and collapse.

Overdose: There is an omnipresent risk of overdose in the addict. In a confused, irrational, or reckless state as a result of taking the drug, an addict may then accidentally or deliberately take a lethally large dose.

The outlook for an addict: Unless a hardened drug addict takes steps toward self-help, the chances of regaining normal health and lifestyle are not very good. Apart from the obvious danger of dying from an overdose, there are the risks of diseases connected with frequent use of the same needle. Ulceration, abscesses, hepatitis, and blood poisoning are common; meningitis, kidney disease, and tetanus are less so, but must be considered. AIDS is also a serious risk.

A survey followed the histories of 108 known drug addicts. After seven years, 25 were off drugs altogether. Thirty-five were still receiving drugs, but in a clinic. Twenty-nine were possibly in the process of giving up their drug habit and 19 were dead. These statistics illustrate just how

important it is to seek medical and psychological help from a doctor or a hospital clinic if a person has a drug addiction problem.

Barbiturates

Abuse of barbiturates, which are essentially sedatives and sleeping pills, has on occasion caused as much physical suffering as misuse of opiates.

The danger associated with barbiturates is tolerance. Even those who use them responsibly to help them go to sleep sometimes find that they begin to lose their effectiveness over time. When a heavy user stops taking them, there may be mental disturbances, which in turn lead to a further loss of sleep. It is for this reason that barbiturates, useful as they are in treating certain conditions such as epilepsy, are generally being prescribed less and less today.

A person who seriously abuses barbiturates takes them by injection. This usually causes elation and removal of inhibitions, but then gives way to confusion, lack of coordination, slower breathing, and even unconsciousness.

Withdrawal symptoms start about a day after the addict stops taking the drug. Sleep is disturbed, there is anxiety, uncontrollable movements of the limbs, and even convulsions.

Cocaine and crack

In recent years there has been a large increase in the illegal use of cocaine and its derivative, crack. Cocaine gives its users a high, making them feel energetic and lively. Mental dependency can result, though actual physical addiction does not occur.

Stimulants

The stimulant drugs have the opposite effect of barbiturates and other depressants, and are generally referred to as amphetamines. They have the ability to make the user more alert, less susceptible to tiredness, and lift the mood. Tolerance can develop very rapidly.

The amphetamine abuser may take the drug by injection to produce a considerable feeling of elation, but this gives way to depression, feelings of persecution, and hallucinations. Although there are no physical withdrawal effects, ceasing to take amphetamines may give the addict psychological problems, including severe agitation and depression.

Drugs that distort the senses

Some drugs are not addictive drugs in the strict sense, but they distort the senses and people may develop a mental dependence on them. In addition they carry special physical dangers.

Marijuana stays in the body for an especially long time after being taken and causes lethargy in the user.

The other drug that distorts the senses, LSD (lysergic acid diethylamide), is potentially dangerous because some people react to it in disturbed ways, becoming violent, experiencing feelings of persecution, or developing strange and possibly disastrous beliefs, for example, that they can fly.

Inhalants, cigarettes, and alcohol

From time to time there are trends for glue-sniffing, or similar activities, especially among teenagers. A variety of substances are used to produce this type of kick: dry-cleaning fluid, paints, sprays, and petroleum-fuel products. In general they give a disappointing short-lived high, a typically fuzzy or confused state. Like the sense-distorting drugs, inhalants are not actually addictive but their physical effects can be devastating. Accompanying or soon after the so-called high there is likely to be slurred speech, stupor, and a general state of confusion. Heart, liver, and brain damage are real dangers.

And of course this picture would not be complete without alcohol and cigarettes, which are potent addictive drugs that cause widespread health and social problems (see Alcoholism and Lung and lung diseases).

Duodenum

Q I have heard duodenal ulcers described as an executive disease. Are all executives likely to get them?

A It is true that duodenal ulcers are common in people who drive themselves hard at work, but executives are by no means the only people to get duodenal ulcers. Recent surveys have shown that ulcers—which are up to 12 times more common in men than in women—affect people in all walks of life, but are most likely in those who are overconscientious and anxious. The stress of being laid off, in addition to the stress of actual work, can help to cause a duodenal ulcer.

Q Do children ever suffer from duodenal ulcers?

A Only occasionally, but adolescent boys who are particularly prone to worry about such things as finding a job, passing exams, or achieving sexual maturity do sometimes develop duodenal ulcers.

Parents who suspect that their son is in danger of developing such a condition should try to ease his worries as much as possible. They should make sure that he eats regular meals, and sees a doctor if he has abdominal pains, particularly if they occur between meals, since these can be a symptom of a duodenal ulcer.

Q My husband has a duodenal ulcer and is frightened that it will lead to cancer eventually. Is there any possibility of this occurring?

A No. Although cancer can occur in various parts of the alimentary canal, cancer of the duodenum is extremely rare. It is known that stomach ulcers can lead to cancer if they do not receive prompt medical treatment, but the same is not true of duodenal ulcers—which is, perhaps, some consolation for those who suffer from them.

This does not mean, however, that a duodenal ulcer should be ignored, because it can lead to severe complications, such as internal bleeding.

The duodenum, a small section of the alimentary canal, plays a vital part in the digestive process by neutralizing the acid in partially digested food.

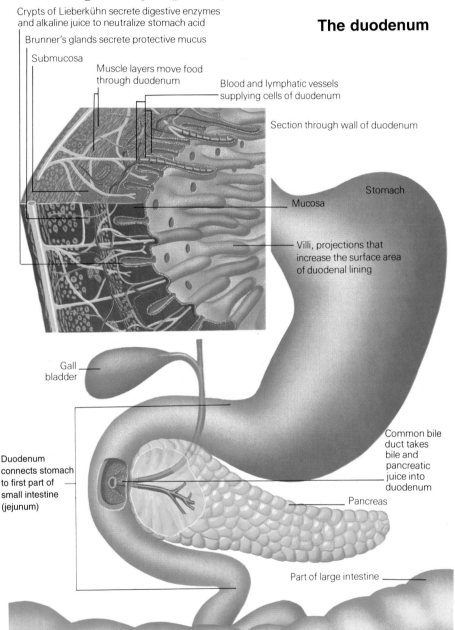

The duodenum

Crypts of Lieberkühn secrete digestive enzymes and alkaline juice to neutralize stomach acid

Brunner's glands secrete protective mucus

Submucosa

Muscle layers move food through duodenum

Blood and lymphatic vessels supplying cells of duodenum

Section through wall of duodenum

Stomach

Mucosa

Villi, projections that increase the surface area of duodenal lining

Gall bladder

Duodenum connects stomach to first part of small intestine (jejunum)

Common bile duct takes bile and pancreatic juice into duodenum

Pancreas

Part of large intestine

Venner Artists

The duodenum is joined to the lower part of the stomach. It is the first part of the small intestine and is vitally important in the efficient digestion of food. It is a horseshoe-shaped tube about 10 in (25 cm) long, and is curled around the head of the pancreas.

Structure and functions

Two layers of muscle in the wall of the duodenum alternately contract and relax and so help to move food along the tube during digestion. Between the muscle layers is the submucosa, containing many glands, called Brunner's glands, which secrete protective mucus. This helps to prevent the duodenum from digesting itself and from being eaten away by the acid mixture arriving from the stomach.

In the innermost layer of the duodenum, the mucosa, are glands that secrete an alkaline juice containing some of the enzymes needed for digestion. The juice also works to neutralize stomach acid.

The cells of the mucosa are in constant need of replacement. They multiply faster than any other cells in the body; of every 100 cells, one is replaced every hour throughout life.

Digestion

The partially digested, liquefied food reaching the duodenum contains hydrochloric acid from the stomach. This acidity is neutralized in the duodenum by the secretions of the duodenum itself, and by the actions of bile and the pancreatic juices that pour into the duodenum from the gallbladder and pancreas, through the common bile duct. These juices continue the process of digestion.

Duodenal ulcers

The most common problem of the duodenum is the formation of ulcers—an eating away of small patches of the mucosa. Duodenal ulcers are usually called peptic ulcers because they involve the combined corrosive action of hydrochloric acid and the enzyme pepsin. Pepsin breaks down proteins and, with ulcers, instead of working on food, it acts on the mucosa.

Peptic ulcers in the duodenum are most commonly caused by the overproduction of hydrochloric acid and pepsin in the stomach. They may also be due to lowered mucus production, which can be caused by, among other things, reduced blood supply to the duodenum, or drugs such as aspirin, which are thought to alter the mucus chemically. This will, of course, have the effect of reducing the degree of protection the mucus gives.

Who is at risk?

Duodenal ulcers are up to 12 times more common in men than in women and characteristically occur between the ages of 30 and 40. Women generally develop ulcers later in life, usually between the ages of 45 and 60.

There is evidence, although it is not clear-cut, that duodenal ulcers tend to run in families, and strong statistical proof that people whose blood type is O are more likely to be affected than those with A, B, or AB blood. Studies suggest that people who are anxious, overconscientious, and ambitious are more likely to develop duodenal ulcers, particularly if they eat hurried, irregular meals. Both anxiety and bad eating habits tend to increase the amount of acid and pepsin produced in the stomach at times when there is no food present for these substances to work on.

Heavy drinking is more likely to be the cause of duodenal ulcers than hot, spicy food. Alcohol, especially in large amounts, is known to impair the efficiency of the digestive process; conversely, those individuals with ulcer-prone personalities tend to drink to relax and to reduce the effects of stress.

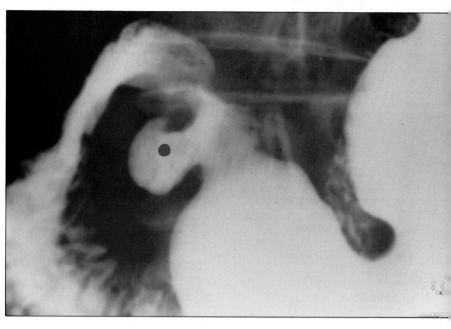

A light coating of barium makes the pouch caused by this duodenal ulcer (the red dot) clearly visible when it is viewed on an X ray.

Symptoms

The symptoms of a duodenal ulcer include pinching pain in the abdomen, or sometimes in the back—where its precise position varies with the position of the ulcer. The pain, accompanied by a feeling of fullness and discomfort in the abdomen, occurs between meals, usually between two and three hours after eating. It can be eased by eating and by alkaline indigestion medicines. There is rarely a loss of appetite and sometimes the first sign of an ulcer is the sudden vomiting of blood or the appearance of black feces, black indicating the presence of blood.

Treatment and diet

Anyone who fears they may have a duodenal ulcer should see a doctor without delay. If one seems to be present, the doctor will refer the patient to a hospital for various tests, probably including an X ray. Other investigations may include chemical examination of the blood and feces, and an endoscopy—the insertion of a flexible, lighted tube into the duodenum so that the ulcer can actually be seen. (Endoscopy of this sort involves an injection to make the patient sleepy and so a short stay in the hospital is necessary.)

The treatment of duodenal ulcers has changed considerably over the last few years. This is because there are new drugs available that stop the stomach from secreting acid. Several different classes of drugs decrease acid production, while others increase the duodenum's defense against acid. Any indigestion that occurs during treatment can usually be easily controlled with one of the many antacid tablets or liquids that are available. However, in some cases surgery may be necessary.

As far as diet is concerned, doctors no longer consider that complicated diets of milk pudding and other invalid foods have any value. The patient should, however, try to eat small, regular meals frequently. The only foods that should be avoided are highly spiced foods, large amounts of alcohol, and anything known to have given the patient indigestion in the past. The patient is also advised to stop smoking.

Other problems

Other problems of the duodenum occur if the pancreas or gallbladder, whose secretions are essential to digestion, are not working properly. Problems can also occur if the duodenum lining is irritated by the toxins produced by food-poisoning bacteria; this usually produces the symptoms of vomiting and abdominal pains. When the duodenum is irritated in this way, its muscles contract while those of the stomach relax. As a result, partially digested food that has already passed through the stomach is pushed back again and this helps to trigger vomiting. As for all intestinal infections, the best treatment is to take nothing but fluids for 24 hours and to see a doctor if the patient finds that the condition has not improved within a couple of days.

Dwarfism

Q My 13-year-old son is shorter than the other boys in his class. Should I take him to the doctor?

A The reason may be simply that his classmates are growing more quickly than he is. In any class of adolescents, there will be a wide difference in height and maturity. At this stage, there is a spurt in growth when both height and weight increase rapidly. This acceleration may not start until the boy is 16; then he will rapidly catch up in stature. However, if your son has not grown for three to six months, there may be something wrong and he should be taken to the doctor. Remember, the average rate of growth at this age is about 2 in (5 cm) a year and growth should be fairly constant.

Q Why are most women shorter than men?

A After the growth spurt in adolescence, the long bones effectively stop growing and there is no further increase in height. Because girls mature physically before boys, they have their growth spurt on average about two years earlier, so they have two years less growing time before their adult height is established.

Q In fairy tales, dwarfs are always portrayed as being rather intelligent. Is it true that they are exceptionally bright?

A There is no evidence that stature and intellect are related. Although some forms of dwarfism are associated with mental impairment, most carry normal intelligence. Short people are as likely to be exceptionally bright as people of normal stature.

Q Can two unusually short people have a baby who will reach a normal height?

A This depends on the cause of their condition. If it is due to a glandular deficiency, the answer is yes. But this type of glandular trouble also gives rise to infertility. If shortness is due to an inherited cause, then the condition is likely to continue in the children.

An individual's height is determined by his or her heredity, but if growth is disturbed by some physical cause, early detection can often correct the problem.

People who are short of stature do not appreciate being labelled dwarfs. In any case, their lack of height is not a disease, but simply shows that one or more of the factors that contribute to height have somehow been thrown out of balance.

Height is only relevant when compared with the average height of other individuals from a similar background. For example, an average European male would be considered short compared with a Masai warrior from Africa, yet the same man would appear a giant next to a member of a pygmy tribe. People of similar ages vary greatly in height; it is only when height falls very much below the expected level that it gives cause for concern.

Factors influencing height

Height is determined by the length of the long bones in the body and the spine; anything that affects the growth of these bones will influence the height a person finally reaches. At birth, there exists a program that indicates a person's potential physique. This program is in the genes inherited from the parents. If a baby passes through childhood untroubled by serious disease and is adequately fed, then he or she will probably achieve this potential stature.

One condition where this probability does not apply is called psychosocial short stature. This happens when a child is deliberately denied or deprived of its mother's love. Physical growth can stop, but when the child is put into a healthy emotional environment, normal growth will resume.

Another cause of dwarfism is due to a condition called achondroplasia. This is an abnormality in the formation of the long bones, so that although these individuals have an average-sized trunk, their arms and legs may be as little as half the length of normal limbs. It is rare to find such people over 4 ft (1.2 m) tall. The condition is passed on through the parents, so producing whole families of shorter people, who marry into their own community and so perpetuate this set of characteristics.

In developed countries, failure to grow in height is not usually due to malnutrition, but can be caused by disease preventing full use of the food that is eaten. A prolonged disease contracted in childhood, such as diabetes, severe asthma, or kidney and heart conditions, can also cause growth to be stunted. Fortunately, however, children have an impressive

A severe deficiency of the hormone thyroxine at birth leads to hypothyroidism, a condition that is characterized by stunted growth and mental retardation.

ability to catch up in growth, once the underlying problem has been addressed.

How growth is controlled

A person's rate of growth is controlled by various hormones, notably the growth hormone from the pituitary gland at the base of the skull, thyroxine from the thyroid gland in the neck, and the sex hormones. The pituitary and thyroid hormones are particularly important; if the slow growth is recognized as being due to a deficiency of one of these, they can then be augmented. This is particularly important in infancy, because brain development is partly dependent on the thyroid hormones and replacement therapy can halt the mental retardation that could result from such a deficiency.

Dysentery

Q I'll be going to South America this summer. Is there a drug I can take with me in case I get amebic dysentery?

A The most sensible course of action would be to try to prevent the disease in the first place. Avoid food prepared with local water, such as fresh salad or washed fruit; drink bottled water or canned drinks; and eat only canned meat and vegetables and fruits that can be peeled or boiled. It is not a good idea to take any drugs for a stomach upset until the cause has been identified, because this may make accurate diagnosis more difficult and could result in inadequate treatment.

Q Is typhoid the same as dysentery?

A No, although there are some similarities between the two. Both are transmitted by contaminated food and water, but typhoid is a form of gastroenteritis (inflammation of the intestines), caused by bacteria belonging to the Salmonella family. The incubation period for typhoid is longer, usually seven–14 days.

Q I work as a cook. Could I be a carrier of dysentery without knowing it?

A It is possible. If you are a carrier you are potentially infectious, particularly because of the nature of your job. If you have some reason to think you are a carrier, you should go to your doctor who will send you for tests. In some countries dysentery is a notifiable disease. This means that the doctor will have to tell the health authorities and can insist that you stop work until you are fully recovered.

Q Can sufferers die from dysentery?

A Dysentery can cause death by dehydration in the very young, the very old, and the very sick. This is far more likely to occur in communities that lack medical facilities and where people have been weakened over a long period by malnutrition.

Wherever there is poor sanitation or the chaos following natural disasters, dysentery can be a major health hazard

Dysentery is a general term for an intestinal infection that causes severe diarrhea and abdominal discomfort. Amebic dysentery that is left untreated can lead to abscesses of the liver. In rare cases the infection may spread to other organs of the body.

Causes
Bacillary dysentery is caused by one of four different bacteria belonging to the Shigella family. Amebic dysentery results from an infection caused by a different tiny organism, the protozoan *Entamoeba histolytica*.

Both diseases are commonly found in tropical countries, but bacillary dysentery can occur worldwide. They are transmitted by food or drinking water that has been contaminated by feces, either directly or by flies and other insects.

Epidemics of bacillary dysentery often occur where there are crowded conditions with poor sanitation. They often follow in the wake of major disasters such as earthquakes and hurricanes, but sometimes occur in schools and institutions.

Amebic dysentery does not cause epidemics, but tends to be prevalent in the homosexual community.

Symptoms and side effects
The incubation period of bacillary dysentery lasts from 12–36 hours. Symptoms include abdominal pain and profuse diarrhea with mucus or blood.

Amebic dysentery develops more gradually. It causes bloody diarrhea, abdominal pain, and flatulence. An occasional side effect of bacillary dysentery is arthritis affecting the knees or ankles. This can last for months or years afterward.

Treatment
Bacillary dysentery is treated with kaolin (kaopectate) or codeine to reduce the diarrhea and abdominal pain. The patient must drink large quantities of liquid to prevent dehydration. Flagyl is used to treat amebic dysentery, and patients should drink plenty of fluids.

Outlook
The outlook is good for adult sufferers who are otherwise healthy. Patients with bacillary dysentery usually recover within a week. Amebic dysentery is difficult to get rid of and occasionally an inflammation of the colon will lead to a blockage some years later. Usually, however, a complete recovery is possible.

Types of dysentery

Bacillary dysentery

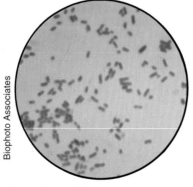

Biophoto Associates

Incubation period
12–24 hours, sometimes three days

Symptoms
Abdominal pain, profuse diarrhea containing blood or mucus. Symptoms last four–7 days

Treatment
Drink plenty of liquids. Take codeine or kaolin (kaopectate) to reduce diarrhea and pain. Take cipro antibiotics

Amebic dysentery

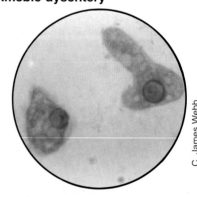

C. James Webb

Incubation period
Onset of the disease is very gradual

Symptoms
Abdominal pain, profuse diarrhea, flatulence. Symptoms last until the disease clears up

Treatment
With emetine, or flagyl and chloraquine. Drink plenty of liquids

Dyslexia

Q My son is dyslexic and left-handed. Is there a relation between the two?

A Yes. Left-handed people are more likely to be dyslexic, but the two do not necessarily go together. This combination may occur because the left half of the brain controls most of the speech processing mechanisms and the actions of the right hand. If there is some brain malfunction in the left half of the brain, the speech process may be affected, leading to dyslexia. At the same time, the right hand may lose its dominance, inducing left-handedness or ambidexterity (the ability to use both hands equally).

Q My daughter has always had difficulty reading, although she tries hard. Could she be dyslexic?

A Dyslexia often includes being a bad reader, among other things. Do not assume that she is dyslexic, however. She may have faulty vision or hearing, so have these checked. Alternatively she may be a late developer, have emotional problems that interfere with her concentration, or not have had enough exposure to reading and writing.

Once you have eliminated these possibilities, find out what types of reading mistakes she makes and try to get an assessment of whether these mistakes are of the type associated with dyslexia. Ask whether she is receiving remedial reading at school and if not, ask for this to be arranged. If she is dyslexic, special lessons will help, but occasionally not everything she has missed can be made up and she may have to learn to live with this fact.

Q My wife and I both always misread certain words. For example, we always read *methodical* as *mythical*. Is this an example of dyslexia?

A No. This kind of slip is due to a chance original misreading which you found amusing. Thereafter, you remembered the event and locked the two words together in your memory.

One of the first real tasks children are faced with at school is learning to read and write. Most manage fairly well, but some do not. One possible reason for this is that they may be dyslexic.

Ray Green

Helping dyslexic children as much as possible will insure that they become more competent readers.

Dyslexia is extreme difficulty with reading and writing; *word blindness* is just one of the terms used to describe its many facets. It affects about one in ten children, is more prevalent among boys than girls, and is caused either by a small number of faulty cells in the brain, or by a delayed or incomplete development in one part of the brain.

If untreated, its consequences are serious, because they will affect the child's progress in school, which in turn will create difficulties in adult life. Fortunately if dyslexia is recognized early, there is much that can be done to remedy the problem.

Causes

Dyslexia is caused by a localized brain lesion (an area of scar tissue) that can arise from either a brain injury or incomplete brain development. However, dyslexics should never be thought of as brain-damaged because this implies that the whole brain is seriously affected, which is not the case.

Dyslexia may be inherited; in about half of all cases it runs in families. It may strike both male and female members of the family, but it need not affect all members. It may produce different effects in different members of the same family, or affect them to very different degrees.

Yet whether the hereditary theory is valid or not, it is evident that in dyslexia something goes wrong in the perception of words or letters. There is nothing wrong with the dyslexic's hearing or vision. The information goes into the brain satisfactorily, but something goes awry at the recording or playback stage, or at the stage that converts marks on a paper to sound, or vice versa.

Symptoms

As it is a symptom of a small and localized brain malfunction or incomplete development, dyslexia can take many forms. Sometimes it is confined to difficulty in reading and affects the person's ability to understand not only long or complex words, but also words of one syllable. Often writing is affected, either because

Last Monday we went to the zoo. We spent much time in front of an iron cage which held seven monkeys. They made us laugh when they put out their paws for nuts.

This is a sample of writing from dictation of an 11-year-old dyslexic. Note the variety of errors in spelling and use of words and punctuation.

the child has difficulty in forming letter shapes or because spelling is affected.

Sometimes an inability to do arithmetic is involved, though the difficulty may largely be to do with problems of writing down numbers correctly. Some children with this form of dyslexia perform fairly well with verbal questions. If asked to write down the answer, however, they reverse the correct order of the numbers or even include a completely irrelevant number. Alternatively, there may be difficulties in touch recognition, where the child fails to recognize the shape of an object that he or she handles, or cannot tell the identity of a letter or number traced with the fingers. However, a dyslexic may have only one or a combination of these difficulties.

Dangers

Although dyslexia affects one ability, albeit an important one, many people believe that other skills are affected too, which is untrue. Thus dyslexics may be labeled as lazy, wilfully disobedient, or dumb, and typecast as not being worth worrying about or bothering with.

Consequently the child may be relegated to a slow-learning group, and being often otherwise bright and intelligent, will become bored by school, come to dislike it, and start playing truant. He or she will fail examinations, be left further behind, and if the dyslexia is untreated, the child will not be able to catch up.

Treatment

Once the problem has been recognized, there are remedial programs for both children and adults, some of which may have to be tailored to the individual. This special program will not only help with the general difficulties of reading and writing, but will also teach the speedy

recognition of road signs and essential words such as danger, fire, no entry, caution, and so on.

Released from the pressure of achieving a normal reading competence, the child may start to feel confident in other fields. Oral instruction, tape-recorded notes, films, pictures, or video tapes are other alternative learning methods the child can use to minimize reading difficulties and boost word recognition.

Outlook

Dyslexia sometimes improves and even disappears by itself. This is either because the brain has finished its delayed development, or it has found some alternative way of achieving the necessary processing, for example, through bypassing the brain lesions that originally caused the trouble. In other cases skilled help with reading and writing problems will minimize, or even eliminate, the deficiencies that the child would otherwise retain.

The most common kinds of mistakes that are made by dyslexics

Confusion of letters similar in shape: d and b, u and n
Confusion of letters similar in sound: v, f, and th
Reversals: was and saw
Transposals: left and felt

Reading
Difficulty in keeping place on a line
Difficulty in switching from end of line to start of next line
Mispronunciation: "rember" for remember, "merains" for remains
Intonation in the wrong place

Writing
Shortening: rember for remember
Letter fusion: "up" for up, "and" for and
Repetition of a word or words
Capitals in the wrong places
Difficulty keeping on the line

Remember:
Every child makes these kinds of mistakes when first learning to read. Do not label a child as dyslexic just because these mistakes occur

---

Helping young dyslexics

Do
- Praise the child when possible; dyslexic children are ashamed of their difficulty and suffer from doubts and uncertainties about their other skills
- Concentrate on the child's strengths; this will build confidence
- Help with longer words by dividing syllables with a pencil line
- Teach correct pronunciation
- Give the child plenty of time with any reading done with your help. Dyslexic children may not understand what they have read, or they may read something correctly one day but then get it wrong the next

Don't
- Ridicule the child about lack of reading skill
- Give the child long lists of words to learn
- Compare him or her with other children, especially siblings
- Overdo remedial work; dyslexics tire more easily than other children when trying to read
- Try to make the child tidy or neaten his or her writing style
- Think the child is dreaming if he or she looks away from reading material; there may be difficulty focusing on the page or finding the place he or she last stopped

Ectopic pregnancy

Q A friend of mine had an ectopic pregnancy a few months ago. She was told it was possible for her to have a normal pregnancy afterward, but it might take her longer to conceive. Why is this?

A When a fertilized egg gets implanted in the fallopian tube, it may be necessary for a surgeon to remove all or part of that tube. However, as long as the tube and the ovary on the other side of the body remain unharmed, there is no reason why she should not be able to go on to have a perfectly normal pregnancy.

One reason it may take longer for conception to take place is that the eggs are usually released from alternate ovaries in alternate months, so an egg will pass down the remaining fallopian tube only every other month.

Q I had an ectopic pregnancy while I was using an IUD. How could this happen?

A The IUD does not prevent fertilization from taking place; it just prevents the fertilized egg from implanting in the uterus. It is therefore still possible for the egg to implant in ectopic sites.

Q I once heard someone claim a baby was born as a result of an ectopic pregnancy. Can this be true?

A Yes, on very rare occasions. In one case, recorded in 1965, a surgeon opened the abdomen of a woman seven-and-a-half months pregnant, who had suddenly experienced severe abdominal pain. To his amazement, he found a 4 lb 6 oz (1.9 kg) baby not in her uterus, but in her abdominal cavity. Both mother and baby survived and the baby was completely normal and healthy.

It is sometimes possible for a case like this to occur because the embryo and its surrounding tissue works through the wall of the fallopian tube and is then free to find a better site for development. The potential danger in this situation is that the fetus will be poorly protected without the wall of the uterus around it.

Occasionally a fertilized egg begins to grow in the wrong place in a woman's body. Such a pregnancy needs to be detected early and treated promptly.

Pregnancy outside the uterus

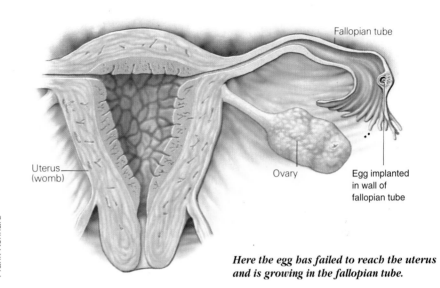

Uterus (womb) · Fallopian tube · Ovary · Egg implanted in wall of fallopian tube

Frank Kennard

Here the egg has failed to reach the uterus and is growing in the fallopian tube.

An ectopic pregnancy is one in which a fertilized egg implants itself outside the uterus. There are four places where this usually happens: in a fallopian tube, an ovary, the abdominal cavity, or the cervix. However, the last three are extremely rare sites for implantation and an ectopic pregnancy usually means that the egg lodges in a fallopian tube.

How it happens
Normally, an egg is released from one of the ovaries and begins traveling down a fallopian tube toward the uterus. The egg is fertilized in the tube and then continues down the remainder of the tube, embedding itself after about a week in the lining of the uterus.

With an ectopic pregnancy, the fertilized egg is delayed on its journey to the uterus and becomes embedded in the wall of the fallopian tube. It then begins to develop just as if it were in the uterus. A placenta starts to form, but it lacks the nutritious blood supply of the uterus and it has no room to grow.

Symptoms
In the early stages of an ectopic pregnancy, there is rarely any reason to suspect that anything is wrong. The first signs of trouble usually occur between the sixth and the 12th weeks. Severe pain is felt in the lower part of the abdomen, often down one side, and is sometimes so intense that it makes the woman faint.

There is no bleeding at first. This pain may be mistaken for a miscarriage, but the difference between the two is that in a miscarriage pain always follows bleeding, whereas in an ectopic pregnancy, pain comes first.

The pain is actually caused by the growing embryo stretching the fallopian tube so much that it triggers contractions of muscles in the wall of the tube, or because the embryo has grown so big that the fallopian tube bursts open.

Treatment
Any woman who experiences pain in early pregnancy should go to her doctor as soon as possible. If it is an ectopic pregnancy, the embryo may burst through the fallopian tube, leading to severe internal bleeding.

If there is no doubt about the diagnosis after examination, then an abdominal operation must be performed to remove the whole or part of the bleeding fallopian tube, together with the pregnancy. If there is a doubt, laparoscopy (where pelvic organs are viewed through a laparoscope inserted below the navel) may be performed to check.

Outlook
Statistics show that there is a 10 percent risk of having a second ectopic pregnancy. So if there has been a previous ectopic pregnancy, a woman should have a check-up as soon as she knows she is pregnant.

Eczema

Q My five-year-old son has had eczema for a year now. I'm told it may get better as he gets older. Is this true?

A Half the children who suffer from eczema when they are very young have grown out of it by the time they are six, and in most of the others it will have cleared up by their teens. However, eczema is notorious for disappearing and reappearing without obvious cause. It does sometimes return in adolescence or adulthood, especially at times of stress.

Q If I touch or sit near someone with eczema, will I catch it?

A Definitely not. Eczema is not infectious and cannot be passed from person to person. Scratching inflamed skin may make the sufferer prone to infections, but this does not make eczema in any way a contagious disease.

Q I have heard that sunshine will do my eczema good, so should I sunbathe while I'm on vacation?

A Generally, sunshine, or to be more exact, the ultraviolet rays in sunlight, is good for the skin and will improve eczema. But some sufferers are very sensitive to sunlight, and their eczema gets worse if it is exposed to strong sun. So if your eczema seems worse while you are on vacation, stop sunbathing immediately.

Q Is it safe for people with eczema to swim in the sea or in public swimming pools?

A Eczema sufferers should take care swimming, not so much because of any risk of infection to them or other people, but because it tends to make dry skin even dryer. Ointments and creams protect the skin against drying out and sufferers who like swimming can use them.

Q Will breast-feeding stop my baby from getting eczema?

A This is possible, though it has not yet been proven.

Eczema is an irritating and unsightly skin condition, but it is a nuisance rather than a danger and can be controlled by simple treatment.

Eczema is a skin complaint that affects about one person in 12 at some point in their lives. It is an unpredictable and rather puzzling disease, often caused by allergies, but just as frequently brought on by emotional upsets or by no obvious cause. It can be distressing, not only because it is irritating and itchy, but also because it affects many visible parts of the body.

The most familiar form of eczema, the scientific name is *atopic dermatitis*, is closely related to asthma and hay fever. It is quite common for people who have it to have one or both of these other complaints, too. Hay fever is clearly an allergic disease, usually brought on by exposure to pollen. Asthma and eczema also can be caused by an allergy to inhaled substances, such as pollen, or by an allergy to a particular food, notably eggs and cow's milk. However, this is not always the case; attacks often occur at times of stress (see Allergies).

Eczema usually makes its first appearance during infancy or early childhood and tends to fade away as the child gets older. Sometimes, however, it appears in an adult who has not suffered from eczema as a child. Most people who get it come from families with a history of eczema, asthma, or hay fever, although it is common for one child in a family to be affected while the others escape it altogether. Babies may suffer from eczema because they are allergic to cow's milk, and recent research suggests that babies from families with a tendency toward eczema have a better chance of avoiding it if they are breast-fed for at least a few months.

Symptoms

The most typical sign of eczema is an inflamed area of skin that becomes dry and cracked or covered with tiny red pimples or blisters. The most annoying symptom is an itch. Scratching the irritating area aggravates the condition, causing wet, bleeding sores, and increasing the risk of infection spreading to other parts of the body. Eczema usually appears first on the face and scalp, and then spreads to the hands and limbs, especially to places where the skin folds or is rubbed by clothing. Much of the discomfort of eczema is caused by the scratching of patches or the rash, rather than by the eczema itself.

Cotton mittens will prevent a young child from scratching the eczema itch to ease the irritation, which can make the affected patches of skin very sore.

Precautions

Eczema in itself is not dangerous or in any way a threat to life. The main problem for the parents of a child with eczema is to discourage him or her from making the condition worse by scratching the affected skin. Young babies with eczema often rub themselves on their bedclothes in a vain attempt to make the itch go away. Little children can be protected from hurting themselves if they wear cotton mittens in bed (and also during the day, if necessary) to prevent them from scratching the itchy skin.

It is essential that eczema sufferers should not come into direct contact with anyone who has cold sores (herpes simplex), because eczematous skin is very vulnerable to the herpes virus, and is liable to widespread infection if it is exposed to it. Obviously friends or relatives with a cold sore should not kiss anyone with eczema.

People who suffer, or who have suffered from eczema in the past, are more sensitive than most to irritant chemicals, so it would be wise for them to avoid jobs that involve exposure to these substances. The risks are considerably reduced by taking such simple precautions as wearing gloves and a face mask, but young people with eczema should think twice before accepting a job where it would be difficult to avoid well-known irritants, such as resins, shampoos, and caustic chemicals.

Treatment

If the eczema can be traced to an allergy, clearly the particular cause (the allergen) should be avoided. Breast-feeding disposes of the problem of an allergy to cow's milk in young babies, but if the mother cannot breast-feed, or if the child has to be weaned early, there are alternatives. Goat's milk does not cause allergic eczema as often as cow's milk and there are also artificial milks based on soya that provide a nutritious diet for babies. It is important to talk to the doctor before giving a baby either goat's or soya milk.

Dealing with an allergy is often only a part of the problem; other measures are necessary to relieve the eczema and prevent it from getting worse. First, materials such as wool that can irritate sensitive areas should be kept away from the skin. If skin is dry and cracked it should not be washed too often, since this will tend to dry it even more. Obviously it should be kept clean to discourage infection, but in place of soap, people with eczema should use aqueous cream or emulsifying ointment, both available from drugstores.

Alternatively, bath products containing mineral oil, when added to the bath water, prevent the skin from drying out;

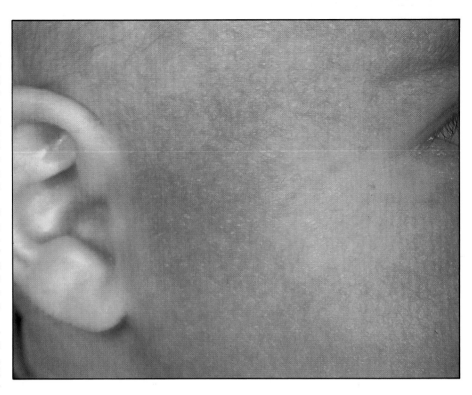

various brands can be bought from drugstores or obtained on prescription from the family doctor.

Medical help

There are a variety of medicines to control the inflammation and itching of the skin. Zinc paste and coal tar are old and tried prescription remedies, sometimes applied in specially prepared bandages that are laid on the skin and covered with a protective layer of cotton. Creams containing small amounts of steroids, such as hydrocortisone, can reduce inflammation and itching, but they should only be applied for limited periods and on a doctor's advice; their continual use could damage the skin.

Creams containing urea are sometimes prescribed to increase the water content of the skin to counteract the dryness of eczema, and an antihistamine drug can control the itching and burning sensations. A drug called sodium cromoglycate, also used in the treatment of asthma, has proven useful in controlling the effects of food allergies and can be prescribed in pill form by a doctor.

Because people with eczema have an often irresistible temptation to scratch their skin, they should keep their fingernails short, smooth, and clean. Where possible, they should wear cotton gloves or even mittens, because these prevent independent finger movements.

Eczema is generally not serious enough to require hospital treatment. However, in certain cases, children seem to benefit

Eczema usually appears first on the face and scalp. The skin is inflamed, dry, and cracked or covered with tiny red bumps.

from getting away from their home environment. This is particularly the case when they are upset or worried by some aspect of home life or school, even though the cause of their distress may not be obvious to the rest of their family, teachers, or other outside observers.

Outlook

The chances are that children with eczema will grow out of it after a time. Fifty percent of children who suffer are free of it by their sixth birthday, and only 10 percent still have it by the time they reach their teens.

However, like most allergic complaints, eczema has a habit of vanishing only to make an unwelcome return in adolescence or adulthood. Emotional stress seems to be the main cause of its reappearance; exams, job worries, and moving to a new house are typical triggers.

Uncomfortable and unsightly as eczema can be, it is not something to brood over. Parents who worry about their child's skin will make the child worry also, and that is more likely to aggravate the condition than it is to improve it. Although eczema cannot yet be cured, it can be relieved and controlled by medicines and ointments and so it should be seen as a nuisance, and probably a passing one, rather than a cause for alarm.

Edema

Areas of swelling indicate a fault in the body's drainage system. It is usually due to heart or liver disease but can have other causes.

Q Is there any connection between varicose veins and edema?

A Yes. The veins in our legs have valves that prevent blood from moving back toward the ankles. Varicose veins are veins that have become swollen and stretched so that the valves cannot stop the blood from slipping back. This leads to a rise in pressure with swelling as a result. Varicose veins that cause problems can be treated by surgery.

Q Why do pregnant women sometimes get edema?

A This happens because their blood volume increases as a result of retaining more salt than normal. Salt retention is due to a rise in certain hormones, especially estrogen and progesterone, which increase during pregnancy.

Q If I am cured of edema, will the skin around my ankles be loose and flabby?

A No. The skin is usually very tight and will not become loose once the edema goes away.

Q I have swollen ankles because of a leg thrombosis that happened three months ago. When will they get better?

A It sometimes takes many months for ankle swelling caused by damage to deep veins to heal completely. The swelling can be controlled by wearing an elastic stocking and by sitting with the legs propped up.

Q I have been given water pills by my doctor and he says I must take potassium pills with them. Why?

A Water pills stop the kidneys from reabsorbing the salt they filter out. Through the loss of salt and water, the volume of blood falls and the swelling subsides. As these pills remove potassium too, it is sometimes necessary to take extra to make up the loss, otherwise symptoms of potassium deficiency may occur.

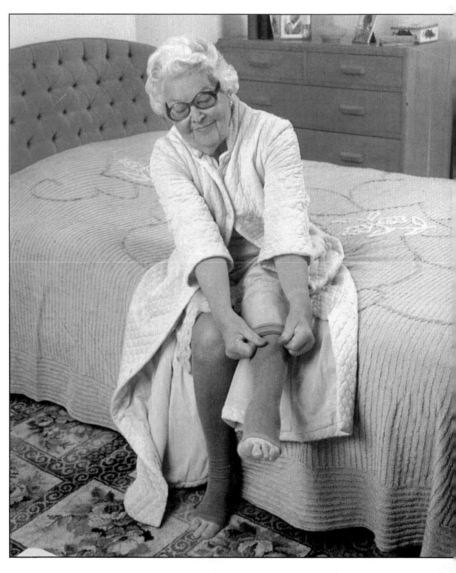

It is normal for blood vessels to leak a small amount of fluid. This fluid is usually removed by an efficient drainage system, the lymphatic vessels (see Lymphatic system). Sometimes the drainage system fails, however, and the fluid builds up in a condition known as edema.

Causes
Fluid leaks out of blood vessels because their walls are thin and the blood that circulates around the body is being pumped by the heart under considerable pressure. Fluid returns to the blood vessels by a process known as osmosis.

Osmosis takes place when fluid passes from a weak solution to a strong solution

Mild edema that leads to swollen ankles can be helped by elastic stockings that squeeze fluid out of the affected area. Any swelling of the joints, including the ankles, however, should be reported to your doctor.

across a semipermeable membrane. The walls of blood vessels form semipermeable membranes. Inside the vessels flows a strong solution of proteins, the natural constituents of blood. It is these proteins that suck back in a lot of the fluid that has seeped out.

Malnutrition or liver disease can cause a lack of protein in the blood, and this is a common cause of edema. Fluid may also accumulate because the drainage

460

system—either the lymphatic vessels or the veins—is obstructed and pressure builds up. This is why thrombosis and varicose veins sometimes cause ankle swelling. Heart failure can lead to a back-up of blood in the veins.

When the kidneys fail to remove excessive salt from the blood, or if we eat too much salt with fluids, the volume of fluid in the blood vessels increases greatly and so does the rate at which fluid leaks out.

If the kidneys are working properly, the rate at which salt is passed into the urine is regulated by the adrenal hormones. The balance of these hormones changes during pregnancy and menstruation and at these times salt retention may result in slight edema.

Special types of edema
Gravity determines where any edema occurs. The most common place is around the ankles. After a patient has spent a long period in bed, however, edema fluid may collect around the buttocks or at the base of the spine.

Severe heart failure, liver failure, or obstruction of any of the large veins in the abdomen cause fluid to collect inside the abdominal cavity. This is known as ascites.

Fluid also accumulates in the lungs if the left side of the heart fails. This causes severe breathlessness with a cough and frothy sputum (spit), and requires emergency attention.

Symptoms
Ankle edema is easy to see if the ankles are grossly swollen, but slight swelling can be more difficult to detect. Fluid tends to collect first on the inner side of the ankle, just behind the ankle bone.

Breathlessness at rest is a symptom of pulmonary edema, when the lungs become filled with fluid.

Dangers
Ankle edema is not dangerous in itself, but it may be a symptom of a more serious condition such as heart disease, which requires treatment.

Severe pulmonary edema is a medical emergency. If it is not treated quickly, the patient will become extremely short of breath, as if he or she were drowning in the body's own edema fluid. Prompt treatment with drugs usually leads to recovery.

Treatment
Edema caused by leakage from aging and thin blood vessels can be controlled by wearing elastic stockings, which squeeze the fluid out of the ankles.

If the fundamental cause of the edema is heart failure, however, the main treat-

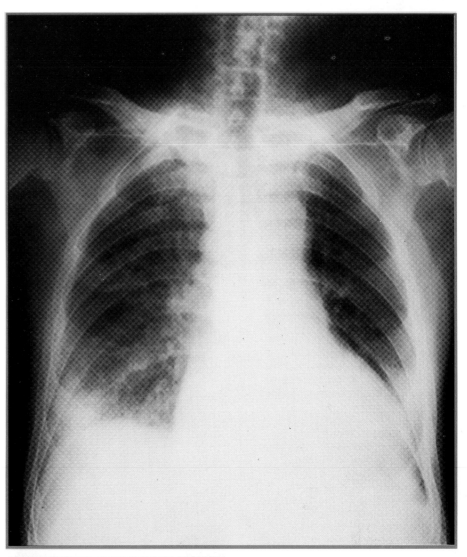

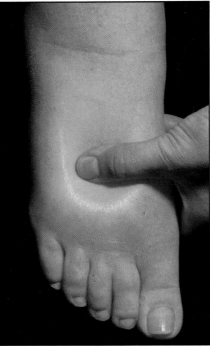

The X ray (above) shows lungs containing fluid as a result of pulmonary edema. This condition is treated by a diuretic, injected into the vein.

Edema of the foot and ankle (left) leads to a swelling pronounced enough for a dent to be left after finger pressure is applied.

ment is to lessen the strain on the heart by reducing the volume of blood circulating around the body. This is done by taking pills called diuretics, which make the patient urinate, therefore reducing the level of salt in the body. It is also helpful to limit salt in the diet, and sometimes it is necessary to take a potassium supplement.

Pulmonary edema is treated with a fast-acting diuretic, which is given intravenously. Oxygen given through a mask may also be needed.

The treatment for thrombosis of the veins involves thinning the blood by using anticoagulants. Varicose veins can be removed surgically.

Elbow

The elbow plays a vital and complex part in a whole range of intricate movements, yet its structure is based on two simple joints: the hinge, and the ball-and-socket.

Because the elbow is vital to movements of the arm and hand, it is one of the most important joints in the body. Any injury to it can be painful and debilitating.

Structure

The elbow is the meeting place for the ends of the three main bones in the arm: the humerus (the single bone in the upper arm), the radius, and the ulna (the two bones of the forearm). These three bones are connected in two joints, each making a different range of limb movements possible.

Between the ulna, which is the longer of the two forearm bones, and the humerus bone of the upper arm, there is a hinge joint that allows the elbow to be bent up and down; this action moves the hand from the shoulder down to the side of the body and back again. In this joint, a rollerlike extension called the trochlea at the lower end of the humerus, moves within a hollow near the head of the

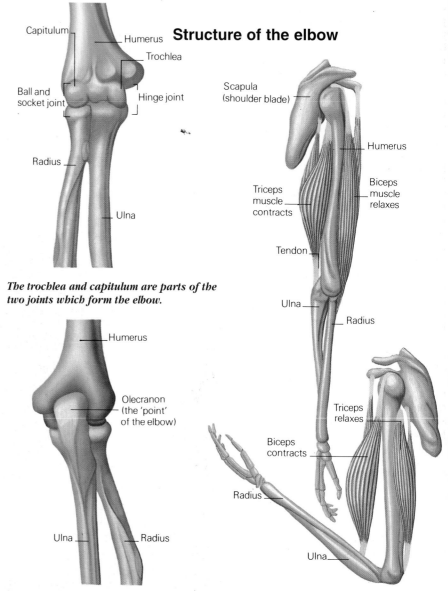

Structure of the elbow

The trochlea and capitulum are parts of the two joints which form the elbow.

The olecranon, the bony projection beyond the hollow at the head of the ulna, forms the point of the elbow.

The biceps muscle runs from the shoulder to the top of the radius; the triceps from the shoulder to the humerus and ulna.

ulna. Beyond this hollow is a projection of bone, the olecranon, which forms the point of the elbow.

Between the radius and the humerus there is a ball-and-socket joint, the socket lying on the radius, the ball part formed by a spherical projection of bone on the outer end of the humerus, the capitulum. This second joint is also involved in bending movements, but its main function is to make possible the rotation of the elbow so that the palm of the hand faces outward, although the extent of the movement is rather limited.

Movement

During movements of the elbow, the radius and the ulna always move together, because they are joined just below the elbow itself and at the wrist. When the palm is facing outward, the two bones lie parallel to one another, but when the back of the hand is uppermost—its most usual position—the bones are crossed over one another.

If the arm is held straight down and the elbow is then turned so that the palm of the hand faces outward, the part of the arm below the elbow automatically moves outward at an angle from the side of the body. This angle, formed by the positioning of the bones in the elbow, is known as the carrying angle and it is vital to prevent the arms from banging into the sides of the body when it is in motion. The angle also helps to increase the precision with which a tool can be held in the hand while the arm is being straightened out.

To allow smooth movement, the ends of all bones that meet in the elbow are covered with translucent hyaline cartilage (connective tissue) that provides a low-friction surface. The synovial membrane, the lining of the elbow, secretes a clear liquid called synovial fluid, which lubricates the whole joint. Covering the membrane is a capsule of fibrous tissue; surrounding the elbow, and between the tissue and the membrane, are several small pads of fat that help to cushion the joint against injury.

If it were not well supported, the elbow would be in danger of dislocation every time the arm moved. It is kept in place by strong ligaments that join the humerus with both the radius and the ulna, and bind the latter two bones together.

Movement of the elbow is made possible by a variety of muscles, joined to the bones by tough, sinewy tendons. These are protected by sacs, called bursae, which lie between tendon and bone and prevent friction. Not only are the bursae similar in structure to the capsule joint of the whole elbow, but fluid also flows between them.

Injuries

The most common wear and tear injury is called tennis elbow. This is a form of bursitis, in which the bursae in the joint become inflamed and produce too much fluid. Like other joints, the elbow may be affected by osteoarthritis (degeneration of the cartilage lining the joint, and of the bones themselves); it is most common in people who have put great strain on their elbows in the course of a lifetime. For example, men who have regularly used pneumatic drills are particularly prone to osteoarthritis of the elbow.

Damage to the elbow is very likely to result from falls or other accidents. It may involve tearing or rupturing of the tendons, ligaments, or muscles; dislocating the bones, so that they are moved out of their correct positions; or fracturing the ends of the bones that form the joint.

Since the injured elbow may have to be manipulated to get the bones back into their proper positions, all such injuries need prompt medical attention. If the ends of the bones have been broken, surgery may be required to pin the bones back into place. Whatever the injury, it is usual for the elbow to be immobilized in a plaster of paris cast until it has healed. This is followed by physiotherapy to help get the joint mobile again.

Even with expert medical attention, elbow injuries often result in permanent stiffness of the joint. One cause of this is that, for some unknown reason, injury to the internal tissues of the elbow is often followed by an abnormal growth of bony tissue within the joint, at the site of the injury. This growth, called the myositis ossificans, is difficult to treat; if it is removed surgically, this simply serves to stimulate the abnormal bone growth again and it soon reforms.

In children, a fracture of the elbow is serious. The break, which occurs near the top of the humerus, is usually the result of a fall onto outstretched hands. The danger of the injury is that it may cut off the blood supply to the forearm and also damage the nerves of the arm.

Treatment

If there is severe swelling and the injured elbow cannot be moved, the patient should be taken immediately to the hospital emergency room for treatment. Even if the elbow injury does not seem serious, the pulse in the wrist should be checked and if it is weak or absent, the patient should be taken to the hospital at once. If there is any chance that the circulation in the arm has been impeded, it will be necessary for the patient to stay in the hospital until the surgeon is absolutely sure that all is well.

One form of bursitis (inflammation of the bursae protecting the tendons that join muscle to bone) is called tennis elbow.

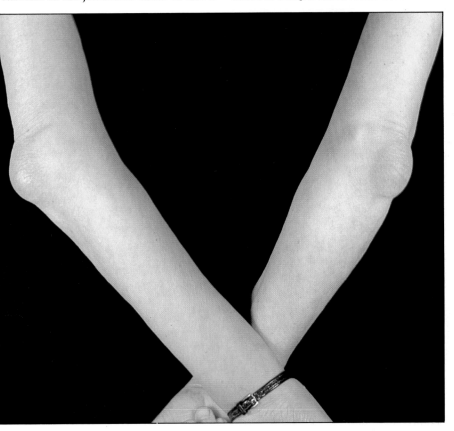

Electric shocks

Q I have always been afraid of being struck by lightning. If I were caught in a violent electrical storm, where is the best place to take cover?

A If you are indoors, stay there. Inside, keep away from windows, open doors, fireplaces, metal pipes, sinks, and plugged-in appliances. Remember that electricity always flows toward the earth and that metal and water are good conductors. If you are outdoors, stay away from metal fences or other metal structures, tractors, power lines, isolated trees, and hilltops. Do not hold onto metal objects such as umbrellas, golf clubs, fishing lines, or bicycles. Seek shelter in a building or if there is none, at least avoid water; find a valley and lie down. If you are in a closed-top car, stay inside.

Q A friend who is a handyman tells me that I can test whether an electric outlet is live by touching it with the back of my hand. Is this dangerous?

A Yes, extremely so. If the outlet were live, the shock would make your arm jerk away. But any attempt to touch a live wire carries too much risk of damage and this test should never be tried.

Q I have only one electric outlet in my room. Is it safe to use several electric appliances on it?

A This is not advisable. A single socket with a lot of appliances has to cope with a power demand for which it was not designed. However, you can use a multi-plug bar in one outlet because they are wired for extra input.

Q My father had to have his arm amputated after a severe electric shock. Why was this necessary?

A Electricity can kill tissues, both directly by burning and indirectly by interfering with their blood supply. After a severe shock, the arm might have contained so much dead tissue that it no longer functioned as a limb.

Most accidents involving electricity need not happen. Countless lives could be saved if just a little extra care were taken—especially in the home.

It is not easy to describe an electric shock to someone who has not experienced one. The effect varies from a mildly unpleasant tingling to severe muscle spasms, destruction of tissues, and failure of heartbeat and breathing. Even low-voltage electricity can harm or kill if the current goes through important parts of the body. The duration, degree, and area of contact affects the intensity of shock, and so do the resistance of clothing and of different tissues.

The greatest dangers

Electricity enters a moist body far more easily than a dry one. It travels readily along blood vessels and nerves, but badly through bone. What the victim is touching affects how the electricity will flow through them. A person is in more danger when barefoot or touching metal pipes than when wearing rubber-soled shoe or standing on a thick carpet or rubbe mat, because these substances are poo conductors of electricity.

Another important factor is the natur of the current. A direct current, like on from a battery, flows in one directio only. It stimulates muscles to contract a the moment it makes contact, for exam ple, when a live point is touched, or at th moment contact is broken. In between, i does not stimulate muscles, though i may burn.

An alternating current is one whos direction is repeatedly changing. It i used for most industrial and domestic purposes. Unfortunately, this frequency i most dangerous to nerves and muscles The fast changes of current act as if th electrical contact were constantly being made and broken. The muscles, therefore

Statistics of deaths in the home

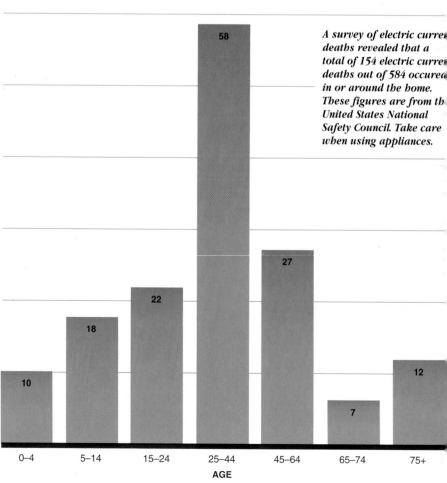

A survey of electric curren deaths revealed that a total of 154 electric curren deaths out of 584 occurred in or around the home. These figures are from th United States National Safety Council. Take care when using appliances.

Emergency treatment for electric shock

FIRST AID

- Call the ambulance as soon as possible and watch for signs of collapse (paleness and sweating of the skin)
- Never rush to touch the victim, or you may be electrocuted too. He or she must first be released from the current before any rescue measures can be safely performed
- Switch off current immediately. If there is no way to do this or if it cannot quickly be done, try to disconnect the current by pulling out the plug or pulling on the insulated cable
- Do not move the victim unless necessary for resuscitation, since there is a danger of fractures if the victim fell or was thrown
- Look for burns and wounds and cover them with dry dressings
- It is quite safe to attend to a person struck by lightning, because the current will have passed to the earth
- If you cannot switch off the current, knock the victim from contact using dry a nonconducting material, e.g. a wooden broom, wooden chair, or thick coat. Or pull with a rope or pole hooked in the victim's armpit. If you are desperate and you are wearing dry shoes, kick hard very quickly
- Once the current has been interrupted, it is safe for you to touch the victim. Give artificial respiration and heart massage if needed and if you are properly trained. Resuscitation may have to be continued for a prolonged period before the victim resumes normal breathing
- If the victim is breathing, put him or her into the recovery position—lying on one side with the lower arm and leg stretched out straight

go into strong spasm. If a person picked up an electrically faulty skillet or an iron with a current leaking through the handle, the muscles working the fingers would close the fist firmly and the person would not be able to let go.

Effects

Electricity may leave a dark mark when it enters the body, often pitting the skin. The size of the injury can be misleading and is no indication of how the current may have fanned out deeper down, killing a large section of tissue. The larger blood vessels may be severely damaged and liable to bleed days after the accident. Clotting may occur in smaller vessels, blocking the flow of blood. Electricity through the brain and nervous system may cause loss of consciousness and paralysis.

The current can disrupt the working of the heart muscles. Instead of the strong beat that makes the blood circulate, there may only be a feeble trembling.

Alternating current through the chest can cause spasms of the rib muscles and diaphragm, so that breathing ceases. If limb and body muscles contract violently, the victim may be thrown, thus creating other injuries, including broken bones.

In milder cases of electric shock, the victim may feel only slightly shaken at the time. He or she may congratulate him- or herself on having escaped lightly, but may collapse later. This could be due to burns and also to damage to the nervous system. In any but the slightest electric shock—the kind that leaves no mark on the skin and gives only a brief, slight tingling—get medical help immediately.

Safety in the home

Unless it is properly safeguarded, the bathroom could be a danger area. It should feature no socket outlets (except for those designed for electric razors); neither should any electrical apparatus be brought in from another room. Electric heaters should be placed away from the bath and out of reach, high on the wall.

In the kitchen, do not handle switches, plugs, or appliances with wet hands. Do not use appliances while standing on a wet floor or while touching metal pipes. Switch off and disconnect any apparatus before filling, pouring, cleaning, or adjusting. Fill electric jugs away from electric rings, and never pour fat from an electric skillet while it is switched on or even plugged in. Never poke a utensil into the toaster while it is plugged in.

Make sure that plugs are securely connected to the wire; replace them if they are damaged. If a plug or outlet becomes warm or hot when in use, have an expert check it. Avoid overloading outlets with adaptors; try to have one appliance per outlet. Use shuttered or covered types so that children cannot poke objects into them. Switch off all apparatus, including the television, when not in use, and

With a little common sense, electrical household appliances are safe to use.

Brian Nash

Danger watchpoint

The high voltages of power plants and of their overhead wires are extremely lethal. The electricity may flash out toward anyone approaching the live equipment before he or she has made direct contact. Rescue is risky. Keep at least 20 yd (18 m) away from the electricity source until the current has been stopped. Only attend to a victim who has fallen completely clear of the site.

unplug any appliance before making any repairs.

Fuse wire must be the right grade for the required load; the local electrical company will give advice on this. Do not replace a blown fuse without first switching off the supply at the fuse box.

Electric cords should be as short as possible and should never be patched together with insulating tape. If the cords are frayed anywhere, they must be replaced; no bare wire must ever show. Do not run cords under carpets, and avoid kinked or trailing cords.

When buying appliances, avoid cheap bargains or secondhand items. Faulty wiring in appliances is the cause of many household fires. For example, electric blankets must be of an officially approved design. You must always follow any instructions for use, and have the blanket serviced regularly.

Electrically powered lawn mowers and garden tools must be used with care. Avoid trailing cords and cables lying across the machine's path as the blades can cut into the cord and give the user an electric shock. Do not use in wet conditions, and keep children away at all times. Older children should be warned about climbing trees whose branches may hide dangerous overhead power lines.

Electrocardiogram

Q My father died of a heart attack last year. Should I have an ECG to make sure that I don't have heart disease?

A An ECG can never rule out heart disease. If the test shows positive features, then some sort of heart disease is probably present in the patient.

However, the test can look normal even when there is some sort of heart trouble. For instance, people with quite severe blockages of their coronary arteries (the arteries that supply blood to the heart) may have a normal ECG.

There is no need to visit the doctor unless you are actually getting symptoms, such as pain in the chest. The best preventive measures you can take are to quit smoking and cut down on the amount of animal fat in your diet.

Q I am a very nervous kind of person and I have to have an ECG. Will my nervousness affect the reading taken by the machine?

A No, it should not make any difference. Just occasionally, people can be so shaky that the electrical activity of their muscles shows up on the recording as a wobbly line. This makes it difficult but usually not impossible to interpret the ECG.

Q I have started getting terrible palpitations when I have to run to catch a bus. Do I need to have an ECG to make sure my heart is all right?

A If the palpitations are really worrying you, it is worth having an ECG done to see if there is any disorder of the heart rhythm. However, it is quite normal to feel your heart beating forcefully in your chest after heavy exercise.

Q It always looks very frightening to see someone with wires attached to them. Are there any dangers to having an ECG done?

A No, none whatsoever. Having an ECG is painless, totally safe, and reliable, which is why it is such a widely used test.

Commonly known as an ECG, an electrocardiogram is a recording of the heart's electrical activity, taken to see if there is any disorder in the heart rhythm.

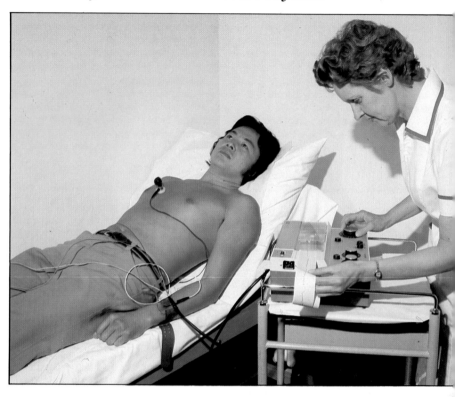

The patient is wired up to the electrocardiograph, which plays out a reading of his heart's electrical activity.

The heart is like a muscular bag that pumps blood by contracting and relaxing. Messages for the muscle to contract (shorten) are carried electrically from one part of the heart to another, and it is this electrical current that can be recorded on a medical instrument called an electrocardiograph.

The reading the instrument gives, called an electrocardiogram (ECG), is extremely useful in diagnosing many heart complaints. The process is totally painless and has no known side effects.

When you might have an ECG

If a person visits the doctor with severe chest pains, it is quite likely that he or she will be advised to have an ECG taken either at the doctor's office or in a hospital. This is used to help the doctor diagnose a wide variety of heart troubles, such as a hole in the heart, a heart attack, or a disorder of heart rhythm (arrhythmia).

Sometimes insurance companies insist on a person having an ECG if they require further information after an initial checkup. Airline pilots, whose jobs involve risk to many others, often have an ECG as a routine part of their yearly medical examination.

How the ECG is taken

Early ECG recordings were made by putting both the patient's arms and one of his or her legs in buckets of salty water (which conducts electricity) and putting a wire from a galvanometer (an instrument for measuring changes in electric currents) into each bucket.

Modern electrocardiographs basically consist of a more sophisticated galvanometer. Instead of putting limbs in buckets of water, the patient sits or lies on a couch and electrodes are attached to each wrist and ankle. These are metal plates held in place by rubber bracelets.

Another electrode is stuck to the front of the chest with a suction cup. This electrode is moved across the chest so that several readings can be taken from various points on the chest. Inside the galvanometer, there is a voltage-sensitive needle with paper passing underneath it. Each time the heart beats, the flow of electricity makes the needle move and the heartbeats are traced on the paper as a series of humps and spikes.

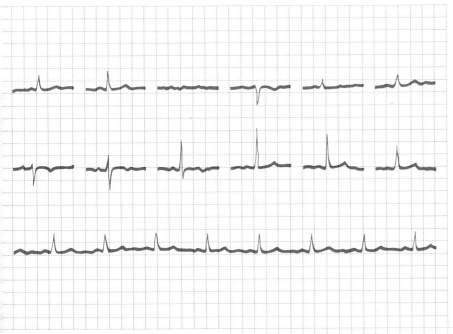

Normal and abnormal ECGs

The tracing of a normal, healthy heart (left). The tracing below shows an abnormality which records as an irregular electrocardiogram pattern.

during physical exercise. This is known as exercise or stress testing.

Other faults

One of the most frequent heart problems is that the atria stop contracting properly and start uncoordinated activity, known as fibrillation. Then the ECG shows no P waves but instead, a wavy line with irregular ventricle spikes.

Since the ventricles are working properly, this is not a serious problem, although patients may experience palpitations (throbs), or the heart may beat too

ECG patterns

The heart has four chambers, two upper, smaller ones known as the left and right atria and the larger, lower chambers, the left and right ventricles. The atria are receiving chambers and the ventricles pumping chambers (see Heart).

The heart must have a sophisticated timing system for it to pump at a regular rate of around 70 beats per minute, with a faster rate if exercising. The timing for the ventricles—the two main pumping chambers—comes from the atria, the thin-walled chambers that collect blood from the lungs and the rest of the body.

Each cardiac (heart) cycle starts with the two atria contracting (getting smaller); then after a small pause, the ventricles contract together. Then they relax and a new cycle begins. This process shows up on the ECG as a small hump known as the P wave, which represents the atria contracting, followed by spikes, which are the ventricles contracting. The spikes are known as the QR and S points.

Most of the electrical activity that the ECG picks up comes from the major thick-walled pumping chamber, the left ventricle, because this contains most of the heart muscle. The major spikes on the recording come from the voltage change as the left ventricle contracts. The ventricles then relax and recharge, shown as the T wave, before the cycle starts again.

The shape of the spikes and waves is different according to which part of the chest they are recorded from.

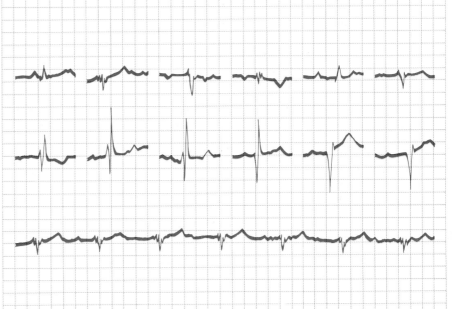

Diagnosing heart attacks

The most important use of the ECG is to show whether a person has suffered a heart attack, or if there is lack of blood

supply to the heart muscle, which can be a cause of both angina and heart attacks.

The change in the pattern will be in the T wave part of the ECG. Subjects with an acute heart attack show an abnormal pattern between the QRS spikes and the T wave. As recovery takes place, the T wave turns upside down. When no heart attack has taken place, but there is lack of blood supply to the muscle, there are often minor changes that are picked up on the ECG while the patient is lying still. These changes may be accentuated if another ECG is taken during or immediately after some form of exercise.

Sometimes the changes are not present at all on the ECG taken at rest, but they become apparent when the ECG is taken

fast. The problem can be solved by giving drugs to slow down the heart rate. There are many other forms of disordered heart rhythm that can be seen from an ECG, some minor and others more serious.

An ECG can also show if the left ventricle has too much work to do, for example, in the case of high blood pressure. When this happens, its muscular wall becomes thicker; this creates a greater flow of current, which in turn will make the spikes larger on the ECG reading.

After the ECG

If the ECG is taken at a doctor's office, the result will be available immediately. Hospital results take slightly longer, after which the doctor can start treatment.

John Hutchinson/Ken Moreman

Electroencephalogram

Q I have had several epileptic attacks and my doctor has asked me to have an EEG. Why is this?

A Epilepsy is a tendency to have seizures due to abnormal electrical activation of the brain. It is classified into groups, according to what sort of attacks a person has. Diagnosis is carried out by observing the pattern of the seizures on an EEG. The EEG also identifies any abnormalities of the brain that may be the trigger for the epileptic attacks, such as lesions. Once the EEG has been carried out, the doctor can prescribe treatment.

Q I am going to have an EEG test and feel very tense and nervous. Will the machine be able to detect this?

A The activity of the relaxed brain is called the alpha rhythm, with waves occurring from eight to 13 times per second. If someone is very nervous, the EEG will show a desynchronized, low voltage, aroused pattern. However, the pattern will appear the same as that for a calm person who is, for example, doing some simple mental arithmetic. The EEG cannot distinguish what is arousing the brain, only that it is aroused.

Q Are EEGs used in the diagnosis of schizophrenia or other mental disorders?

A No. The EEG of someone mentally disturbed is usually normal. This is ironic, since the test was invented by a psychiatrist and was at first used most widely in psychiatric hospitals. Once again, it is the quantity, not the quality, of brain activity that is being recorded.

Q Would having an electroencephalogram test give any indication of a person's mental ability?

A No. The EEG is only a relatively crude test of the quantity and distribution of a brain's electrical activity and in no way relates to the quality of that activity. It is not possible to distinguish the normal EEG of a genius from that of someone less gifted.

The electroencephalogram records the brain's electrical activity, tracing signs of Alzheimer's disease and epilepsy.

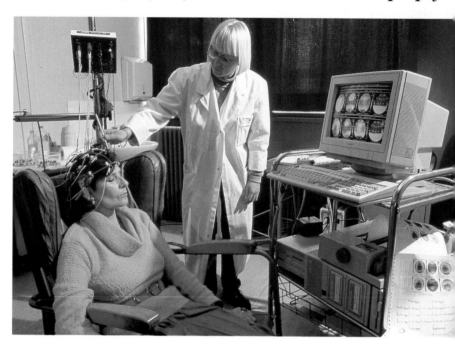

The amount of electricity produced by the brain is very small, and much is lost in conduction through the skull and scalp. Special amplifying equipment—the electroencephalogram (EEG)—records the brain's electrical activity by causing an ink pen to move over a roll of paper.

How the EEG works

The electricity from the brain is picked up by special silver electrodes, placed on the skin of the scalp. They are joined in pairs over adjacent parts of the brain, so that if the charge detected by one electrode is different from that detected by its partner, voltage difference will move the pen.

If one electrode is over a negatively charged part of the brain and its partner is over a positive charge, the pen will move down; if the situation is reversed, then the pen will move up. If there is no charge, or if both parts of the brain under the two electrodes have the same charge, the pen does not move and the paper records a flat line.

Eighteen or more cords are connected by their electrodes to the scalp to cover the whole of the top of the head. The highly trained technician who fixes the electrodes in place uses a special conducting jelly and a harmless removable glue. The machine then records from pairs of electrodes in various combinations, so that the activity of the entire brain may be seen.

Recent electroencaphalography (EEG) tests revealed that one particular electronic signal is especially disturbed in patients with Alzheimer's disease.

There are usually eight pens in a row, recording the reading simultaneously. The final set of lines measures both the strength of fluctuating voltage differences (in microvolts, each one millionth of a volt), and their frequency.

The recording session

The session—entirely harmless and painless—lasts between 45 and 75 minutes and produces about 15 minutes' worth of brain waves on paper. Once the wires are in place, the person being tested relaxes on a couch. During the session, he or she will be asked to blink and to breathe heavily and strobe lights may be flashed before the eyes. These methods can help a doctor to detect abnormalities in the EEG recording that might be missed if the patient was relaxed.

Uses of the EEG

The EEG is used mainly to investigate epilepsy and Alzheimer's disease, and to point out those who should have further tests to see if brain disease is a possible cause of epilepsy. Most people who have convulsions have no brain disease, but their EEG record may show that some drugs might be more effective than others in controlling the attacks.

Electrolysis

Q I am tired of plucking my eyebrows. Can I have them permanently reshaped with electrolysis?

A This can be done, but it is inadvisable for the following reasons: first, the muscle structure under the eyebrows is extremely delicate; second, the bone is close to the skin, making it difficult to insert a needle.

Q My mother says she had some veins treated by electrolysis. What does she mean by this?

A She means that she had some broken veins or spider veins on the surface of her skin treated to make them less obvious and to prevent them from spreading. This is a secondary use of electrolysis and is quite safe.

Q I have very hairy legs and am considering having the hair permanently removed by electrolysis. Is this a good idea?

A It depends. If you have all the time and money in the world, then there is no reason why you shouldn't go ahead. Electrolysis is slow and very expensive, so you have been warned!

Q I have hairs growing from a mole on my face. For years I have been clipping them off, since I read somewhere that it could be dangerous to pluck them. Could I have them removed by electrolysis?

A Check with your doctor first. If he or she says you can go ahead, then that's fine. But you were quite right to be careful not to pluck them before getting advice: in very rare cases, if the cells in moles are disturbed, they can become malignant. But if you are given clearance, electrolysis will solve the problem permanently.

Q Can I get an electric shock from electrolysis?

A No, it is quite safe. A very low voltage is involved and the equipment is carefully insulated, so there is no danger at all.

Of the many ways now available for removing unwanted hair, the safest and most permanent is electrolysis.

Electrolysis is a cosmetic technique most commonly used for removing unwanted hair from the upper lip and the chin. However, it can also be used on other parts of the body, particularly the chest and stomach. It is safely performed only in clinics by fully trained technicians.

However, it is not suitable for all types of unwanted hair. If growth is the result of glandular disturbance, new hairs will grow as fast as the old ones are removed, so a doctor or dermatologist should always be consulted before beginning a course of electrolysis. Neither should hair be removed from moles, growths, or any other birthmark without first consulting a doctor.

The procedure for removing hair by electrolysis is extremely simple. A fine needle is inserted into the hair-bulb until it touches the root. A small current of electricity is transmitted to heat the tip of the needle, so that it destroys the area where the hair grows. The hair can then be lifted out with tweezers. If the hair remains difficult to remove, then the root has not been completely destroyed, and the treatment must be repeated.

Little discomfort is involved in professional electrolysis. Some people report light, prickling sensations.

The length of time electrolysis takes depends on how many hairs are being removed at any one time. Up to 700 can be treated per session. A gap may have to be allowed between treatments before going over the same area again, because the skin may be slightly inflamed.

A certain amount of regrowth is inevitable; if the root has not been destroyed, a new hair can reappear within weeks. Even if the old hair has been destroyed, activation of the root may stimulate new hair to grow.

Aftercare

After treatment, the skin should be kept dry to allow it time to recover. Cream rather than water should be used for cleansing, and avoid using astringents, or makeup. A soothing lotion, such as calamine, should be applied to blemishes.

How electrolysis is done

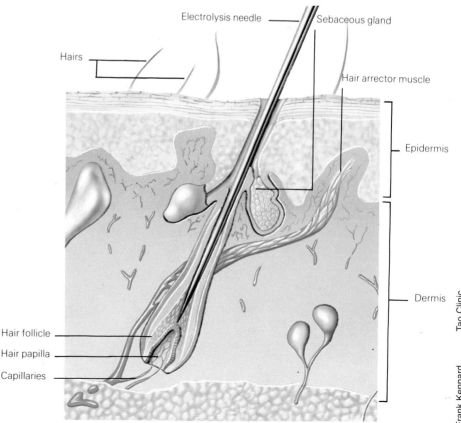

Electrolysis needle — Sebaceous gland

Hairs

Hair arrector muscle

Epidermis

Dermis

Hair follicle

Hair papilla

Capillaries

Tao Clinic

Frank Kennard

Elephantiasis

Q My mother has a swelling in her legs which the doctor says is edema. Is this a form of elephantiasis?

A Edema of the legs is a sign that fluid is trapped in the tissues, but it happens as a result of high pressure in the veins (as in heart failure) or when the blood proteins have fallen to a low level (as in liver failure). The resulting swelling is similar to, but not the same as elephantiasis, which is caused by blockage or damage to the lymph system.

Q My husband's job sometimes takes him to tropical countries and I am worried about him catching various diseases. Can he be inoculated against elephantiasis?

A Elephantiasis is hardly a disease that should worry you; it is rare for an American to catch it if staying in reputable, clean places. However, it is one of the tropical diseases against which, for technical reasons, people cannot be immunized. Your husband should take all the sensible precautions, including sleeping under a net and using insect repellent.

Q I have a mild swelling as a result of radiotherapy, and understand that this is an early stage of elephantiasis. Will exercise cure it, or should I rest?

A As you say, elephantiasis can be quite mild or hardly noticeable. In a severe case, with pain and inflammation, rest is usually advised. But with a condition like yours, gentle exercise is often advised since it encourages a flow of lymph to develop in new, unobstructed channels.

Q My sister has just come back from a tropical cruise and I think she was bitten by mosquitoes. I know these can cause diseases such as elephantiasis, but is there a way of testing?

A Tests can be done for elephantiasis, but they do not provide absolute proof. She should see her doctor for advice.

Elephantiasis is usually caused by a parasitic worm and it occurs mainly in tropical countries, but due to improved hygiene and insect control, it is slowly becoming easier to keep in check.

The rather worrying name elephantiasis is given to any swelling in the body that has been caused by a blockage in the vessels of the lymph system. These vessels form the body's drainage system, carrying away from the tissues any of the large amounts of water and waste products they contain.

In Western countries, elephantiasis is rare. However, cases do occasionally occur as a result of the lymph system being blocked by cancer cells, or being damaged by radiotherapy treatments.

Tropical elephantiasis

In tropical climates, elephantiasis is caused by worms, the most common of which is called *Wuchereria bancrofti*. This condition is also sometimes described as a filarial infestation.

To understand how the worm can get inside the human body in the first place, it is necessary to understand its life cycle. To reproduce, it lays eggs that hatch into tiny, immature forms of the adult called larvae. Mosquitoes carry the larvae, and deposit them into the human body when they bite.

The larvae then find their way into the lymph system, where they slowly develop into mature adults. The adults may, after a period of as long as a year, also enter and be detected in the bloodstream, but the worms do their actual damage in the lymph channels.

Blockage

In these locations, the worms actually block the lymph channels and cause an inflammatory reaction. This causes large, painful swellings that are usually in the lower legs and genitals.

Symptoms

The first sign that a patient may recognize as being a symptom of the disease will probably be painful swellings. This can occur any time from three months to two years after the person is bitten. A simple method of testing for the disease is simply to press on the swelling; if affected, it will dimple.

If the genital area is affected, which is likely, urination may be difficult. In time the blockage makes the skin thick, irregular, and discolored. The underlying tissue will also become very tough and fibrous like elephant hide.

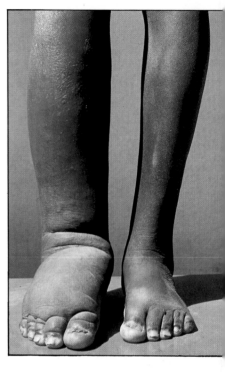

Elephantiasis is the swelling caused by a blockage of the body's drainage system.

Treatment

Unpleasant as it is, tropical elephantiasis is not a threat to life. The worm can be killed by a drug called diethyl-carbamazine. The swelling can be reduced by raising the limb to encourage drainage, and by using compression stockings to squeeze lymph past the obstruction.

Other causes

When caused by cancer, the cancer cells block the lymph vessels. If caused by radiotherapy (one of the treatments for cancer), the vessels are damaged rather than blocked, but with the same result.

Prevention

Controlling the spread and breeding of larvae-bearing mosquitoes is the most effective way of preventing elephantiasis. Anyone visiting or living in a danger area, usually in the tropics, should take all the normal precautions of sleeping under mosquito nets and using insect repellent. In general, an American is unlikely to be infested if he or she keeps to hotels and other places which maintain a good standard of cleanliness.

Emergencies

Q Should people who have been in an accident be given any fluids to drink?

A No one who is likely to need hospital treatment for injuries should be given anything to drink or eat until they have been to the hospital. Even a few sips of water may be dangerous if an anesthetic has to be given.

Q If I find someone collapsed in the street, how can I tell if it is something serious, or if the person has just fainted?

A Very easily. People who faint are unconscious for a few seconds. Their pulse is slow rather than rapid. When they regain consciousness, they will probably remember feeling giddy before blacking out. Anyone who remains unconscious for more than a few seconds has collapsed for some other, more serious reason.

Q If someone's heart stops beating, how much time is there to get it going again by artificial means?

A The brain can only survive undamaged for about three minutes without a proper supply of oxygen from the blood; therefore, it is vital to act quickly. Effective cardiac massage and mouth-to-mouth resuscitation can keep someone alive for more than an hour, so this allows plenty of time for help to arrive.

Q What should I do if my toddler accidentally swallows some iron pills?

A Induce vomiting by gently inserting a finger toward the back of the throat. Then take the child to the hospital at once.

Q My father is prone to epilepsy. What should I do if he suddenly has a fit?

A Simply make sure that he sees a doctor or goes to the hospital without delay. Try to prevent him from injuring himself. Do not try to pry open his mouth if it is closed, or physically restrain him when he is having a seizure.

Anyone can suddenly and unexpectedly find him- or herself faced with a medical emergency. Correct action, taken calmly and promptly, can save lives.

Tony Stone

An emergency is any situation in which immediate, expert, medical attention is essential. The priority in any emergency is to summon the emergency services immediately by calling 911. While waiting for help to arrive, you may be able to take some steps to help the victim.

The first thing to do is to find out what happened. Look around for obvious clues and talk to any people who may have witnessed the accident or incident. A quick assessment of the situation must then be made and the appropriate action taken without delay.

First questions
If the patient is conscious, ask about any pain and find out where the injuries are; the clues are bleeding, tenderness, and any limb or part of the body that is not its usual shape.

Ask the patient what he or she thinks may be wrong. Also ask about any previous illnesses that may be relevant.

Signs to look for first
Note whether or not the patient is breathing well, especially whether the breathing appears to be rapid, irregular, or unusually noisy.

Then feel the pulse, noting both its rate and its strength. Look at the skin and note sweating, unusual paleness, or any blue tinge. A blue hue, especially in the lips, suggests breathing difficulty.

Next look for signs of shock. Every severely injured person develops this condition, which always requires urgent

Prompt action is essential in an emergency, whatever the weather conditions.

treatment in the hospital. The signs are: cold, sweaty, and pale skin, which may have a bluish tinge; a fast, weak pulse; and rapid, shallow breathing. A person with shock is anxious, agitated, and often thirsty, but as shock progresses becomes apathetic and listless.

Shock usually results from severe blood loss that may be external or internal (in which case, it may not be immediately apparent). It can also be caused by damage to the heart and circulation, and should be distinguished from the understandable emotional upset of being involved in an accident.

Unconsciousness
If a person is unconscious, check immediately to see whether or not he or she is breathing. Feel for the pulse, then look for any signs of an injury, bleeding, or head injury.

If no obvious cause for the unconsciousness can be found, remember that people undergoing treatment for an illness that causes blackouts often wear bracelets or pendants giving details of their illnesses. Sugar lumps or glucose tablets in a pocket suggest that the patient may be a diabetic.

Action
Act quickly but calmly. If it is certain that there are no broken limbs, and especially that there is no damage to the spine,

Common emergencies and their treatment

Where	Type of emergency	Treatment
IN THE HOME	BURNS AND SCALDS	Immediately douse with plenty of cold water. Do not burst blisters. Go straight to the hospital for anything worse than a trivial burn
	ACCIDENTAL POISONING	Make the patient vomit by putting a finger into the back of the throat. Go straight to the hospital. If a corrosive poison—for example, a household cleaning agent—has been swallowed, do not make the patient vomit
	DEEP CUTS	Control bleeding with direct pressure
	FALLS	Broken hip bone common in the elderly following fall. Go straight to the hospital
IN THE STREET	AFTER A TRAFFIC OR OTHER ACCIDENT:	
	BLEEDING	Control with direct pressure
	FRACTURES	Put limb in comfortable position, otherwise do not move the patient. Call for help
	HEAD INJURY	It is best not to move the patient. Call for help
	CHEST INJURY	Anyone with a steering wheel injury to the chest may require mouth-to-mouth resuscitation, so check for breathing difficulties
	COLLAPSE	Roll the patient onto his or her side
AT WORK	CHEMICAL SPILLAGE ON PART OF BODY	Wash off with plenty of water
	SMOKE OR TOXIC GAS BREATHED IN	Lung damage may be delayed and not immediately obvious, so take the patient straight to the hospital
	ELECTROCUTION	First turn off the electricity. Causes burns and heart failure, so treat the same as for these
	INJURIES FROM MACHINERY	Crush injuries are common. Stop bleeding by applying pressure. Do not move fractures. Make sure severed limbs are taken to the hospital with the patient
AT PLAY	DROWNING	Clear out the mouth with your fingers. Begin mouth-to-mouth resuscitation. Keep the patient warm
	FRACTURES	Same as for fractures in the street
	DISLOCATIONS	Same as for fractures. Do not try to put the bone back in the joint
	ANIMAL BITES	Wash thoroughly. Control bleeding by direct pressure. Serious infection may follow deep bites, so check that the patient is protected against tetanus. If in doubt, go to the hospital
	SNAKEBITES	Even with bites from the most poisonous snakes, there is always time to get hospital treatment, so reassure the patient. Tell the patient to lie still

gently move the patient to a safe place—preferably one that is sheltered and away from the scene.

Check whether the patient is breathing, and if not, start mouth-to-mouth resuscitation at once. If there is no heartbeat, start cardiac massage, too, if you know how to do this.

If the patient is unconscious but is still breathing, roll him or her onto their side. This makes the tongue fall forward, allowing any saliva or vomit to drain out through the mouth; this is vital to prevent the patient from choking on their vomit.

Bleeding
Even the most terrifying amount of bleeding can be controlled by firm, direct pressure on its source; preferably with a sterile gauze pad, but otherwise using any soft, clean, and instantly available piece of cloth.

Shock
Make sure that the patient is lying comfortably. His or her head should be flat, and the legs raised slightly. Do not give the patient anything to drink.

General precautions
Cover wounds and protect the patient from cold. Loosen clothing at the neck. If in doubt whether the patient is alive, continue resuscitation until help arrives.

Emetics

Q How long after poisoning can an emetic be useful?

A As a rule, anything ingested passes through the stomach within four hours and is then irretrievable by means of an emetic. Some drugs, such as aspirin, tend to slow down stomach activity, so the time limit can be extended in an aspirin overdose.

Q My baby has swallowed a button. Should I give her an emetic?

A It is not necessary. Provided that it is not too large and smooth, it should reappear within a few days in your child's feces. If it does not, tell your doctor.

Q My sister says it is safe to use salt water as a home emetic in an emergency; I disagree. Who is right?

A You are. Salt water often fails to induce vomiting unless a large quantity is used, and this can be dangerous. Instead, put a finger down the throat in an emergency; if this fails, get medical help.

Q I am considering aversion therapy to give up smoking. Are emetics ever used?

A Yes, sometimes. Aversion therapy involves conditioning the patient to associate a formerly pleasurable habit with great unpleasantness, so that it appears and feels less desirable. An emetic is given, which makes the patient feel sick, while he or she is shown pictures of diseased lungs or ashtrays, or is encouraged to chain-smoke. After a while the patient psychologically links the habit with the unpleasant physical sensations, and with luck, stops smoking.

Q My brother vomits whenever he eats eggs. Why is this?

A This may be a food allergy. The protein can act as an emetic by stimulating an allergic response in the gut wall. Most children grow out of food allergies, so it may be a short-term problem.

Vomiting may be unpleasant, but in some situations, such as drug overdoses, it can save lives. In these cases an emetic is often used to induce the process.

Brian Nash

An emetic is a substance which, when taken by mouth, causes vomiting, the body's natural reflex action to rid itself of its stomach contents (see Vomiting).

Uses

Emetics are usually used to eliminate poisons taken either accidentally or deliberately. This is done by first increasing the intake of fluids, and then using an emetic to empty the stomach. Where an emetic is not appropriate, a stomach pump (gastric lavage) is used.

Immediate treatment is vital. If there is any doubt as to whether a poison has been taken (as in the case of small children), the induction of vomiting, termed *emesis*, is usually safer than waiting.

However, an emetic should not be used if a corrosive poison such as bleach has been swallowed; the lining of the stomach may be burned and vomiting could cause perforation. In the case of a patient who is drowsy or unconscious, the protective cough reflex may be impaired and although the emetic may still work, vomit may be inhaled, causing pneumonia.

Some drugs, such as travelsickness pills, are antiemetic. In a case of overdose, an ordinary emetic would not be effective, so a stomach pump would be used instead.

It is wise to know emetic techniques in case of an emergency, such as when a child eats poisonous mushrooms or berries.

Types and techniques

Vomiting can be induced in a variety of ways; the first involves mechanical means. The Romans used a feather to tickle the back of their throats; today a finger is best used. Both techniques work by stimulating the gag reflex, which encourages regurgitation.

Unless the patient is a very young child, use his or her finger rather than your own, otherwise it may get bitten. Gently insert a straight index finger down into the mouth until it touches the back of the throat, causing the patient to gag and retch. If vomiting does not occur, repeat the treatment until he or she does vomit, encouraging him or her to bend forward with the head down to allow the stomach contents to run out.

Ipecac syrup is the safest emergency emetic. This works by stimulating the stomach and vomiting center of the brain. The exact dose depends on the formula, indicated on the bottle. Once the dose has been given, the patient should drink several glasses of water, so as not to retch on an empty stomach. It is advisable to consult a doctor before using ipecac.

Emphysema

Q My doctor says that my emphysema has been caused by smoking. Why is this?

A Smokers are much more likely to get emphysema than nonsmokers, but since only a minority of smokers develop severe emphysema and a few sufferers have never smoked at all, additional factors must be involved. In nonsmokers, this is thought to be the lack of a substance in the blood called alpha$-_1$ antitrypsin, which helps protect the lungs from damage done by the accidental release of elastase, an enzyme that can destroy them.

Q When I run for a bus, I often get breathless. Could I have emphysema?

A You are probably just out of condition. Get more exercise, cut out cigarettes, and see if your breathlessness improves. If it does not, or it gets worse, see a doctor.

Q Is emphysema dangerous for someone with a heart condition?

A Yes. It may also cause heart conditions. The heart has to pump harder to force blood through blood vessels in the lungs, whose functional powers have been reduced, and over time this strains the heart. Also, because the lungs lose the ability to exchange oxygen for carbon dioxide in sufficient quantities, the body is deprived of oxygen and the heart has to pump more blood through the lungs. In the worst cases, the additional load on a malfunctioning heart may eventually lead to death.

Q My daughter recently had whooping cough and has now been diagnosed as having emphysema. Why is this?

A Your daughter has interstitial emphysema, a less serious condition in which air bubbles appear in the chest. These resulted from the sharp intake of breath preceding each cough, which ruptured some of the alveoli in her lungs, causing a release of air. The bubbles may cause discomfort, but she should make a full recovery.

Lung diseases are always distressing, particularly when the sufferer is perpetually short of breath, as with emphysema. Since damage is permanent, the best approach is to try to avoid the disease in the first place.

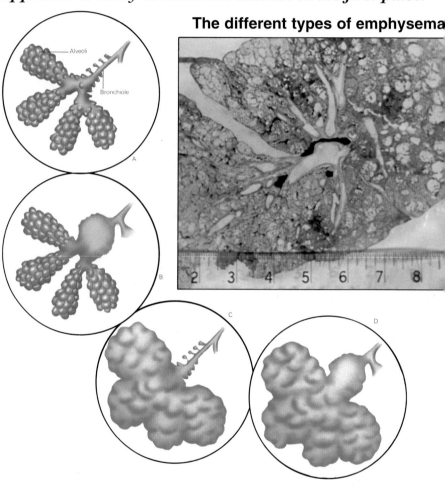

The different types of emphysema

(A) shows normal bronchioles and alveoli. In pulmonary emphysema, often suffered by coal miners, the bronchioles may be distended (B) and sometimes the air sacs (C).

Occasionally, as in alpha$-_1$ antitrypsin deficiency emphysema, both are swollen (D). This paper-thin section of lung (inset) shows emphysema and bronchitis.

Pulmonary emphysema is a serious and debilitating lung disease. The tiny air sacs in the lungs (the alveoli) and the narrow passages leading to the air sacs (the bronchioles) become permanently distended with air. The lung tissues lose their elasticity and the number of blood vessels is reduced. As a result, the lungs' ability to supply the blood with oxygen is progressively decreased and the patient becomes breathless with the slightest exertion.

Pulmonary emphysema is less frequent in women; there may be a hormonal factor that protects them from the disease. It rarely appears before the age of 40, but if it occurs in middle age it causes disability and eventually death.

Causes

Smoking is undoubtedly the greatest contributory factor in most cases of emphysema, but continuous exposure to dust or high levels of air pollution may bring on various forms of the disease. Many people with chronic bronchitis also suffer from emphysema, which is made worse by smoking.

However, although smoking is a cause, not all smokers contract emphysema, and it also occurs in nonsmokers. One theory put forward to explain this is that a substance called elastase is produced by the white cells in the lungs. Smoke or dust particles may interfere with the cells, releasing elastase. Unless it is inactivated by a blood substance called alpha-$_1$ antitrypsin, it will attack the lung tissue. People who lack alpha-$_1$ anti-trypsin are particularly susceptible to pulmonary emphysema; if they smoke, they are likely to develop a severe form of the disease.

Chronic bronchitis may also be a contributory factor. The airways of the lungs are blocked by mucus, produced as a response to irritation by smoke or other pollutants. To breathe in, a person must make a great deal of effort to overcome the resistance of the mucus, and the inspiration of air may result in the distension of the alveoli. Bacterial infection, which is common in chronic bronchitis, may contribute to the process by weakening the lung's elastic tissue.

In addition to pulmonary emphysema, there is focal dust emphysema (coal worker's pneumoconiosis), caused by coal dust covering the walls of the air passages leading to the lungs' air sacs. Subcutaneous emphysema may result from whooping cough or a broken rib that punctures the lungs.

Symptoms
The most obvious symptom of emphysema is breathlessness, followed by coughing, which can be brought on by the slightest exertion, such as talking or laughing.

Chewing and swallowing may also be difficult because of the breathlessness, and there may be discomfort after a meal because the lungs have expanded, pushing the diaphragm into the stomach. Loss of appetite and weight loss may occur.

In severe forms of the disease, lung enlargement may cause the chest to expand into a barrel shape. Lack of oxygen in the blood may produce cyanosis, a blue coloration in the skin that is most noticeable on the lips and under the fingernails. Because the disease is progressive, these symptoms will get worse.

Dangers
The loss of elasticity of the lungs and the presence of mucus in the airways may result in carbon dioxide no longer being efficiently eliminated from the lungs and insufficient oxygen being breathed in. The patient may have to make strenuous efforts to breathe and may rapidly become out of breath.

In some patients, large holes develop in the lung tissue and large air bubbles called bullae appear on the lung surface. Coughing may burst the bullae, causing the release of air into the chest. In severe cases the lungs collapse and an operation may be required to remove the air.

Emphysema can also affect the heart. The loss of blood capillaries and thickening in the alveolar walls greatly increases the resistance of the lungs to the flow of blood. The heart has to pump much harder to force blood through the lungs and it also has to pump a greater volume of blood when the patient exercises to deliver the amount of oxygen required. In time this can cause the heart to become strained and begin to fail.

Treatment
Although pulmonary emphysema cannot be cured, its progress may be slowed. The most important thing to do is to stop smoking. Some patients, particularly those who also have chronic bronchitis, may benefit from using bronchodilator drugs, which help to clear the airways. Breathing pure oxygen from a cylinder allows enough of the gas to enter the blood; portable cylinders can be used for short trips outside the home.

Operations to cut out the bullae can be performed. Weight loss can be combated with small, frequent, high-energy meals. Mild exercise may help maintain patients' muscle tone and prevent them from becoming housebound. Lung volume-reduction surgery is a new, experimental treatment where parts of both lungs are removed, decreasing the hyperinflation of the chest and improving breathing.

Outlook
If smokers give up their habit and treatment is given, emphysema can sometimes be slowed. Unfortunately there is no way of repairing lung damage that has been done already. This is why it is so important not to begin smoking.

How the lung tissue of smokers may be damaged by emphysema

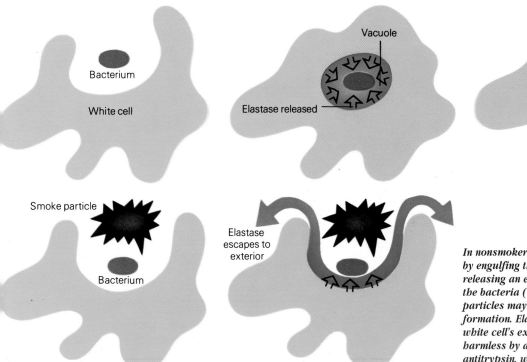

In nonsmokers, white cells destroy bacteria by engulfing them in a vacuole and then releasing an enzyme, elastase, which digests the bacteria (above). In smokers, smoke particles may interfere with vacuole formation. Elastase may then leak to the white cell's exterior, and unless it is made harmless by a substance in blood, alpha-$_1$ antitrypsin, which some people lack, it may damage the lung tissue (left).

Encephalitis

Q My son has measles. Is there any way in which I can make sure that he does not also get encephalitis?

A Encephalitis is an extremely rare complication of measles, but there is no way to predict who will get it, or to prevent it from occurring. If you are worried, keep a close eye on him; if he appears very drowsy, has a high fever, and perhaps convulsions, call your doctor immediately.

Q Can vaccination cause encephalitis?

A Encephalitis can occur as a result of a vaccination, but this is very rare and the risk of it happening is probably less than that of contracting the disease for which the vaccination was given. It is routine practice not to give a vaccination to those who have an abnormal immune system, since these people have an increased chance of getting encephalitis. This includes people with many allergies, or who are on drugs that suppress the immune system.

Q My uncle has cancer. Could encephalitis occur as a further complication?

A Yes, there is a slight possibility of this. Some types of cancer, particularly those of the lymphatic system, are uncommonly complicated by a form of chronic encephalitis. This may be caused by an otherwise harmless virus being allowed to create trouble because the immune system is weakened by cancer.

Q I seem to remember reading that encephalitis is always associated with permanent brain damage. Is this so?

A No. Although there is a substantial risk of this occurring, some people may have a less severe illness from which they make a complete recovery. It is probable that many people have slight bouts of encephalitis with viral infections, which they may not even have reported to their doctor at the time, having dismissed them simply as a bout of flu.

Commonly—and inaccurately—referred to as sleeping sickness, encephalitis is a rare disease that can strike people of any age. Early diagnosis is vital.

Encephalitis is an inflammation of the brain. It is usually due to an irritation in the brain caused by a virus; however, it may also be due to meningitis, a bacterial or viral infection of the brain's lining membrane. Rarer kinds of encephalitis are caused by abnormal reactions of the body's immune system to common viruses, such as measles, or when the body's immune system has been altered by cancer or certain drugs.

Acute encephalitis can occur as a rare complication of many common viral infections—again, including measles—or as a result of the herpes simplex virus. Chronic encephalitis usually occurs in people who have an abnormal immune system that cannot deal with viruses in the normal manner.

Symptoms and treatment

Acute encephalitis may start suddenly, completely out of the blue, or it can sometimes follow the onset of a common viral illness. The patient has a headache, a high temperature, and becomes drowsy or confused. Often there are convulsions. In addition, there may be a particular trouble with speech (aphasia), or a general weakness and twitching of the limbs. As the condition worsens, drowsiness gives way to coma.

Chronic encephalitis is much rarer. About one in a million children who have the measles develops a form of encephalitis. The child's behavior starts to deteriorate and all brain functions become damaged. Unconsciousness and convul-

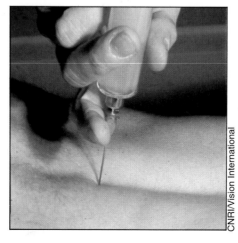

A sample of cerebrospinal fluid, taken by a lumbar puncture, will help to identify the virus that is causing encephalitis.

sions occur, then death. Other forms of chronic encephalitis cause a gradual deterioration in the intellect, often with muscle twitching (myoclonus) and convulsions. The cause of the illness may be identified by an electroencephalogram, brain X-ray scan, lumbar puncture, or

Lumbar puncture technique

A lumbar puncture consists of passing a special needle into the central canal of the spinal cord and drawing some fluid into a syringe.

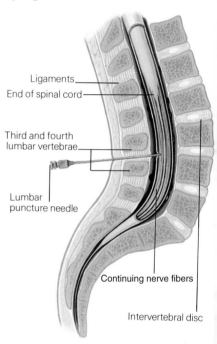

Ligaments

End of spinal cord

Third and fourth lumbar vertebrae

Lumbar puncture needle

Continuing nerve fibers

Intervertebral disc

brain biopsy. Treatment with drugs will depend on the cause of the encephalitis. Treatment must be started as early as possible to avoid the danger of permanent brain damage. Convulsions must be treated with anticonvulsant drugs, and if the patient is very ill or in a coma, expert nursing will be needed. In all cases of encephalitis, convalescence is prolonged.

Outlook

As with any brain damage, the eventual outcome depends on the extent of the disease and also the area of the brain that has been affected. With acute encephalitis, there may be a complete recovery, but often there is a long-term effect. In the case of chronic encephalitis, the outlook is less optimistic.

Endocrine system

Q My teenage sister is very fat. Are her glands faulty?

A Probably not; most adolescents put on a little puppy fat, or it could be that she is simply eating too much or is not active enough. A number of hormone conditions can give rise to obesity; two of the best-known are an underactive thyroid and overactive adrenals. In the case of the thyroid, weight gain is not a particularly common feature in the few young people who get this disease. The overactive adrenal is a very rare condition and is always accompanied by other signs.

Q I have heard about hormone replacement therapy. What does this mean?

A Some hormones are essential for life. If, for some reason, a hormone-secreting gland is removed or is underactive, then the hormone concerned must be replaced. In the case of thyroid and cortisone, pills can be given by mouth. Insulin, which comes from the pancreas, has to be given by injection. It is very rare for the parathyroid glands to be removed or to stop working, but when this happens, the level of calcium in the blood can be controlled with extra vitamin D. The phrase *hormone replacement therapy* is often used to refer to giving female sex hormone preparations to women when their natural production decreases after the menopause.

Q I am 18 and have started developing hair on my face and around my nipples. This is embarrassing and I am sure it is my glands. Can anything help?

A This is always a difficult problem. The growth of hair on the face and body is, of course, a response to male hormones. In the majority of cases, there is no definite abnormality in the hormone balance, since it is not only normal, but desirable for girls to have small quantities of male hormones circulating in addition to female ones. If hairiness is excessive, however, there may be a definite hormone imbalance that can be treated medically.

The body is like a finely tuned musical instrument, with the glands of the endocrine system keeping all the parts working in harmony with each other.

Many of the vital functions of the body are controlled by the endocrine system, which consists of glands that secrete hormones (chemical messengers) into the bloodstream. Hormones are concerned with metabolism (the many processes by which the body is kept functioning), and

The pituitary gland apparently controls its own hormone level, in addition to those of other glands.

tend to interact. They are are responsible for balancing the levels of basic chemicals like salt, calcium, and sugar in the blood. They are also essential to the reproductive system, controlling ovulation, menstruation, pregnancy, and milk production in women and sperm production in men. They are critical to the growth of children and their development during puberty.

Other glands, for example, the sweat glands in the skin and the salivary glands

Major hormones secreted by the endocrine system

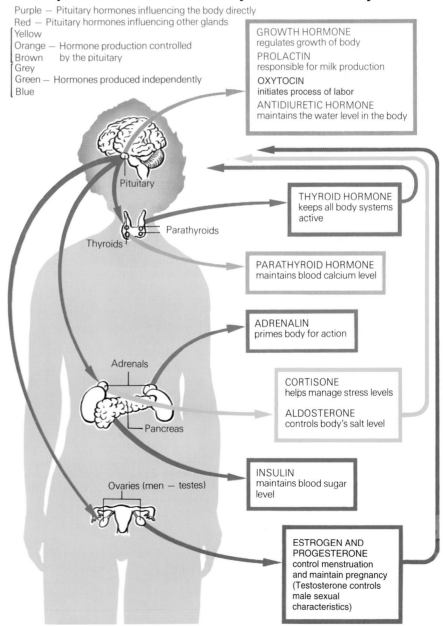

Purple — Pituitary hormones influencing the body directly
Red — Pituitary hormones influencing other glands
Yellow
Orange — Hormone production controlled
Brown   by the pituitary
Grey
Green — Hormones produced independently
Blue

GROWTH HORMONE
regulates growth of body
PROLACTIN
responsible for milk production
OXYTOCIN
initiates process of labor
ANTIDIURETIC HORMONE
maintains the water level in the body

THYROID HORMONE
keeps all body systems active

PARATHYROID HORMONE
maintains blood calcium level

ADRENALIN
primes body for action

CORTISONE
helps manage stress levels
ALDOSTERONE
controls body's salt level

INSULIN
maintains blood sugar level

ESTROGEN AND PROGESTERONE
control menstruation and maintain pregnancy
(Testosterone controls male sexual characteristics)

Pituitary

Parathyroids

Thyroids

Adrenals

Pancreas

Ovaries (men — testes)

Frank Kennard

The feedback mechanism

When the level of thyroid hormone is low (left), the pituitary gland secretes TSH (thyroid-stimulating hormone) which sets off its production. When there is enough thyroid hormone (right), the pituitary stops producing TSH.

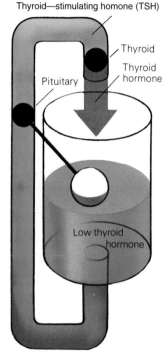
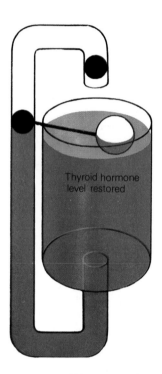

in the mouth, open onto an organ's surface and are known as exocrine glands. The pancreas, however, is a gland that has both endocrine and exocrine activity, since it secretes hormones into the blood but also produces alkali and other digestive substances that are secreted directly into the intestine.

Overall control

A small gland in the base of the skull, called the pituitary, is responsible for controlling much of the hormone system. It acts as a conductor, secreting hormones that turn the other glands on and off. The pituitary interacts with three important groups of glands. The first, the thyroid, is situated in the neck just below the voice box. The pituitary also directs the activities of the two adrenal glands, which are found in the abdomen lying just on top of the kidneys, and affects the sex glands, the two ovaries in a woman and the two testes in a man.

The pituitary gland exerts its control in a very simple process called feedback. An example of this occurs in the thyroid gland. When the gland is stimulated by TSH (thyroid-stimulating hormone) made by the pituitary, it produces the thyroid hormone. When this hormone's level in the blood rises, the pituitary turns off the

secretion of TSH. But when the level of thyroid hormone starts to fall again, TSH is produced once more. In this way, a relatively constant level of thyroid hormone is maintained in the body. This may be raised or lowered by the pituitary, which is itself controlled by the part of the brain immediately above it, the hypothalamus.

The pituitary controls the adrenal cortex (part of the adrenal gland), where cortisone production is stimulated with ACTH (adrenocorticotropic hormone). The action of the ovaries is controlled with FSH (follicle-stimulating hormone) and LH (luteinizing hormone) and that of the testes with ICSH (interstitial cell-stimulating hormone). The balance of the ovarian hormones, estrogen and progesterone, affects a woman's menstrual periods.

Apart from its role in controlling other endocrine glands, the pituitary secretes a number of other important hormones, including the growth hormone, which is essential for normal development in children, and prolactin, which plays some role in the production of breast milk.

All these hormones come from the front part of the gland, or anterior pituitary. The back, or posterior pituitary, secretes only two hormones: oxytocin, which causes the womb to contract in labor, and ADH (antidiuretic hormone),

which is concerned with maintaining the correct amount of water in the body.

Acting independently

Various other glands and their hormones act more or less independently of the pituitary. Perhaps the most important of these is the pancreas, which secretes insulin. Insulin controls the sugar level in the blood; a lack of insulin causes diabetes.

Also important are the four tiny parathyroid glands, each about the size of a pea, that lie behind the thyroid gland. These control the level of calcium in the blood, which is essential to good health.

Finally there are the hormones secreted by the walls of the gut and by the pancreas that direct the processes of digestion. Many of these gut hormones have only recently been discovered and there is obviously a very complicated system of hormone-controlled mechanisms that affect such things as acid production by the stomach, alkali secretion into the intestine by the pancreas, and bile excretion by the gallbladder.

The precise way in which the various gut hormones work is still being investigated by scientists. Perhaps one of the best-known and most understood is the hormone gastrin, which is secreted by the pylorus and causes acid to be produced in the stomach.

Problems and their treatment

The endocrine system can go wrong in many ways, but luckily most endocrine diseases can be cured or at least alleviated. The two main problems are over- or undersecretion of hormones.

Excess hormone production is probably commonest in the thyroid gland, but the reasons for this are still being researched. In other glands, excess production of hormones is usually the result of a tumor. Since these tumors are usually benign (not cancerous), surgery is often very successful in curing these endocrine conditions.

Underactivity can be dealt with by giving replacement doses of the relevant hormone by mouth. This is particularly successful in failure of the adrenal glands (Addison's disease).

Pituitary gland problems

When the pituitary gland causes trouble, the situation can become rather complicated because the failure of hormone secretion leads in turn to a failure of the thyroid and adrenal glands. Nowadays, however, medical investigation is more straightforward than it was in the past, although many blood tests may be required to measure the levels of the various hormones in the body.

John Hutchinson

Endometriosis

Q When I make love with my boyfriend I sometimes feel a pain deep inside me. Could I be the wrong shape?

A No woman is the wrong shape, since the vagina stretches during intercourse to accommodate the penis. It is more likely that you have a physical problem that is stopping you from enjoying intercourse. As the pain does not occur every time, it is more likely to be due to endometriosis than another common cause, such as a tipped uterus; however, see your doctor to be sure, and to rule out the possibility of a pelvic infection.

Q My doctor said that I was suffering from mild endometriosis because my periods were heavy and frequent, and I often had pain in the pelvic region during intercourse. She warned me I might find it difficult to conceive, but I am now pregnant. I enjoy making love more than ever because the pain has stopped. Does this mean that my endometriosis is cured?

A Unfortunately not. The pain has stopped because your periods have stopped. Once the baby is born and your periods restart, it is likely that the endometrial cysts will start to act up again.

Q I suffer from frequent nosebleeds. Could endometriosis be the cause?

A It is extremely unlikely; endometriosis of the lining of the nose is very rare. If your nosebleeds coincide with your monthly period, however, then it is worth checking with your doctor.

Q Why does a hysterectomy cure endometriosis?

A The growth of endometrial tissue is governed by the hormones progesterone and estrogen, which are in turn controlled by the ovaries. If the ovaries are removed (as in a complete hysterectomy), the body no longer prepares for pregnancy and the levels of these hormones stop fluctuating. The endometrial tissue therefore does not grow.

In this fairly rare condition, the tissue that forms the lining of the uterus is also found in other areas of a woman's body.

The tissue that forms the endometrium, the lining of the uterus, provides a home for a fertilized egg. The endometrium nourishes the egg until the placenta develops to take over this function.

During the first half of a woman's monthly cycle, the ovaries secrete higher levels of the hormones estrogen and progesterone. This causes the endometrium to grow and thicken. It stops growing when an egg is released, and begins to secrete nutrient-rich substances. If no fertilized egg implants in the uterus, the hormone levels fall, and the tissue shrinks. The endometrium is expelled during the menstrual period and the cycle starts again.

Normally this monthly shedding and renewal of endometrial tissue inside the uterus does not cause any problems. However, the same tissue is occasionally found in other areas of the body, usually on the ovaries, inside the fallopian tubes, on the outside of the uterus, elsewhere in the abdominal cavity, or in the bladder. In very rare cases it may be found on the surface of the stomach, arms, or legs, on the lining of the nose, or inside the lungs.

What causes endometriosis?

This misplaced tissue occurs during the development of the fetus, when its reproductive organs form. Some experts believe that the condition can also devel-op later on if menstrual blood containing endometrial tissue backs up in the uterus and flows back up the fallopian tubes, leaving deposits on the ovaries.

The misplaced tissue is also controlled by the hormones, and grows and bleeds with the woman's monthly cycle. There will be a small loss of mucus and surface tissue as well as blood. Tissue growing on the outside of the body, usually in spots on the stomach area or arms and legs, will swell and bleed with the woman's periods. It may look odd and will need to be covered while it is bleeding, but it does not lead to other problems. If the tissue is on the lining of the nose, the shedding will seem like a light nosebleed. However if the tissue is growing inside the body, the blood cannot drain away and instead accumulates around the site of the tissue deposits.

Potential problems

Endometriosis of the ovaries is particularly likely to cause problems, including ovarian cysts that can grow to such a size that they can make the sufferer think that she is pregnant. In addition to causing pain, endometriosis of the fallopian tubes can cause scarring, which can in turn

A laparoscope shows an ovarian cyst caused by endometriosis. The cyst is the swollen white area at center left.

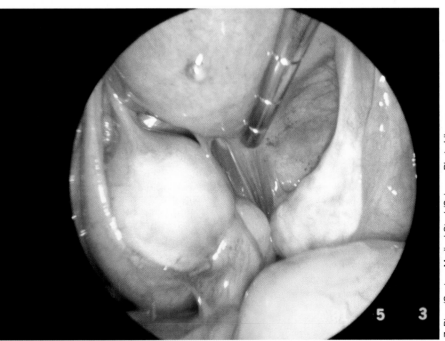

ENDOMETRIOSIS

The blue patches show the areas where endometriosis can develop.

lead to infertility because the tubes are no longer able to transport a fertilized egg to the uterus. The problems get worse because the body responds by trying to wall off the spots of alien tissue to stop them invading other areas. As a result, blood-filled cysts form. These cysts grow bigger with each cycle.

Diagnosis

Endometriosis is most commonly diagnosed in women in their late 20s, when the cysts have grown big enough to be uncomfortable or obvious. Younger women with a more severe form of the condition may be diagnosed earlier.

In other cases women may suffer from mild endometriosis, which does not need treatment during their fertile years. However they may find that the cysts become worse during menopause, when hormone levels fluctuate to a much greater extent.

The symptoms vary in severity, depending on the amount of endometrial tissue and its location. They include: pain in the pelvic area, especially during intercourse; very short menstrual cycles; painful periods; and infertility. When there is no monthly bleeding, such as during pregnancy or menopause, the symptoms do not appear.

A doctor who suspects endometriosis will carry out an internal examination to check for tender nodules, but the condition is difficult to diagnose accurately without a laparoscopy. This is carried out in a hospital, under a general anesthetic. A hollow needle is inserted into the abdomen just below the navel, and carbon dioxide is pumped through it into the abdominal cavity, to expand it and move the intestines out of the way. The surgeon then inserts a viewing tube (the endoscope) to inspect the ovaries and fallopian tubes.

Endometrial cysts are a dark bluish-purple, and may be as small as a pinhead or as big as a walnut. Some women may have only one or two cysts, others may have up to 100.

Treatment

Treatment will depend on both the severity of the problem and the age of the sufferer. If cysts in the pelvic cavity are not too numerous and widespread, they can be treated by laser during a laparoscopy without affecting the uterus, fallopian tubes, or ovaries. Hormone treatment can also be effective. In the past women who did not want a hysterectomy were often advised to take a high-progesterone contraceptive pill continuously, so that nor-

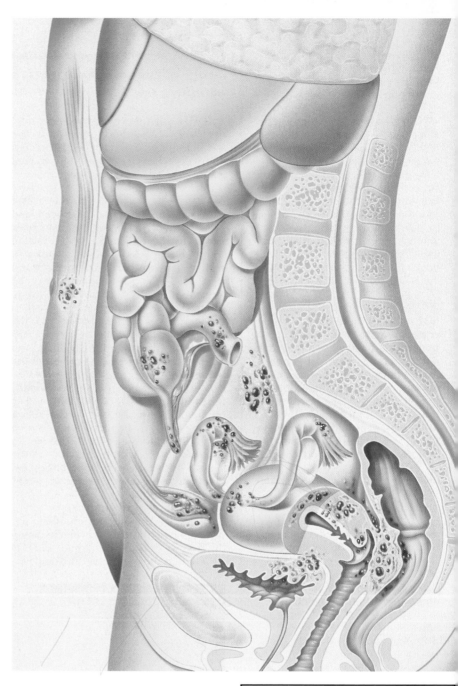

mal hormonal activity was suppressed and the monthly bleeding stopped. However, the newer, safer generations of contraceptive pills contain a lower level of progesterone and doctors are reluctant to prescribe high-dose versions, so other hormones may be prescribed instead.

Major surgery will generally be delayed for as long as possible if the woman wants to have children in the future. However, if the disease is widespread and the symptoms are causing a lot of pain, or if the woman has completed her family, the doctor may recommend a complete hysterectomy (removal of the uterus, fallopian tubes, and ovaries) so that the monthly cycle no longer occurs.

Symptoms

The symptoms of endometriosis are vague and can point to other disorders. However, if you experience any of the following symptoms, it is worth speaking to your doctor so that they can be investigated further:

- Chronic pain in the lower abdomen
- Occasional or regular pain during intercourse
- A very short menstrual cycle (under 25 days)
- Very heavy, painful periods
- Difficulty in conceiving a baby

Endoscopy

Q Can an endoscope ever get stuck when it is being used to look inside you?

A When used correctly endoscopes never seem to get stuck. The older endoscopes were straight, but usually tapered, so withdrawal was simple. With the more modern, fiber-optic types, the tubes tend to be smaller and more flexible, so the withdrawal of the instrument is never difficult.

Q I have to have an endoscopy. Can I watch what is happening inside me?

A Yes. Some fiber-optic endoscopes do have a side-viewing attachment that is used by medical students or for taking photographs of the condition seen. If you are not sedated or no anesthetic is used, then it may be possible for you to see, for example, your stomach. To watch a minor operation down an endoscope is also possible, but most people prefer not to.

Q I have a relative who had an endoscopy and an X ray. Why would this be necessary?

A There are some areas where endoscopes cannot go. In such cases they are used to site a fine tube that feeds into the entrance of a complicated organ, such as the pancreas. Dye is then injected into the organ and an X ray is taken. The fine pattern of ducts and connections within the gland become visible and this can help diagnosis in some conditions.

Q I have a stomach ulcer and my surgeon keeps asking me back for a gastroscopy. Is this usual?

A Gastroscopy is so safe that many doctors use it as a tool to review a case's progress. It is the only instrument that allows the surgeon to look at the ulcer directly. With ulceration of the stomach, it is sometimes difficult to decide whether to give prolonged medical treatment or to operate. Your surgeon is probably observing the ulcer at regular intervals to keep the options open on your behalf.

One of the most advanced methods of diagnosing disease in a body organ is through endoscopy. The procedure is painless and can be used on its own or with X rays.

Endoscopy is a procedure in which a doctor looks down a tube into a hollow part of the body to search for illness or disease. The instrument used to perform an endoscopy is called an endoscope.

Types

Individual endoscopes have been developed for many different parts of the body, including the abdominal cavity, esophagus, rectum, bladder, lungs, stomach, intestines, uterus, and knee joints. In spite of their similarity of function, they are named differently, depending on the part of the body they are designed to examine. As long as there is space within an organ to maneuver the instrument without causing damage, an endoscope can be used. However, organs like the liver and brain are too solid to safely insert an endoscope.

Early endoscopes were called sigmoidoscopes. They consisted of a hollow tube made of metal, often with a light bulb so doctors could see into organs. They are still in use today and are very effective for some diagnoses. More sophisticated endoscopes have since been developed, including the fiber-optic endoscope, which consists of hundreds of small bundles of glass fibers, down which a light is shone. The image is reflected up inside the bundles, which act like a tubular mirror, so that the image appears at the eyepiece. Since the glass rods are so thin, they can bend easily, making the endoscope flexible enough to wriggle around any organ.

For example, a fiber-optic colonoscope can be threaded along the bends in the colon (part of the large intestine). By using a kind of pulley, the tip of the scope can be maneuvred around the curves, so that the whole length of the colon can be examined. This is a great improvement on the straight sigmoidoscope, which could only see as far as a straight rod could be placed without causing damage.

Some advanced endoscopes have steering mechanisms, clearing mechanisms, and surgical attachments with which to perform minor operations. The only limitation to endoscopes is that they cannot see into the walls of organs or into solid organs, but as miniaturization continues, more useful scopes will be developed.

A gastroscope is used to look into the stomach to try to find evidence of an ulcer, bleeding, or a tumor.

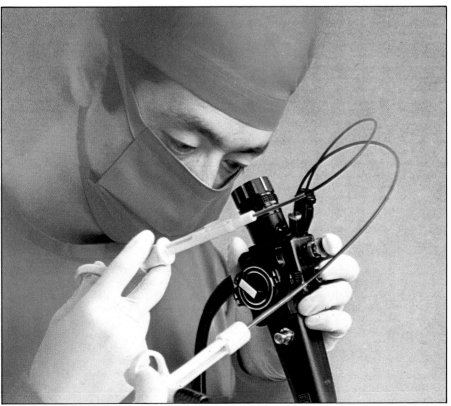

Olympus/Key Med

Types of endoscopes and their uses

Endoscope	Site	Anesthetic	Reason
Gastroscope	Stomach	Sedation	Ulcers, bleeding, tumors
Colonoscope	Colon	Mild sedation	Tumors, polyps, ulceration
Colposcope	Uterus	Sedation or general anesthetic	Abnormal bleeding or tumors
Cystoscope	Bladder	General anesthetic	Tumors, stones, ulcers, and any other abnormalities
Bronchoscope	Bronchus	Sedation or general anesthetic	Removal of foreign bodies, diagnosis of lung cancer, cysts
Laparoscope	Abdomen	General anesthetic	Gynecological conditions, damage from injury, abdominal pain sterilization in women
Arthroscope	Joint	General anesthetic	Torn and damaged cartilage
Amnioscope	Uterus	Sedation	Suspected fetal abnormalities

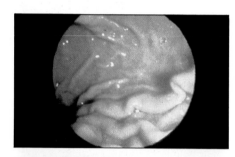

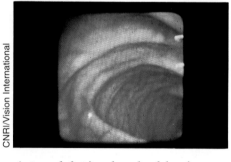

A stomach (top) and a colon (above), viewed through endoscopes.

CNRI/Vision International

Uses

Endoscopes are used primarily as diagnostic tools to allow a doctor to look directly into an organ and see abnormalities and the causes of disease. Larger endoscopes have several channels in the cylinder; air can be blown in to distend the organ and improve viewing.

Some endoscopes have attachments that can be used in performing minor operations. A biopsy attachment to an endoscope enables a piece of tissue to be removed, or to pass an electric current to seal off a point of tissue that is bleeding. Others have specialized attachments. The cystoscope, which is used for looking into the bladder, has refined attachments that can cut away a bladder tumor or remove small stones.

The most common endoscopies are performed on the stomach (via the mouth) and large intestine (via the anus). In cases of severe injury or pain in the abdomen, a laparoscope can be passed through the wall of the abdomen to look for bleeding or damaged organs. Where a bladder abnormality is suspected, a cystoscope can be passed up the urethra.

In exceptional circumstances, it may be necessary to look into the uterus of a pregnant woman and check the development of the baby. This is known as amnioscopy. Alternatively, in cases of ectopic pregnancy where the fetus develops outside the uterus, usually in one of the fallopian tubes, a laparoscope can be used to look into the abdomen to confirm the diagnosis. Performing an endoscopy during pregnancy is often safer than an X-ray examination, which may harm the developing fetus.

Exploratory procedures

Endoscopy is a harmless and painless procedure. By giving a direct view of the organ concerned, it can save patients from complicated and often inexact investigations, and from exploratory surgery.

For instance, in the case of peptic ulceration of the stomach, the patient may complain of typical ulcer symptoms, although there may be other causes. A physical examination may not be helpful because there are no physical findings specific for ulcers; X rays, using a barium meal, can be misleading. A gastroscope, however, lets the doctor to look directly at the lining of the stomach wall. Any ulcer can be clearly seen, and in some cases, a small piece may be taken for laboratory tests. The only alternative would be to open the stomach surgically, but the gastroscope makes this unnecessary.

Treatment

The most common endoscopy that needs hospital admission is gastroscopy, where a fiber-optic endoscope is passed down the esophagus into the stomach. Having fasted for eight hours so that the stomach is empty of food, the patient is given some sedation, either by pills three or four hours in advance, or by injection directly into the vein.

The endoscope is lubricated with jelly and placed in the patient's mouth. The patient then swallows it—vomiting is prevented because of the sedation—and the tube is fed down the esophagus into the stomach. This may be uncomfortable but it is not painful.

The surgeon then connects the light source, the room is darkened, and the inspection of the esophagus and stomach begins. The patient may be asked to lie in different positions to bring areas into view. In many cases, the procedure is so comfortable that the patient goes to sleep. When the investigation is completed, the surgeon slowly withdraws the instrument. The patient goes home when the sedation wears off.

Other endoscopies are more complex procedures, in particular laparoscopy, which is used to sterilize women, and cystoscopy. These may be done under a general anesthetic. Provided endoscopies are performed by a doctor, there is no danger of damage to an organ or tissue.

Enema

Q I had always thought that laxatives were the best treatment for constipation, if a change of diet was not sufficient. Isn't this the case?

A Yes, oral laxatives are the best kind of treatment. But if they fail to get things moving, even with the additional help of suppositories, after a few days the hardened feces may cause a blockage. In such a case an enema is the only way to break it up.

Q Do I really need to have an enema when I go into labor? It sounds awful!

A Enemas are no longer given routinely in labor. However they can be very helpful in some cases for clearing the rectum without the mother having to bear down. Defecation normally takes place automatically as the baby's head travels down the vagina, so if you don't like the idea of this you may prefer to request an enema.

Q My grandmother had an enema many years ago and said it was really painful. Is this still true?

A No. Modern enemas are given through soft tubes made of a nonirritant material, and although they may be a little uncomfortable, pain is a thing of the past.

Q I have to have a barium enema X ray. Will I need an ordinary enema beforehand?

A Yes, this is normal practice. The large intestine will need to be cleared to receive the barium enema, so you will be given laxatives a few days before and any residual feces will be washed out with a saline enema just before the X ray; this will insure that the pictures are not obscured.

Q What happens if an enema doesn't relieve constipation?

A In rare cases of enemas failing to break up a rock of feces, it may have to be removed by hand. This is usually done by a nurse, after the patient has been dosed with painkillers.

Whether it is a problem of constipation, the need to clear the large intestine before an operation, or the only way to treat a medical condition, enemas are easy to give, quick-acting, and totally painless.

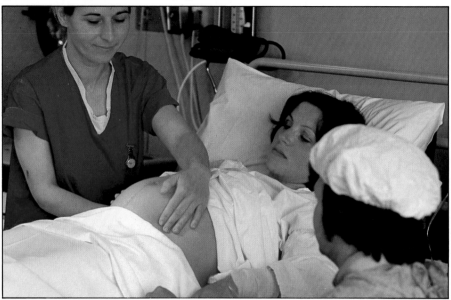

Mike St Maur Shiel/MC Library

An enema is sometimes given in early labor to make the birth easier.

The most common reason an enema is given is to relieve constipation when all other forms of treatment have failed. Severe constipation often occurs after rectal surgery (for hemorrhoids), but it can happen suddenly for no apparent reason. The feces form such a hard mass that they obstruct the rectum; an enema will soften the obstruction and allow it to be passed easily and painlessly.

An enema is sometimes given to women in the early stages of labor or to surgical patients who have to undergo a procedure concerned with the large intestine. It can also be used to diagnose or treat diseases relating to the intestines.

Barium enemas are used as an aid to diagnosis in radiology. The barium shows up the large intestine in contrast to the surrounding tissues on the X ray.

Certain diseases can be treated using enemas containing drugs. For example a steroid enema may be used to combat the intestinal inflammation in Crohn's disease (ileitis) and ulcerative colitis.

Treatment

The old method of giving an enema was to irritate the lining of the large intestine with 1 pt (0.47 l) of soap solution. This stimulated movement of the muscles, which broke up and lubricated the feces.

A safer treatment runs a dose of 3.75 to 5 fl oz (111 to 148 ml) of an olive and arachis (peanut) oil retention enema into the patient, who must then lie quietly.

Later, a second enema of 5 fl oz (148 ml) of saline solution allows for easy defecation.

Phosphate enemas—dosage 3.75 fl oz (111 ml)—draw fluid into the large intestine from the surrounding tissues. The fluid softens the feces and encourages movement in the intestines.

If an X ray of the large intestine is required, a barium enema is run into the colon. The volume used and the position of the patient is varied, depending on what the radiologist is trying to see.

Enemas are administered at hospitals or at home by a nurse. But a caring relative could quickly learn the technique to treat a housebound patient.

The solution is put in a plastic container attached to a plastic tube; this is no more than 6 in (15 cm) long with the diameter of a little finger.

The patient lies on the bed with his or her head slightly down and knees drawn up to raise the buttocks and expose the anus. The tip of the tube is then lubricated with KY jelly and while the patient is encouraged to relax, the tube is inserted into the anus. The enema is then administered by squeezing in the contents of the container, while the patient resists the natural inclination to defecate. Once the tube is removed, the patient can be transferred to the bathroom to await the effect of the treatment.

Environment

Q We are thinking of moving from the city to the country. Will this provide a better environment in which to raise our children?

A In some ways your children will certainly benefit from a move to the country. They will breathe cleaner air, have more space in which to play, and will be subject to less irritating noise. Before you make such a move it is important to weigh up all the advantages and disadvantages.

In the country your children may have to travel a long way to school, which may affect their grades. They may miss having friends nearby and find it more difficult to pursue their hobbies. The most important consideration is to provide your children with a stable family environment, and if you really believe your move will help to achieve this, then it is probably a good idea to go ahead.

Q I have given up smoking but am worried that my health is still being damaged by breathing in other people's cigarette smoke. Is this likely?

A Yes. Recent studies have shown that it can be damaging to breathe in other people's smoke. This is just one reason why environmentalists devoted to improving the conditions of life for everyone are anxious to ban cigarette smoking from buses, trains, theaters, restaurants, and other public places.

Q Our house is on the flight path to an international airport and I am finding it increasingly difficult to sleep because of the noise. What should I do?

A The most simple solution to your problem would be to move to another location, but if this is not possible, then try wearing earplugs at night. If this does not help, it would be wise to consult your doctor, since it is known that a lack of sleep and constant bombardment of the ears by aircraft noise can have damaging effects on one's physical and mental health and well-being.

Research has shown that though heredity is important, the physical and emotional situation in which people are brought up plays a vital role in their development.

At this age, a child is dependent on his parents to provide stimulation and dictate the nature of his environment

The environment is an all-embracing word used to describe the ingredients of a person's surroundings and experiences. This includes not only the physical environment, whether town or country, tropical or temperate climate, but also the social situation in which he or she lives. Scientifically, the adjective *environmental* is used to describe any influence on a person's life that produces effects that are not inherited.

The problem of studying the effects of the environment on human life is that usually the situation is not clear-cut. It is hard to make a clear distinction between the effects brought about by inheritance and those that can be attributed to the environment. This is why scientists have found it very useful to make studies of identical twins to distinguish between the effects of nature (inheritance) and those of nurture (environment).

Identical twins are invaluable in such research because they are known to have exactly the same hereditary material. When identical twins are formed, a single egg in the mother is fertilized by a single sperm from the father, but the egg then splits into two, so that the cells of each twin have exactly the same chromosomes. These chromosomes contain identical genes—the inheritance factors that carry the program for each individual and determine not only the details of body structure, such as eye and hair color, but also, to some extent, their personality and intelligence (see Genetics).

To find out the effects of the environment on identical twins, research concentrates on cases in which twins have

Studying identical twins has taught researchers much about the relative importance of environment and heredity.

been reared in separate families. These studies have provided particularly useful statistics for those trying to assess the influence of nature versus nurture.

Studies of twins

In their analysis of identical twins, scientists have examined both physical and mental differences and similarities. They have compared the twins not only with each other, but with brothers and sisters brought up in the same family, and also with nonidentical (fraternal) twins who are totally unrelated to them.

Studies of height and weight indicate that the environment does have a marked effect, although this is stronger where weight rather than height is concerned. It seems that what a person eats has more effect on his or her weight than height, although in some of the identical twins reared apart it was shown that the children who were given the better diet, including more protein, grew taller than those on poorer diets.

Statistics have also been gathered that reflect the influence of the environment on an individual's physiology. The figures demonstrated that identical twins have very similar amounts of sugar in their blood, for example, and that female twins begin menstruating at almost exactly the same time. These statistics show that these traits are affected more by heredity than by environment.

Intelligence and personality

The effect of the environment on mental abilities, particularly on human intelligence, is a matter of much controversy. Again, studies of identical twins have been conducted to try to work out the environmental element in intelligence.

The results so far show that identical twins do have much more similarity in mental abilities, even when they were brought up apart, than their brothers and sisters or nonidentical twins.

But the environment also has an enormous effect on achievement, since figures compiled on identical twins who had been brought up separately showed that nearly all those who received the most years of education scored highest in intelligence tests.

Identical twins have also provided evidence for the influence of the environment on personality, but again the results are not entirely clear-cut. One recent set of studies sought to bring together identical twins separated from each other soon after birth, some of whom had even grown up on different continents. These pairs of twins, meeting for the first time in middle age, found they had the same tastes in dress, in the partners they had married, and that they suffered from the same fears and phobias. One pair of twins even discovered that they had both had major depressions at the same time as a result of marital problems.

The family situation

Parents striving to bring up their children in the best possible way often worry about providing the perfect environment for their families. In doing the best for one's family, it is important to remember that the environment is very complex and consists not only of tangible items, such as food, clothes, and housing, but also of intangibles like love, security, friendship, and affection.

As far as home environment is concerned, parents ideally should adopt a well-balanced attitude. It is essential to protect children from disease, for example, by insuring that the home is clean and that food is not contaminated by disease-carrying organisms. However, it is possible to become overly obsessed with dirt, to the extent that children suffer because they are not allowed to express themselves for fear of getting dirty or making a mess. Similarly it is very important for a child to learn self-expression through creative play, but not necessarily with expensive toys or games.

Finally it is important to remember that the total environment, for children and adults, depends not only on the individual, but on the attitude of the whole community towards such matters as hygiene, pollution, and the allocation of basic resources like education. It is important to try to achieve a good balance.

A child's environment begins to change when he or she reaches playschool age.

485

Enzymes

Q I have stomach ulcers. Do enzymes have anything to do with them?

A Yes. When food enters the stomach, the stomach wall secretes two substances—pepsinogen and hydrochloric acid. These combine to form a powerful enzyme called pepsin that helps to digest the food. Ulcers are caused when pepsin begins to digest the stomach wall itself. This happens after excessive acid secretions have destroyed the protective lining of mucus. Stress and smoking are thought to be largely responsible for increasing acid secretion. Stomach ulcers can usually be relieved by resting, not smoking, and using drugs that either neutralize or suppress acid secretion, or help to protect the stomach lining. However, in some cases, surgery may be necessary.

Q My daughter was born with an enzyme deficiency called phenylketonuria and must follow a special diet. If we have more children, will they be affected?

A Any further children you and your husband have will have a one-in-four chance of being affected by the condition. But hospitals routinely screen for the deficiency at birth and if it is present, the child only needs to be put on a diet that cuts out those proteins that contain the substance phenylalanine. However, do consult your doctor before you decide to have another child or if you become pregnant again.

Q I use biological detergents for washing clothes. Can the enzymes they contain damage my hands?

A Certain detergents contain protease enzymes, which help to dissolve stains containing proteinaceous material, such as blood or egg yolk. If you handwash clothes, the detergent removes the protective layer of oil on the skin. The enzymes may then attack skin proteins, causing irritation or even damage, particularly if skin is cut or chapped. Avoid this by rinsing both clothes and hands thoroughly after using such detergents.

Enzymes are the body's catalysts, which means that they make certain vital processes, such as digestion, growth, and reproduction, possible.

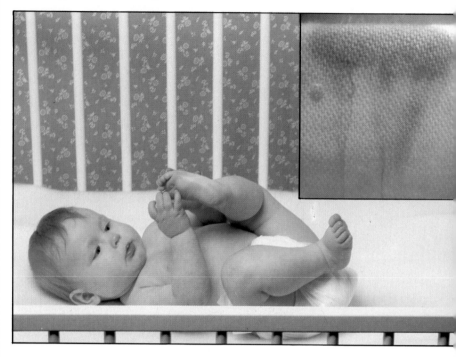

Enzymes promote all the various important chemical transformations that allow any living organism, including humans, to function normally. Enzymes speed up some of these chemical reactions several thousand-fold.

Enzymes activate processes that create and sustain life. Here (inset) it is possible to see their action in a biological detergent, digesting a bloodstain.

The role of enzymes
Enzymes are found throughout the body and come in hundreds of different varieties. Each variety promotes a different chemical transformation. These transformations are of two main types: those that involve the breakdown of large molecules to produce energy and smaller molecules, which are the building blocks of life; and those that use the building blocks and energy for growth, reproduction, and defenses against infection.

Each cell in the body manufactures all the enzymes it needs to perform its usual functions. Some enzymes are so important that they are produced by every cell; these enzymes are usually used within the cell itself. Others are produced only by specialized cells; these may be secreted and used outside the cell, for example, enzymes involved in the digestive process act outside cells, in the gut itself.

Problems
Some substances can deactivate enzymes by occupying their working areas. Cyanide has this effect on an extremely impor-

tant enzyme called cytochrome oxidase, which is involved in the production of energy, and small quantities of cyanide can cause death in a very short period of time.

Many disorders are caused by enzyme deficiencies. For example, albinos lack an enzyme called tyrosinase, which is involved in making the skin pigment melanin. This is why their hair and skin are white in color. Other enzymes convert the amino acid tyrosine to thyroid hormone; if one of these is missing at birth, the child will be mentally retarded.

Enzyme deficiency disorders can be traced back to defects in genes, which determine inherited characteristics. Although not at present curable, in many cases, problems can be alleviated if the missing enzyme is replaced.

Many drugs prescribed by doctors work by altering the activity of enzymes. One of the effects of aspirin is to inhibit the activity of the enzyme cyclooxygenase, which is involved in producing substances called prostaglandins. Certain prostaglandins are thought to be connected with painful inflammation of the joints, so aspirin is a useful treatment for disorders such as rheumatoid arthritis.

Epilepsy

Q I suffer from epilepsy and worry about my children. Can epilepsy be inherited?

A Epilepsy does sometimes run in families, but your children's chances of being affected are only slightly increased—perhaps about five times the national average.

Q Is there any connection at all between mental handicap and epilepsy?

A Yes. Where mental deficiency has resulted from severe brain damage or from an inherited defect of the brain, epilepsy is a common complicating feature. However, epilepsy itself is not a cause of mental handicap and it most definitely is not a sign of any feebleness of mind.

Q Is it true that flashing lights or a TV picture can bring on an epileptic seizure?

A In susceptible people an epileptic seizure may be induced by a bright light flashed at a fixed frequency. A faulty television picture could cause problems, as could some computer games with flashing graphics.

Q Can a person's diet have an effect on epilepsy?

A Research is being undertaken in this area of medicine. Some nutritionists believe that correct amounts of vitamin B_6 and magnesium in the diet of someone who has seizures can reduce the number of attacks. A diet that causes production of ketones (ketogenic diet) may also prevent seizures. Anyone who has epilepsy should ask their doctor's advice about diet; but do not experiment without consulting a doctor.

Q I have recently had a seizure. Do I have to tell the DMV?

A Failure to inform the DMV that you have had an attack is an offense and might automatically disqualify you from insurance coverage. Laws regarding driving with epilepsy vary from state to state.

Epilepsy is a symptom of repeated disturbances in the brain's normal electrical activity. These can be successfully brought under control with drugs, and people with epilepsy are then able to lead normal lives.

Epilepsy involves repeated periods of disordered electrical activity in the brain, beyond voluntary control. It results in a variety of symptoms depending upon the part of the brain involved. The most common are sudden unconsciousness and twitching of the whole body—in other words, a generalized seizure or fit.

The name epilepsy comes from the Greek word *epilepsia*, meaning "taking hold of" or "seizing." It was Hippocrates, the Father of Medicine, who first concluded in the fifth century BC that epilepsy was due to a disorder of the brain, but it was not until 1929 that the coincidence between the attacks and the occurrence of abnormal electrical discharges in the brain was confirmed.

Epilepsy affects about five people in every thousand and is slightly more common in males than females. When epilepsy develops for the first time in both children and young people, a cause is rarely found. When it happens for the first time in older people, it is more serious and may point to a disease of the brain, for example, arteriosclerosis or a brain tumor.

It is vital for a child who has epilepsy to be encouraged to regard the seizures as an inconvenient nuisance that a great many people have to cope with, and not as something shameful or dramatic. If a seizure happens at school, no other child will be harmed by seeing it. The support and acceptance of both adults and children is of great value.

Causes

Epilepsy is divided into two categories. The one in which there is no obvious underlying cause is known as idiopathic epilepsy; the other, in which the cause can be identified, is called acquired or secondary epilepsy. More than three-quarters of all cases of epilepsy belong to the first category.

Idiopathic epilepsy

Epilepsy sometimes runs in families. The relatives of those with epilepsy are between five and 10 times more likely to have fits than other people, and in the twin of an epileptic, the likelihood is increased twenty-fold. However, some believe that this is because of difficulties

If the epilepsy is controlled and there is someone else present, the epileptic can even go swimming.

Spectrum

Areas of the brain associated with epileptic attacks

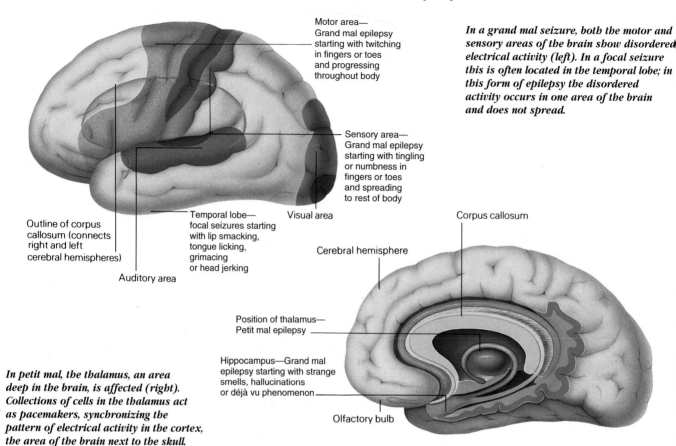

Motor area—
Grand mal epilepsy
starting with twitching
in fingers or toes
and progressing
throughout body

In a grand mal seizure, both the motor and sensory areas of the brain show disordered electrical activity (left). In a focal seizure this is often located in the temporal lobe; in this form of epilepsy the disordered activity occurs in one area of the brain and does not spread.

Sensory area—
Grand mal epilepsy
starting with tingling
or numbness in
fingers or toes
and spreading
to rest of body

Outline of corpus
callosum (connects
right and left
cerebral hemispheres)

Temporal lobe—
focal seizures starting
with lip smacking,
tongue licking,
grimacing
or head jerking

Visual area

Corpus callosum

Cerebral hemisphere

Auditory area

Position of thalamus—
Petit mal epilepsy

In petit mal, the thalamus, an area deep in the brain, is affected (right). Collections of cells in the thalamus act as pacemakers, synchronizing the pattern of electrical activity in the cortex, the area of the brain next to the skull.

Hippocampus—Grand mal
epilepsy starting with strange
smells, hallucinations
or déjà vu phenomenon

Olfactory bulb

---

during childbirth. The symptoms of idiopathic epilepsy show very few constant features.

Acquired epilepsy

After head injuries: Posttraumatic epilepsy can be a complication of a severe head injury, one suffered in an automobile accident for example. In exceptional circumstances the condition can develop months or even a year after the injury itself.

After a high fever: Seizures may be caused in children without epilepsy by a very high fever and the resulting fit is known as a febrile convulsion. Although this is extremely worrying for parents, no damage is done to the child as long as the fever is brought down; usually there will be no further fits.

Arteriosclerosis: Narrowing of the arteries to the brain becomes more common as people age, and when epileptic seizures develop in older people, they are usually due to this. It is not uncommon for a person to have a fit in the course of a stroke, but less common to suffer any trouble once the stroke has happened.

Poisons: Acute poisoning can cause fits. In the past children developed convulsions as a result of lead poisoning caused from licking lead-based paints. These are now banned for household use, but they can still be found on old toys and Victorian furniture.

Fits may also be caused by too sudden a withdrawal from drugs such as barbiturates. For this reason, doctors are being discouraged from prescribing barbiturates for insomnia although they have been one of the mainstays of treatment for epilepsy. Remember, it is the withdrawal from the drug that causes the fit.

Epilepsy with a mental handicap: Epilepsy emphatically does not cause mental handicaps. However in people who are born with very low intelligence due to brain damage at birth or to infections in the uterus like rubella (German measles), the incidence of epilepsy is very much higher.

What happens

Normally the brain controls the functions of the body either by interpreting electrical messages from sensory nerves or by generating electrical impulses for transmission down the motor nerves, to the muscles. This normal electrical activity can be measured by taking an electroencephalogram (EEG), using an instrument called an electroencephalograph.

During an epileptic attack, the electrical impulses recorded by the EEG increase in voltage and frequency, so that what appeared to be a reasonably ordered pattern of electrical activity becomes frenzied. The attack usually begins at one spot and then spreads as the fit develops to involve the whole brain. However, the EEG does not provide a sure diagnosis of epilepsy, because it records normal electrical activity in almost 25 percent of cases, nor does it give much information about the cause of the fit. In a person whose EEG recording is normal, despite a history of recurrent seizures, a doctor may try to induce a seizure by flashing lights in the patient's eyes—a procedure known as photoic stimulation.

Occasionally abnormalities in electrical activity in the brain develop only during sleep. Sometimes EEGs are recorded during natural or artificially induced sleep to chart the abnormalities.

Types of epileptic attack

There are several forms of epileptic attack depending upon the part of the brain in which the abnormal electrical activity starts, and also upon how far the activity spreads.

Q Can epilepsy be cured by alternative treatments like acupuncture, hypnosis, or meditation?

A No. Epilepsy is at present an incurable symptom and unrelated to mental stress, so it is unlikely that these forms of treatment would be any help to an epileptic.

Q Is there anything I can do to prevent myself from having epileptic attacks?

A The only thing that keeps seizures at bay is regular medication. Modern drug therapy is very effective and most people with epilepsy lead full and active lives. However it can be helpful to avoid hunger, fatigue, and stress.

Q My son, who has fits, wants a bicycle for his birthday. Should we get him one?

A A bicycle would not be safe for him at present. Explain this to him, dealing with the situation as a nuisance, not a tragedy. If the seizures disappear entirely for a long time, you can think again about your son having a bicycle, but ask your doctor's advice first.

Q Why do fevers sometimes cause convulsions in young children?

A The brain of a small child may be electrically less stable than that of an adult and more easily irritated by fever. The irritation stimulates the motor nerves, the muscles contract, and the result is a convulsion.

Q How can you protect a child who suffers from epilepsy from the possibility of physical harm during an attack?

A It is important not to overdo protection, so that the child leads as full a life as possible. Bicycling could obviously be dangerous, but swimming is not, so long as there is an adult in charge while the child is in the water. It is a good idea to keep the bathroom door open at bath time in case he or she has a seizure; it is sensible to guard fireplaces and stairwells.

Generalized seizure: This typical epileptic attack, better known by the name *grand mal* (French for "great illness"), follows a fixed pattern and is caused by disordered electrical activity over the whole brain. The attack, which seldom lasts more than a minute or two, may begin with the patient experiencing a strange sensation or smelling an odd and unreal smell. Occasionally there is also the feeling of having been in a particular place or situation before (known by doctors as the *déjà vu*, or "already seen" phenomenon).

This stage of the attack is known as the aura and it is followed immediately by the tonic seizure, during which the muscles contract and remain contracted. The patient loses control and falls rigid to the ground, often sustaining some injury during the fall. (The tonic phase of a seizure accounts for epilepsy being known in the past as the falling sickness.)

The patient may shout and then pass into the clonic phase, when the arms and legs twitch and the breath is held. In both the tonic and clonic phases, he or she may become incontinent and bite the tongue. After the clonic phase, the sufferer will feel confused, drowsy, and may sleep. Paralysis may develop in one or more limbs and last for an hour or more.

Women sometimes have grand mal fits more often before a period, and during pregnancy fits may either increase or decrease in number.

Petit mal ("little illness"): This form of epilepsy develops in children only and rarely persists into adult life. The child with petit mal does not fall down, but loses touch with the world for a couple of seconds. The fits may pass unnoticed at home; at school the child may be labeled as a slow learner or punished for inattention. Some children may have many attacks each day, which will cause them to be confused and forgetful.

A child with petit mal may be speaking at the time of the attack and suddenly stop for a second or two, only to continue after the break as if nothing had happened. In fact, he or she will be quite unaware of the attacks and it will take an observant parent or teacher to spot them. The EEG recording is often abnormal in cases of petit mal, showing some typical changes in electrical activity which are considered to be constant.

Children may easily look vague and far away without having petit mal. A child in a daydream can be brought back to the real world without any difficulty; the child with petit mal is, for just a second or two, quite detached from it.

Focal seizure: This type of fit is caused by disordered electrical activity in one part of the brain, which does not spread. The symptoms depend upon the location of the activity and may show themselves as a twitching of an arm or a leg or of one side of the face.

A common site for the disordered activity is in the temporal lobe of the brain

The electroencephalogram (EEG) records electricity activity in the brain.

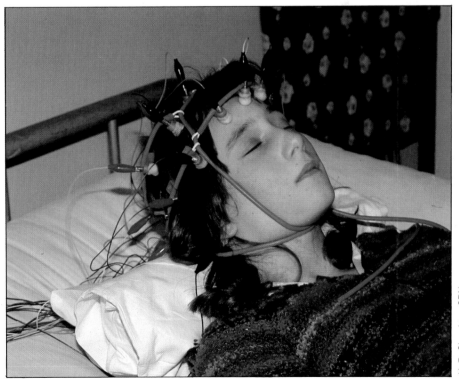

K. R. Slaughter, SRN

Brian Nash

If a person keeps looking at the zigzag pattern made by railings as he or she runs a stick along them uninterruptedly, the brain's electrical activity may become disordered and a seizure may result.

The flashing lights from a video game could cause an epileptic seizure through what is called photoic stimulation.

What to do if someone has an epileptic seizure

- It is not possible to stop an epileptic attack, but it is helpful to protect the person having it from injury while he or she is thrashing around. Make sure that the patient cannot bang his or her limbs against any hard furniture and keep him or her well away from a fireplace. A child having a convulsion should not be left at all until the attack is over

- Do not attempt to push anything into the patient's mouth or to force open the jaws. They are clenched with immense power and it is possible to cause an injury by trying to open them

- When the fit is over turn the patient gently onto one side and loosen the clothes at the neck so that there is no difficulty in breathing

- If the fit has happened in an unsafe place, like the street, get the patient to safety quickly on a stretcher

- If someone in your family has a fit for the first time, give the doctor a careful, detailed account of what happened during the attack and just before it; it will help toward making a correct diagnosis

- A child who has a convulsion because of high fever should not be kept warm. Remove blankets and thick clothing, and if the temperature rises above 103°F (39.4°C), sponge the patient all over with tepid water until it comes down to 102°F (38.8°C)

and this gives rise to temporal lobe epilepsy. The outward signs of this include smacking the lips, making licking movements of the tongue, jerking the head, and grimacing. The aura—the first stage of the attack—is strong; patients often complain that during it they experience unpleasant sensations, smell peculiar smells, and have the feeling that their surroundings are familiar (the *déjà vu* phenomenon).

Status epilepticus: When fits follow one another in rapid succession, persistent holding of the breath may cause brain damage through oxygen shortage. This form of epilepsy is a medical emergency and requires treatment in the hospital as a matter of urgency. A single epileptic attack does not need hospital treatment, but it is wise to let the doctor know when one has happened, in case the particular medication needs adjustment.

Treatment of epilepsy

Grand mal seizures can be treated with a number of different drugs, e.g. phenytoin, sodium valproate, carbamazepine, primidone, or phenobarbitone. Status epilepticus needs to be controlled quickly by the intravenous administration of a drug; the one often used is diazepam.

The antiepileptic drugs are known collectively as anticonvulsants; their effect is to bring the abnormal electrical activity in the brain under control. If this is maintained for a long period of time, the seizures may disappear entirely. All medicines have unwanted side effects and this

is especially true of the anticonvulsants. One of the side effects common to most of them is drowsiness. Skill is needed to balance the benefits of the medicine, in the form of fewer seizures, against the unwanted and uncomfortable effects of an unnecessarily large dose.

Outlook

Fitness to drive: Most states will grant a driver's license to someone who has been free of any epileptic attack, with or without treatment, for one year. A person already holding a license who develops epilepsy must inform the authorities as soon as possible so they may consider the details. A history of febrile convulsions in early childhood may be ignored.

Anyone who has had a seizure at any time since the age of two is barred from working as a driver of a heavy goods truck or a public transporation vehicle.

Hazardous occupations: It is not a good idea for anyone who has epilepsy to work at a hazardous job, for example as a construction worker or a crane driver.

Sports: The only sports which might prove hazardous are swimming, cycling, and horseback riding. If the epilepsy is well controlled, however, the risk is negligible and there should be no problems. If the symptoms are poorly controlled, it would clearly be unwise to participate in any of these sports.

Episiotomy

A minor operation called an episiotomy may be performed on a woman giving birth. Healing can cause discomfort, but it is a small price to pay for a healthy baby.

Q Will I feel any pain after an episiotomy?

A An episiotomy can cause some discomfort (but not actual pain when you walk or sit), which may last for about two weeks. Certain things can be done to help—for example, you can take painkilling pills, sit on a foam rubber ring to relieve the pressure on the stitches, or use a topical anesthetic spray.

Q I have had an episiotomy and am pregnant again. Will I have to have another one when I have my next baby?

A Not necessarily. It will depend on whether the situation which required you to have the first episiotomy recurs. Often the tissues at the opening of the birth canal stretch more easily during a subsequent labor and an episiotomy is unnecessary.

Q Can anything be done to help an episiotomy heal more quickly?

A Yes. Hygiene is very important: wear clean, cotton underpants every day, take frequent baths containing salt, and change maternity pads regularly. An episiotomy usually heals so well that you may find it difficult to even find traces of the scar afterward.

Q How soon after having an episiotomy can my husband and I have sex?

A The scar has usually healed completely within four weeks of the birth. Your doctor will check this, and if all is well, it is quite safe to have sex. Do remember, however, to take the necessary contraceptive precautions.

Q Will I find sex painful once the episiotomy has healed?

A It is very rarely painful. If you have any pain, it is wise to consult your doctor. In rare cases, it may be necessary to perform a small operation to readjust the opening to the vagina. Normally, you will find that there are no problems with sexual intercourse.

Toward the end of the birth process, the baby reaches the lower part of the birth canal, or vagina. This area is surrounded by firm muscular and fibrous tissue that is stretched as the baby passes through. Occasionally the tissue is overstretched by the baby and tears. Tears usually heal very well, but sometimes they may extend into the anal canal and cause problems, such as permanent incontinence. They may then need to be repaired surgically later on.

To prevent this from happening and for other reasons, it may be wise to cut into this mass of muscle, the perineal body. This cut is called an episiotomy.

Other reasons

When a baby is due to be born, the mother helps to push it through the birth canal by bearing down; however, the muscle at the opening of the birth canal, instead of stretching open as it should, may remain firm and unyielding. Widening the opening to the canal with an episiotomy can sometimes help the mother to push the baby out more easily.

Occasionally an episiotomy is performed to reduce the pressure on a baby's head just before it is born, for example, if it is born bottom first, in a breech position, or if it is premature and would suffer too great a trauma from a normal labor.

An episiotomy is almost always performed when it is necessary for an obstetrician (a doctor who specializes in the delivery of babies) to assist the birth of the baby using forceps. Here, an episiotomy is done partly to allow more room in the vagina for the forceps and partly to prevent tissue from tearing.

The operation

An episiotomy is usually done only a few minutes before the baby is delivered. The tissue to be cut is injected with local anesthetic to make it numb. A few minutes later, the cut is made with scissors or a knife. Usually, the cut is made in the perineum (the tissue that lies between the vagina and the anus), slightly off centre. This only takes a few seconds to perform. The cut is sewn up once the baby and the placenta are delivered. The stitches usually dissolve within 10 days.

Risk of tearing

Many women have babies without needing an episiotomy; some may choose not to have an episiotomy even though they risk tearing. Anyone with strong preferences should discuss the matter with the doctor or midwife who is delivering the baby, and have their request written into their hospital notes.

The different types of episiotomy cuts are indicated by the straight and broken lines.

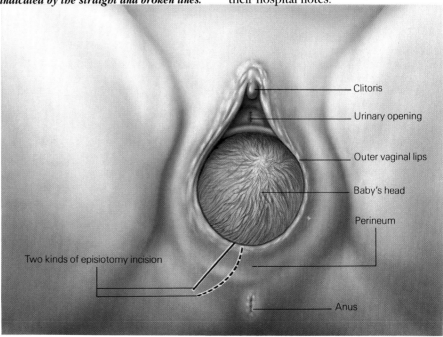

Clitoris
Urinary opening
Outer vaginal lips
Baby's head
Perineum
Two kinds of episiotomy incision
Anus

Frank Kennard

Erection and ejaculation

Q My baby son has erections. Is this normal?

A Yes. This is a reflex erection and no cause for concern. He will not ejaculate, since his internal organs have not yet developed so as to be able to produce sperm.

Q What is a wet dream and why do they happen?

A A wet dream is nature's way of releasing the sperm that has been produced over some days. Most boys start having wet dreams when they reach puberty and they should be reassured that this is completely normal. For some young boys, it can be a worrying experience, especially if they do not understand what is happening to them. It is helpful to discuss it within the context of sex education.

Q Is it possible to climax without ejaculating?

A Yes, but this is very rare. One prominent sexologist found that only 0.4 percent of males have had this experience at some time in their lives.

Q What I can do about premature ejaculation?

A This problem, which usually has a psychological origin, is quite common; anxiety and stress usually only make it worse. One self-help technique to control ejaculation is simple distraction. When you are at the point of orgasm, think of something totally unconnected with sex; this may delay your orgasm.

Alternatively, there is the squeeze technique, developed by the sex therapists Masters and Johnson. When you are at the point of ejaculating, your partner should squeeze the frenulum, which is a thin, triangular mark, located on the underside of the point where the glans or head of the penis meets the shaft. If you are uncircumcised, draw back the foreskin to see it. The pressure should be firm, maintained for three or four seconds, then released. This should stop ejaculation, but if the erection diminishes, your penis may need to be stimulated again.

Many men are unaware of what happens to their bodies when they experience erection and ejaculation. Knowing how the sex organs function is an important aspect of understanding sexuality.

During the sexual process, a man's penis goes from its normal, unaroused state to orgasm, where sperm is discharged. There are four stages in this orgasmic cycle: arousal, plateau, orgasm, and resolution (see Intercourse).

Arousal

Sexual arousal is usually associated with an arousing thought, though physical stimulation is required to actually reach orgasm. The stimulation may be either indirect, by kissing, stroking, or fondling parts of the body that are not specifically sexual, or direct, by touching the penis itself. A nerve message from the brain goes to the base of the spinal cord, which then sends a message of arousal to the genitals.

When a man is not aroused, the penis is flaccid (soft), and the blood vessels within it lie close together. The scrotal sac, which lies beneath the penis and holds both testes, is loose. Each testis continuously produces sperm, ready for ejaculation.

Once the man is aroused, the penis becomes larger and more erect as the blood supply is increased by the action of hormones. A new system of blood flow comes into operation. Blood vessels that have lain close together now expand to allow a generous blood flow to be pumped into the penis. The blood flow out of the penis continues and special veins expand to allow a small amount of blood to flow back into the body without decreasing the erection.

Sometimes men experience erection without any sexual stimulation, either direct or indirect. This is called a reflex erection and can happen after lifting weights, while dreaming, or upon waking. This response is not fully understood.

During the arousal phase, the heartbeat and blood pressure increase, breathing becomes heavier, and the nipples may harden and grow erect; this lasts throughout the cycle.

Plateau

During the plateau phase the penis is fully erect, having increased in both length and width. The glans (head of the penis) darkens in color because of the increased blood flow. The testes increase in size by as much as 50 percent and rise up to enable a more powerful thrust of the penis during intercourse.

A few drops of semen may appear at the opening of the penis and be released. This is one reason why the withdrawal method, or coitus interruptus (withdrawing the penis from the vagina before orgasm), is an unreliable method of contraception; sperm are often present in the seminal fluid that is released initially before proper ejaculation occurs.

The male sex organ

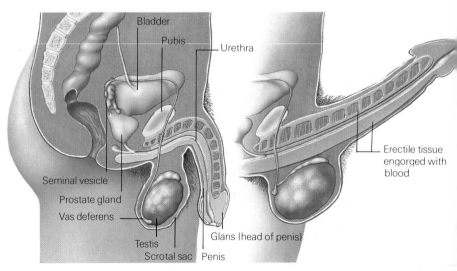

Flaccid penis

Erect penis

Bladder
Pubis
Urethra
Seminal vesicle
Prostate gland
Vas deferens
Testis
Scrotal sac
Penis
Glans (head of penis)
Erectile tissue engorged with blood

Four stages of the male orgasmic cycle

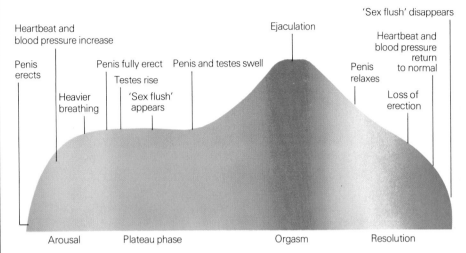

Penis erects

Heartbeat and blood pressure increase

Heavier breathing

Penis fully erect

Testes rise

'Sex flush' appears

Penis and testes swell

Ejaculation

'Sex flush' disappears

Heartbeat and blood pressure return to normal

Penis relaxes

Loss of erection

Arousal   Plateau phase   Orgasm   Resolution

John Hutchinson

Q Can men have multiple ejaculations?

A Some men may feel that they begin to come several times during the course of lovemaking and that they nearly reach the point of climax. Once ejaculation has taken place, it is usually necessary for the man to wait some time before climaxing again. This can range anywhere from a few minutes to a few hours, depending on the magnitude of the state of arousal that the man experiences.

Q How much semen is ejaculated?

A In each orgasm, a man ejaculates anything from 0.07 to 0.2 fl oz (2 to 6 ml) of semen. However, if a man has not ejaculated for some time, he may find that he ejaculates more than if he has had sex in the last few hours. The amount of semen is not an indication of fertility; it is the number and mobility of the sperm it contains that counts.

Q One of my friends claims he can have five orgasms in an evening. I manage one, sometimes two. Is there something wrong with me?

A Not at all. Many men like to think of themselves as studs, or pretend that they are to their friends; in fact, such people are rare. When men are younger they are sometimes able to manage more orgasms, but the frequency usually starts declining in their twenties. The fact that you reach orgasm once or even twice is quite normal. So stop worrying and put the idea of trying to have multiple orgasms out of your mind.

Q Whenever I become aroused, I get a measleslike rash all over my chest. Is there anything I can do about it?

A This rash is what sexologists call the sex flush, or simply a flushing of the skin around the chest, neck, and forehead. Not all men get it, but some do. It is a normal part of the orgasmic cycle, which occurs at the plateau phase and disappears during resolution; it is nothing to worry about.

Orgasm

The ejaculatory climax has two stages. In the first stage, sperm travel up from the testes through the vas deferens (two tubes that carry sperm to the prostate gland) to reach the seminal vesicles which produce the seminal fluid. The sperm and the seminal fluid are mixed together and the fluid then travels to the internal opening of the urethra (the tube that carries urine from the bladder to the penis). Because of the buildup of sperm in the urethral entrance, the man will feel that he is about to come.

In the second stage, the seminal fluid is forced through the urethra by the rhythmic contractions of the urethra's muscles and out of the external opening. There are usually three or four main bursts of semen, followed by weaker, more irregular contractions.

These two stages happen in a matter of seconds, and although they are separate processes, it is impossible to have stage one without stage two. However, some men may ejaculate immediately, while others will exercise control over the timing of their orgasm.

Resolution

After ejaculation, the penis and testes slowly return to their normal size and position. The penis once again becomes flaccid as the blood drains away, back into the body, and the blood vessels return to their nonaroused state.

Some men may find that the head of their penis is particularly sensitive at this time and may not wish it to be stimulated or touched any further. If the plateau phase has been long or the penis remains inside the vagina, the penis may stay erect for a considerable time.

While some men can become sexually aroused again within a few minutes, the time varies from man to man and from occasion to occasion. The amount of semen in subsequent ejaculations is reduced, but this does not lessen the chances of pregnancy; there are millions of sperm in each ejaculation.

Problems

The process of erection and ejaculation will not happen exactly like this every time for every man. Many men find that there are occasions when they experience problems with one or both functions.

One of the most common difficulties is premature ejaculation, in which the plateau phase is very short and ejaculation takes place almost immediately. This is usually due to worry, either about sexual performance or problems within the relationship. Often these tensions have to be worked through before the problem can be dealt with.

Some men find it difficult to maintain an erection or reach orgasm when they are with a partner, but they are perfectly able to do so through masturbation. This is known as impotence. Frequently the reason is psychological; the man may be worried about letting his partner down and failing sexually.

Both premature ejaculation and impotence are usually based on emotional factors rather than physical ones. It is important that any problems of this kind are brought to the family doctor, rather than suffered in silence. The doctor may if necessary refer a man to a psychosexual specialist who can help to overcome the difficulties. Sometimes couples engage in joint therapy to try to work out sexual problems together.

Esophagus

Q If I drink something that is too hot, can I actually burn my esophagus?

A In theory, yes you can; in practice this happens only in very rare cases. The nerve endings in your lips, tongue, and the lining of your mouth would have warned you that the liquid was painfully hot and you would have stopped drinking and spat out any of the drink already in your mouth before it was swallowed.

Q If my baby son accidentally swallows something sharp, like a piece of broken glass, what damage could he do to his esophagus?

A Usually, amazingly little damage is done, even though you would have thought that some drastic disaster was almost a certainty. Sometimes the glass scratches the lining of the esophagus as it goes down and causes a little bleeding, but seldom more than that. If something like this does happen, however, it would be wise to let your doctor know. It may be necessary to follow the foreign body's progress through the gut, and possibly take X rays to see where it is, until it is excreted.

Q Can anything be done for people suffering from cancer of the esophagus?

A Yes, a great deal. There are now many people who survive for years after being successfully treated for cancer of the esophagus. Provided that the diagnosis is made early, and this is the crucial factor, a curative operation is usually possible.

If the cancer is in the lower part of the esophagus, the operation will consist of removing the cancerous section and bringing up the stomach to be joined with the cut end. Growths in the upper part of the esophagus used to be much more difficult to deal with, because there is not so much room to maneuver. Nowadays it is sometimes possible to transplant part of the colon to act as a replacement for the diseased section of the esophagus.

Most food passes down the esophagus so smoothly that we are unaware of its passage. It is only when we eat something too large, too hot, or too cold that we notice this vital link between mouth and stomach.

The esophagus or gullet is the tube that connects the back of the mouth to the stomach. Its only function is to carry food from the mouth to the stomach, where it will be broken down by the various digestive processes and then absorbed into the bloodstream (see Alimentary canal).

Structure

The esophagus is an elastic tube about 10 in (25 cm) in length and about 1 in (2.5 cm) in diameter. It extends from the back of the throat (the pharynx), where it lies immediately behind the windpipe (trachea), down through the diaphragm, and into the upper part of the stomach.

The top and bottom ends of the esophagus are each controlled by a strong muscular ring, called a sphincter, that can open and close to allow for the passage of food.

Like the rest of the alimentary canal, the wall of the esophagus is made up of four layers: a lining of mucous membrane to enable food to pass down easily, a submucous layer to hold the mucous layer in place, a relatively thick layer of muscle consisting of both circular and longitudinal fibers, and finally, an outer protective covering.

Swallowing

When food enters the mouth, it is chewed by the teeth and lubricated by saliva into a smooth, slippery mass called a bolus. This bolus enters the esophagus by the act of swallowing, which is a complex activity involving several different groups of muscles.

The muscles of the throat, or pharynx, contract, forcing the food toward the upper end of the esophagus. At the same time, other throat and face muscles raise the tongue up against the roof of the mouth so that food does not pass back into the mouth; these muscles also move the palate upward to prevent food from getting into the space at the back of the nose, and close the epiglottis (a flap of skin) over the raised larynx so that food cannot get into the windpipe (trachea) and lungs.

Occasionally the epiglottis does not close in time and food or liquid does get into the larynx. When this happens the substance that has been swallowed is immediately expelled by forceful coughing, the sensation we know as food going

down the wrong way. This is a reflex action and is not under our control.

The first part of swallowing is a voluntary act over which we have conscious control. Once the food has passed the

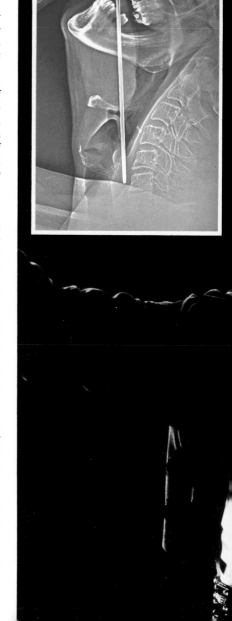

This X ray shows how The Amazing Stromboli swallowed a sword. He kept his epiglottis open to allow the sword into his esophagus without swallowing.

back of the tongue, however, the continuation of the act of swallowing is an involuntary, automatic act that cannot be stopped consciously (see Muscles).

The bolus of food does not just slide down the esophagus into the stomach. It is actively pushed down by a series of wavelike muscular contractions of the esophagus wall, a process known as peristalsis. The passage of food is, therefore, an active process and not just a passive mechanism depending on gravity; which is why we can eat and drink just as well standing on our heads as sitting down.

Common problems

A surprising variety of things can pass down the esophagus without damaging it. People have even been known to swal-

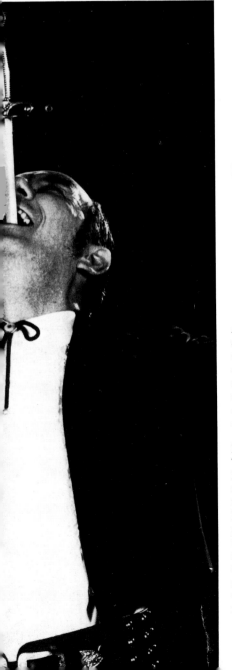

Hiatus hernia and the esophagus

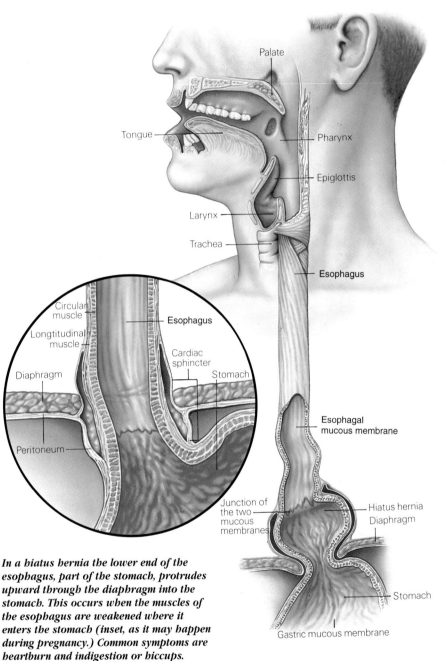

In a hiatus hernia the lower end of the esophagus, part of the stomach, protrudes upward through the diaphragm into the stomach. This occurs when the muscles of the esophagus are weakened where it enters the stomach (inset, as it may happen during pregnancy.) Common symptoms are heartburn and indigestion or hiccups.

low broken glass without being harmed. The esophagus may become blocked, however, if a large object is swallowed, for example, when a child swallows a toy. If this happens swallowed food will be brought back rapidly, and the person will retch persistently and feel pain behind the breastbone. Surgery may be needed to remove the blockage. Similarly if a person swallows a corrosive substance, such as acid or strong alkali like bleach, the esophagus can be seriously damaged and may require surgery to correct it.

Perhaps the most common of all problems in this area is inflammation of the esophagus (esophagitis). This is usually caused by acid passing up into the esophagus from the stomach and it results in a burning sensation behind the breastbone after eating. This condition, which is commonly called heartburn, occurs frequently during pregnancy, and it is a common symptom of a hiatus hernia. The treatment for esophagitis normally depends on antacids and drugs to reduce acid production in the stomach.

Estrogen

Estrogen is a general term for a group of female sex hormones, all with slightly different names (such as estrone or estrol) and all performing essential functions in a woman's reproductive life.

Q I have been taking the Pill for a number of years. Will this upset my sex hormones?

A In some women the Pill does upset the normal estrogen and progesterone levels, and this is probably responsible for side effects, such as cramps, headaches, changes of mood, and fluid retention. These side effects usually disappear when the Pill is discontinued. In a few women the natural cycle is disturbed so much that periods cease and it is difficult to restart them. Fertility, although obviously interfered with by the Pill, usually returns when it is stopped. There are, however, a few women who find it difficult to become pregnant after taking oral contraceptives for a long time.

Q I am just beginning to go through menopause. Will the lack of estrogen in my body cause any physical differences?

A The most obvious difference is the cessation of periods. There are also changes in the breasts, which tend to become smaller and less firm. In some women there are also effects on the vagina, which may become less moist and supple. This situation can be substantially improved by taking synthetic estrogen.

Q Does estrogen have any effect on pregnancy?

A After having stimulated the uterus to prepare for a possible pregnancy, estrogens continue to play an important part in the subsequent pattern of events, though another hormone, progesterone, also has a vital role. Levels of estrogen increase throughout pregnancy, reaching a peak just before birth, but rapidly drop to normal levels immediately after it. Much of this estrogen is manufactured in the placenta rather than in the ovaries. Estrogen does not seem to play a part in the onset of labor, but it is likely that the high levels of estrogen during pregnancy keep the enlarging breasts inactive until the time arrives for milk production.

Estrogens first achieve prominence in a woman's life at puberty. About four years before a girl has her first period (see Menarche) the hypothalamus in the brain begins to secrete substances called releasing factors. These act on the pituitary gland and stimulate it to produce the hormones responsible for a girl's sexual development. One is a growth hormone; two others—the follicle-stimulating hormone (FSH) and the luteinizing hormone (LH)—are responsible for controlling the various changes in the monthly menstrual cycle.

Follicle-stimulating hormone
FSH has the effect of stimulating the growth to maturity of egg follicles (Graafian follicles) in the ovary—all of which have been present since before birth. Only a few follicles grow at first, but as they do, the layers of cells surrounding them begin to secrete estrogen. These follicles produce estrogen for about a month and then fade. Each month, however, more and more follicles are stimulated by FSH until eventually between 12 and 20 become active at a time. Thus, there is a gradual increase in the amount of estrogen circulating in the body and this is what triggers specific changes during puberty.

Effects of estrogen
As the months pass by the amount of estrogen circulating in the body increases more rapidly. This has the effect of stimulating growth in the lining of the uterus, the endometrium, in preparation for its role of accommodating a fetus. Feedback to the pituitary results in it secreting less FSH, with the effect that the ovaries in turn produce less estrogen. Estrogen support for the thickening of the lining of the uterus is withdrawn and it begins to break down and flow out through the vagina as a mixture of blood and debris, the first period (menstruation). During the period the hypothalamus stimulates the pituitary to produce more FSH, which triggers the ovary to mature another batch of egg follicles and manufacture more estrogen; so the cycle is repeated.

The amount of estrogen rises steadily all through the first (or proliferative) phase of the menstrual cycle, during which the lining of the uterus is growing thicker, until by the 13th day after the onset of the last period, the lining is six times its original thickness. Feedback to the hypothalamus and pituitary causes a slowing down in the production of FSH once the estrogen peak has been reached, but also stimulates the manufacture of the other major pituitary sex hormone, luteinizing hormone. This also acts on the ovary, stimulating one of the egg follicles to break open and release its egg, which then makes its way into the fallopian tube where it is available for fertilization. Once this monthly cycle is established, it continues until a woman reaches menopause (see Menopause).

Estrogens are necessary not only to initiate puberty and the succession of menstrual cycles but to maintain the woman's other sexual characteristics. If, for any reason, the supply of estrogen fails, not only do the menstrual periods cease and the fertility rate falls, but the woman may begin to take on what appears to be a more masculine appearance.

The activity of the hypothalamus gland, which is the initiator of the chain of events that results in estrogen production, can be influenced by emotional factors. It is because of these influences that anxiety and depression can affect estrogen secretion and thus both fertility and the cycle of menstruation.

Uses of estrogen
Taking a small daily dose of synthetic estrogen, called hormone replacement therapy (HRT), as a substitute for what the ovaries are no longer producing naturally does much to alleviate the effects of menopause. The sudden discontinuance of such treatment brings about an artificial menstruation, often called withdrawal bleeding. This technique is sometimes used to provoke regular periods in patients when periods are either erratic or absent. One of the changes that sometimes accompanies menopause is a drying up of vaginal secretions, a situation that can often be improved by using estrogen preparations prescribed by a doctor.

Most estrogen preparations taken nowadays are chemically (synthetically) manufactured rather than prepared from natural sources. The most widespread use of these preparations is as a constituent of the contraceptive pill.

Estrogen production and the developing egg

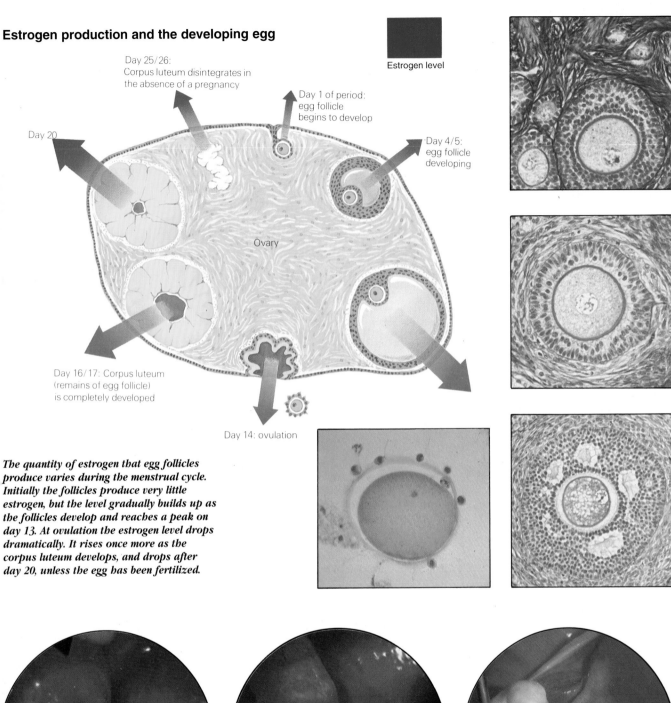

Estrogen level

Day 25/26: Corpus luteum disintegrates in the absence of a pregnancy

Day 1 of period: egg follicle begins to develop

Day 4/5: egg follicle developing

Day 20

Ovary

Day 16/17: Corpus luteum (remains of egg follicle) is completely developed

Day 14: ovulation

The quantity of estrogen that egg follicles produce varies during the menstrual cycle. Initially the follicles produce very little estrogen, but the level gradually builds up as the follicles develop and reaches a peak on day 13. At ovulation the estrogen level drops dramatically. It rises once more as the corpus luteum develops, and drops after day 20, unless the egg has been fertilized.

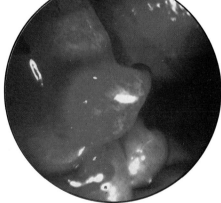

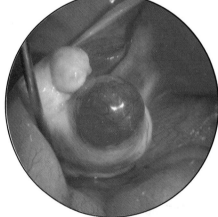

The egg is just beginning to leave the Graafian follicle in which it has been maturing for at least 10–14 days.

The egg is expelled from the ovary toward the fallopian tube. It is surrounded by a jellylike fluid from the follicle.

Here artificial hormones have been used to stimulate ovulation. The egg can be seen lying on a small follicular cyst.

Eugenics

Q My sister has a Down's syndrome son who, despite his handicaps, has a cheerful and affectionate personality and has brought real joy to her family. Why is it that some people think it would be better to have an abortion if it is discovered that a baby will be handicapped in this way?

A Your question raises one of the most argued-over issues of eugenics, namely whether by preventing the birth of handicapped children, people are not only failing in their duty, but depriving themselves of many advantages that are not immediately obvious. Against this view, many people, including some doctors and scientists, feel that letting such children survive increases the number of abnormal genes in a population, so causing the birth of larger and larger numbers of abnormal children. Some parents are also concerned that they will not be able to provide adequate care for a handicapped child.

Q Is it true that in the future it will be possible for a woman to select the sperm of some exceptionally talented or famous man with which she may be artificially inseminated to produce a brilliant child?

A It is true that a sperm bank has been set up in which the sperm of certain famous people has been frozen and preserved for this purpose. But apart from the obvious moral questions this raises, there is no guarantee that if such sperm were used it would result in the birth of children with the exceptional talents of their fathers. This is because the genes or inheritance factors of the mother may come out, in preference to those of the father. Also, environment—in other words, the family and social life and general upbringing of a child—plays a large part in determining whether he or she will be of outstanding, average, or low ability; one could never be certain of how such a child would turn out. Relying on chance to determine the abilities of children is probably a better system than it might appear.

Eugenics is the science which aims to improve the physical and mental standard of populations by preventing certain bad inherited qualities from being passed on. Not surprisingly, it is highly controversial.

A happy family with normal, healthy children: eugenics aims to make this as certain as possible for every couple.

The word *eugenics* was first coined by the English scientist Sir Francis Galton in the early years of the 20th century. Because the term is often misused, it is useful to go back to his original meaning, which was the study of how various factors that happen to be in human control can either improve or worsen the hereditary qualities of future generations.

The idea was based on his belief that because more abnormal children survive as a result of better medicine and living conditions, growing up to have children of their own, the total number of genes —inheritance factors—responsible for producing abnormalities in a population will also grow.

It was a worrying idea, but Galton looked on the bright side, suggesting that if people could make things worse, they could also make them better.

Inherited disorders

Was Galton's premise correct? For the first stage of his thinking, probably yes. Certain inherited physical disorders such as muscular dystrophy, diabetes, and hemophilia, may well be on the increase simply because more babies carrying the genes that produce these diseases survive to have children who are also affected.

It is also possible that the amounts of harmful substances, such as pesticides and atomic radiation, leaking into the environment will produce hereditary diseases in the future.

Improving inherited makeup

The second half of Galton's theory may be attractive, but it has one serious flaw. If human beings could indeed improve their genes, how would they decide which characteristics were desirable for passing on, and which undesirable?

Preventive or progressive

Eugenics is divided into two different branches, in line with Galton's two stages of thought.

Preventive eugenics is concerned with preventing the increase of the genes that cause abnormalities. Progressive eugenics, on the other hand, is concerned with encouraging the increase (or guarding against the decrease) of genes that give normal or desirable characteristics.

In practice, the two branches are the same, because by lessening the number of bad characteristics passed on to children, the proportion of good ones automatically increases. The only difference between them is emphasis.

Modern attitudes

The emphasis of modern eugenics is chiefly preventive and this is achieved mainly through abortion and genetic counseling. If a couple fear they may be carrying genes that could produce an abnormal baby, a genetic counselor will advise about the chances of this occurring by studying the family backgrounds and calling on statistical knowledge built up from the study of thousands of cases.

The amniocentesis test

A genetic counselor or doctor may also suggest that a woman has an amniocentesis test to detect whether her unborn baby has certain abnormalities. The procedure is so-called because a sample of the amniotic fluid surrounding the baby is removed from the mother and studied.

Amniocentesis can detect Down's syndrome (a chromosome disorder that causes mental deficiency), spina bifida (a serious defect of the spinal bones), anencephaly (absence of the brain), respiratory distress syndrome, and abnormalities of the sex chromosomes.

In every case of genetic counseling and after every amniocentesis test, the decision on whether to have an abortion is left entirely to the parents. No pressure or persuasion of any kind is applied.

Dangers of eugenics

At the opposite extreme there are the controversial, even horrifying, consequences of placing too much emphasis on, or faith in, progressive eugenics.

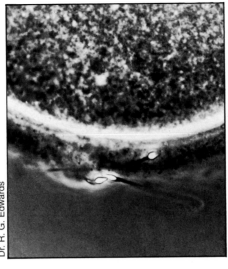

Dr. R. G. Edwards

The moment of human conception, when a sperm fuses with the female egg; scientists can now make this happen artificially.

The best example of this in recent times is provided by the Nazi regime in Germany. This ordered the sterilization and extermination of people considered unfit to breed—mainly Jews—and the use of special groups of so-called pure Germanic women as breeders in an attempt to create a master race.

Sperm banks

This is another form of progressive eugenics, not so disturbing as Nazi methods, but requiring careful consideration. For some years it has been possible to

Scientists created these cloned frogs, all identical to each other. Could they do it with human beings one day?

freeze and store the sperm and eggs of human beings. At present babies cannot be created at will from such genetic material, but the possibility exists. Many people find this idea disturbing because who is to say which sperm and eggs are the most valuable and what if the power to create children artificially were to get into the wrong hands?

Cloning

The technique of cloning involves making an exact copy of a living being via a specially treated egg. Cloning has been done successfully with animals such as mice and sheep and it might be possible in the future to clone a human through its DNA material. The idea of children walking around who are exact replicas of someone else is not only uncanny but worrying, because no one knows exactly what it would be like psychologically for the clone or for society.

Genetic engineering

The other possibility for progressive eugenics is genetic engineering. At present this means essentially the ability to transform naturally occurring substances. Copies have been made, for instance, of the genetic material that forms the hormone insulin, vital for proper utilization of the body's sugar.

In theory this makes it possible to change the genetic makeup of cells and eggs, to improve the quality of the human beings whom they create.

Strict regulations have been drawn up for the practice of genetic engineering, but little is known about what potential this branch of science possesses.

Eugenics in disguise

Before forming any firm opinions on the subject, it is worth bearing in mind that human beings have been using techniques which amount to eugenics for thousands of years. Family planning is the most obvious example. Contraception generally leads to smaller families and this means that there is less likelihood of abnormal children being born.

Equally, many religions forbid marriage between close relations. Behind this is the knowledge that children born to closely related people are more likely to be genetically abnormal.

Finally, arranged marriages, as practiced in a number of religions, could also be regarded as a form of eugenics, because they are an attempt to bring together a suitable man and woman, with a view to producing the best possible offspring.

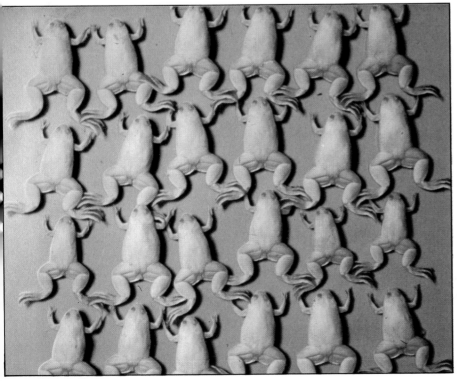

Euthanasia

Q My grandmother, who is a blind and disabled diabetic, often longs to die and begs me to help her. How could it be wrong for me to give her an overdose of insulin?

A To do what you suggest would be murder in the legal sense, even though your grandmother has begged you to end her life. Get as much help as you can for her instead; people in her condition often suffer from depression and treatment can do much to help. People of sound mind can usually find meaning and pleasure in life, even when they are more disabled than your grandmother. Help her as much as possible to do that.

Q My son suffered irreversible brain damage as a result of a car accident. After a time his life-support system was disconnected. Did the doctors do the right thing or could they have tried anything else?

A You can be absolutely sure that your son was treated in the only possible way. Once it has been established beyond all doubt that the brain is dead and that life can only continue through a life-support system, the only sensible, humane decision is to switch off the support.

Q I work in an old people's home and one of the elderly women, who is in great pain, has pleaded with me to put an end to her life. Wouldn't this be a kindness to her?

A No. From an entirely practical point of view, you might fail to kill her and only make her more disabled than ever. You would also be breaking the law and that could have grave effects on the rest of your own life. In addition, if mercy killing were to become widespread, many people, both old and young, might be killed for reasons far less humane than yours. Do all you can to help this woman. Although she says that she wants to die, she may not really mean it and your care and support can help to make her life tolerable. Your attitude will have an effect on her and all the people in the home.

Euthanasia, or mercy killing, involves deliberately putting an end to the life of someone who is ill or injured beyond hope of recovery. There is much debate about the morality of euthanasia and the right to die.

Euthanasia literally means "an easy or painless death." It can also mean mercy killing, the deliberate ending of the life of someone suffering from an incurable disease or the effects of terrible injury. Such a decision could be taken by a doctor or a relative whose motive is to relieve intolerable misery and pain, or not to prolong the life of a body in which the brain is no longer functioning.

There are two main arguments against euthanasia: that severe pain can and should be controlled by drugs, and that if some form of killing by doctors or others were made legal, it might easily be abused and people might be put to death for reasons unconnected with mercy.

However, many people see the argument in terms of their own right to die when faced with the indignity of deterioration, dependence, and hopeless pain.

Doctors do at times deliberately give up trying to keep someone alive for whom there is no hope of recovery. There is a clear difference between giving a fatal dose of a drug to kill a patient and withholding a drug or some other treatment that prolongs life in painful circumstances which cannot improve.

Life-support machines

When a person is so severely injured that he or she is kept alive only by a life support-machine, the decision to withdraw that support is a very difficult one. In most countries it is taken by specialists in the treatment of a particular injury, only after every possible chance for natural recovery has been given, and on the basis of evidence from electrical tests applied to the brain.

The same kind of decision has to be taken over a newborn baby with a severe congenital abnormality; with the parents' consent, the doctors may withhold the facilities of an intensive care nursery in the knowledge that, without these, the baby will die quickly and painlessly.

Living will

Most people have a natural fear of a painful death. Others fear that they will become dependent on other people for every care and unable to commit suicide, even though they are in great pain.

A growing number of people in the United States have prepared a document called a living will, to be placed on their

Sipa Press

American Dr. Jack Kevorkian helps terminally ill patients to commit suicide with the help of a machine they can switch on.

hospital bed for the time when they can no longer take part in decisions on their own future. The document is addressed to their physician, family, attorney, and/or the executor of the will, and states that the patient should be allowed to die rather than be kept alive by artificial means when there is no longer a likelihood that they will recover. Check with the district attorney's office to see if this is legal in your state. Some families have called upon Dr. Jack Kevorkian, a doctor sympathetic to their suffering.

Excretory systems

Q Every time I go to the hospital, I am asked for a urine sample. Why is this?

A Urine can show a number of signs of disease. If there is sugar in the urine, it suggests that the sugar in the blood is raised, which indicates diabetes. Urine may also show protein and blood, indicating kidney or bladder trouble, most commonly due to infection of the urinary tract.

Q I am often constipated and I am worried about poisons building up in my body. Is constipation serious?

A No, but it is a common idea that failure to defecate every day will have serious consequences. Constipation can cause pain and discomfort but it does not lead to poisoning.

Q Every so often I feel sick and have a headache. Years ago I was told these were bilious attacks. Does this mean the flow of bile is obstructed?

A It used to be thought that biliousness was due to a bile disorder. However, doctors do not make this diagnosis anymore. Most people with these kinds of symptoms are suffering from migraine attacks, where the headache is characteristically on one side and is associated with feeling sick.

Q When I became jaundiced because of my gallstones, my urine became very dark and strong. Why was this?

A This is a well-known symptom of certain types of jaundice where the bile duct is obstructed. It means that the bile pigment builds up in the blood and is excreted in the urine.

Q If I use an antiperspirant, am I preventing the body from excreting waste?

A No. The sweat glands under the armpits where antiperspirants are usually applied do not excrete any important waste products.

The human body constantly produces a variety of waste products that have to be gotten rid of if it is to remain healthy. A number of organs throughout the body are responsible for this vital process.

Excretion is the process by which the body gets rid of waste products. The different constituents of the body continuously produce their own by-products. These must be eliminated or the body will effectively poison itself. It is the job of various organs—including the lungs, the kidneys, the liver, and the intestines—to insure that this does not happen.

The function of the lungs

Waste products are produced by the process of body cells burning up fuel with oxygen to produce energy for the body's functions. When glucose, the most common body fuel, is burned, then the waste is the gas carbon dioxide. This dissolves in the bloodstream and is carried to the lungs and exhaled.

It may seem odd to think of the lungs as organs of excretion, but carbon dioxide is the most important waste product to be excreted by the body. If carbon dioxide starts dissolving in the blood in greater quantities than normal, the blood becomes very acid. This in turn puts a stop to many essential chemical activities in the body and death can result. This is known as respiratory failure and may be the final stage in chronic bronchitis.

The kidneys

Most cells in the body use some form of protein in their chemical activities. The breakdown of protein results in waste products that contain nitrogen. The kidneys are responsible for filtering this nitrogen-containing waste, the most common compound of which is urea, out of the bloodstream.

As this child breathes out to make bubbles, he gets rid of carbon dioxide, the main waste product excreted by the body.

Brian Nash

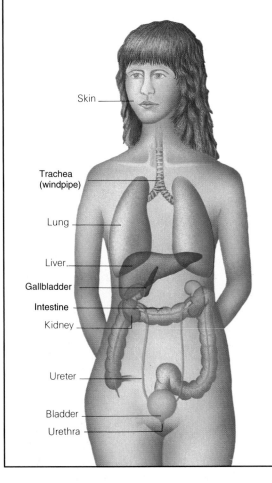

Skin

Trachea
(windpipe)

Lung

Liver

Gallbladder

Intestine

Kidney

Ureter

Bladder

Urethra

Venner Artists

How the body clears itself of waste

These are the methods or systems by which the body rids itself of waste products, which are mainly the result of digestion and various chemical processes necessary to maintain life.

The skin excretes water and salt (derived from food) through the pores via the sweat glands

The lungs excrete carbon dioxide (from the burning of glucose as fuel) and some water via the windpipe (trachea) and mouth

The liver and gallbladder excrete bilirubin (from the breakdown of hemoglobin from red blood cells in the liver) via bile passed out with the feces

The kidneys excrete urea (from the use of proteins by the cells), water, and mineral salts via the bladder and urethra

The intestines excrete feces (the remains of food after the nutrients have been removed) via the anus

The kidneys also regulate the amount of water passed out of the body and keep the correct balance of salt in the body.

The way the kidneys work is complicated. They receive about two pints (one liter) of blood every minute. The blood passes through a filter at the end of each of the two million tubules in the kidneys. The filters separate out the watery part of blood (the plasma), which passes into the tubules, while most of the rest stays in the bloodstream. As the filtered fluid moves down the long kidney tubules, much of the water, salt, and other valuable substances are absorbed back into the bloodstream. Some water, urea, and other waste substances pass (in the form of urine) down two tubes into the bladder.

The kidneys produce urine continually during the day and night. About four pints (two liters) of urine is passed in 24 hours, but this can vary a lot. The body's delicate water balance is controlled by the kidney tubules which absorb more or less of the filtered fluid. If the body is becoming dehydrated, the pituitary gland in the brain secretes the hormone ADH (antidiuretic hormone) to instruct the kidneys to absorb more water. The total amount

of urea passed stays about the same, but it is dissolved in a greater or lesser proportion of water and so leads to weaker or stronger urine.

A similar system exists to manage the balance of salt in the body. A hormone called aldosterone, secreted by the adrenal glands just above the kidneys, sends a message to the kidney tubules to reabsorb more or less salt according to the body's needs.

The liver
The liver is like a high-powered chemical factory and storehouse combined. Its cells are grouped in clusters around veins, into which they pass their waste products. These waste products are excreted in the form of bile into nearby bile ducts. The bile ducts come together into a large duct that drains into the small intestine.

The gallbladder
Bile is stored in the gallbladder, which squeezes it out into the intestines. The reason for this is that bile contains substances that break down large droplets of fat into smaller droplets in a process

called emulsification, which makes them easier to absorb. So the bile system not only provides a useful way of eliminating waste products from the liver, but also plays an important role in the digestion of food.

Bile is green or brown. Its color comes from the breakdown of hemoglobin in the used red cells of the blood, which changes color as it undergoes the breakdown process. It is the bile that gives the feces their brown color.

The bowels
When food enters the stomach, it is churned up and broken down by acid until it is liquid. It then enters the small intestine, where the true process of digestion takes place and all the desirable nutrients in the food are absorbed.

Finally what is left of the digested food enters the colon or intestine. This is a long, wide tube that starts in the lower right-hand corner of the abdomen, then works up and round in a horseshoe shape before coming to an end at the anus. During this passage through the large intestine, the remaining mush gradually solidifies as water from it is

Q What's the difference between excretion and secretion?

A Excretion is the process in which waste products are lost. Secretion, on the other hand, is the process in which glands produce substances that have a particular purpose. The tear glands, for example, secrete tears which lubricate the eyes and to some extent protect them from infection.

Q My grandfather has to get up once or twice a night to urinate. Does this mean he has a weak bladder?

A It is quite normal for many people to urinate once or even twice during the night. It is unlikely to be due to a disease, unless your grandfather has noticed any change in the pattern of urination. If there is a change or he is having any pain or difficulty urinating, he should see his doctor.

Q I take senna pods to relieve my constipation. Is this the best remedy?

A No. Senna and similar laxatives act by irritating the intestine and making it move the feces. It is much better to take the natural approach and give the intestine more work to do by eating plenty of unrefined food like whole grain breads and bran. You should also increase your daily amount of fresh fruit.

Q I find that whenever I eat beets my urine turns red. I thought this was just the color in the beets, but my friend tells me that I may be bleeding from the kidneys. Should I see my doctor?

A No, you are right. It is quite common for food coloring to come out in the urine. This happens with beets and with asparagus in some people. Some drugs may also color the urine.

Q Is my baby's diaper rash due to his urine being strong?

A No, this is an old wives' tale. The most important thing is to change his diapers frequently and use a barrier cream.

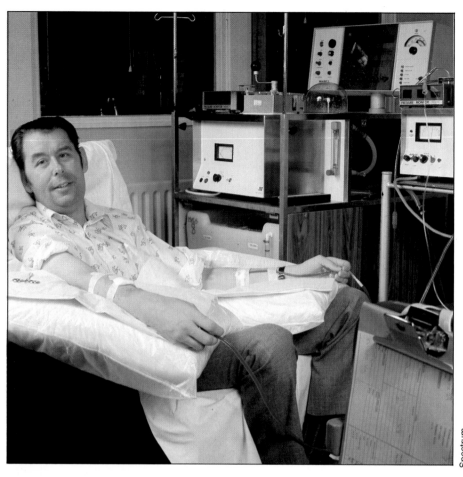

Spectrum

This patient is undergoing dialysis, which means that a machine is taking over the excretory function of the kidneys and removing waste products from his body.

absorbed into the bloodstream through the intestinal wall. The final consistency of the food waste, or feces, depends upon how much water is absorbed.

Most of the substance of the feces is simply food residue after the nutrients have been removed. It is arguable whether this should be called excretion, but the intestine certainly does contain some true excretions, because it contains the waste products of cell chemistry in the form of bile.

The skin
On a hot day the body loses a large amount of salt and water in sweat. Sweat is the product of the sweat glands in the skin and its sole purpose is to regulate the body heat, because heat is lost as the sweat evaporates from the skin.

However, if you did not sweat at all for a day, then any excess salt or water could easily be excreted by the kidneys. So sweat does not fulfill any essential function in the clearing of waste products.

Tests
Many of the widely used blood tests are designed to find out whether the main parts of the excretory process—the lungs, kidneys, and bile systems—are working properly.

Many patients who are treated in the hospital will have preliminary tests to measure the level of urea in their blood. The level of bilirubin, one of the main constituents of bile, is also commonly measured in the hospital.

If either of these substances is present in excess, it is an indication that either the kidneys or bile system is not working fully. This type of malfunction may not produce any symptoms in the patient, but it is essential for doctors to know whether these organs are functioning because all the drugs used in treatment have to be eliminated through the kidneys or the liver, and hence through the bile. If either system is not working properly, drug levels may build up in the system and so smaller doses must be given.

It is slightly more difficult to measure carbon dioxide levels because blood has to be taken from an artery, usually at the wrist, rather than from a vein. However, the level of carbon dioxide can and must be measured when an overall assessment of respiratory function is required in medical tests.

Exercise

Walk up five flights of stairs and if you are out of breath by the fourth, you are unfit. Exercise will not only increase your stamina and improve your health and appearance, but it will also affect the way you feel generally and allow you to enjoy everyday activities more fully.

Q I am considering using a toning machine, the type that gives you small electric shocks. Would it be as effective as taking exercise?

A No. These machines do not provide the same benefit that exercise does, because they do not increase the body's workload. Your muscles will be stimulated to expand and contract rapidly, but this will not make them use up calories or make the heart and lungs increase their output. The only thing that such a machine does is encourage you to be lazy about exercise, and there is not much evidence that it will make you thinner, either.

Q I often feel very stiff in my shoulders and neck after going jogging. Is this normal?

A No. It simply shows that you are not using your arms and shoulders properly. It is fairly common for muscles to get tense in the early stages of a new activity and for you not to notice stiffness until afterward. Try to jog with your shoulders relaxed, and let your arms swing loosely at your side.

Q Why do people get stomach cramps if they swim too soon after a light meal?

A After eating, the stomach and intestines need extra supplies of blood to aid digestion. The muscles also require more blood for swimming. If they don't receive enough they are deprived of oxygen and go into spasms, or cramps. Therefore it is best to take a half-hour rest after a light meal so that the stomach can empty itself.

Q Will some types of exercise give me large, bulky, unfeminine muscles?

A No. Women have less muscle than men and all that exercise does is to firm and tone the muscles you already have. Some women athletes do develop very masculine proportions, but this is only as a result of long and strenuous training in a selected sport.

Good health is not just the absence of disease; it is a state of vitality when all the parts of the body work efficiently and respond easily to a person's needs during work and recreation.

Regular exercise is an essential element of good health. It helps to build and maintain a degree of physical fitness that insures you can perform all your daily activities safely and enjoyably.

Running in place helps to keep the whole body trim and is a simple way of exercising because it can be done anywhere.

Brian Nash

Clothing: The Dance Centre

How much exercise do we need?

The amount of exercise needed to keep fit will vary a lot from one person to another. It will depend on factors such as diet, the type of work you do, normal body weight, metabolic rate, and how well you handle various forms of stress.

Walking, jogging, swimming, cycling, and games such as tennis and squash are ideal forms of exercise for keeping the whole body in shape. Other types, such as yoga and callisthenics (from the Greek, meaning "beauty and strength"), exercise specific areas of the body or are used as part of an overall program.

Some people do exercise more than they need to keep the body working properly. This type of training usually involves increasing muscle bulk and strength and developing the capacity of the lungs and heart. It is vital for any strenuous sporting activity but unnecessary for normal pursuits.

Why exercise?

Being physically fit is not just a question of muscular strength. Someone who is badly out of shape may have an impaired digestion, lowered mental alertness, and shortness of breath, all of which can be improved by exercise.

Our state of mind may also be affected by exercise or the lack of it, because being more fit means being happier too. The immediate effect of exercise is improved muscle tone. Even when the muscles are at rest, a certain amount of tension still remains. This insures that the body is ready to respond to demands.

Occasional bouts of exercise are not the answer. The cumulative effects of regular exercise on the heart and lungs are well known. The right exercise program will strengthen the muscles and increase the ability of the heart and lungs to supply oxygen to the tissues.

Exercise has been shown to reduce high blood pressure and it is recognized as important in the treatment of some heart conditions. Many cardiovascular disorders are caused or aggravated by arteriosclerosis, in which deposits left on the walls of the arteries make them harder and thicker and progressively reduce the blood supply. Exercise increases the force and speed of the circulation, making arteriosclerosis less likely.

It is important to have proper instructions before undertaking strenuous exercise such as step aerobics. The teacher should take you through preliminary exercises that warm up the muscles and you should avoid any overexertion that could cause injury.

Exercise is also a valuable part of any overall plan to lose weight. During increased muscular activity, the body's need for carbohydrates as a source of energy is increased dramatically. If the intake of food is reduced, the body has to rely on stores of fat to meet this, with a resulting loss of weight. If enough exercise is built into a regular reducing program, the need for dietary restriction will be less severe.

Who needs it?

As a general rule planned exercise is good for everyone except very young children and people suffering from serious illnesses or disabilities. However, the degree will vary according to age, sex, and state of health.

Children up to the age of six do not need special exercise. Their natural play is enough and too much activity can wear them out.

For school-age children a planned program is often part of the curriculum. Some naturally take to an exercise routine. Children who dislike such a program are usually unfit to start with and embarrassed by their poor performance. They should be encouraged to enjoy it for its own sake, however, because exercise is

Exercising in water is an excellent way to stay in shape. It is particularly useful for pregnant women or anyone recovering from an injury, because the water supports the body and helps prevent unnecessary strain.

Zefa

Renner/BSIP/Science Photo Library

essential to insure the proper development of muscles, bones, and ligaments in normal growth.

Many women make the mistake of thinking that dieting and calorie control are equivalent to keeping fit. Men, however, are statistically at a much greater risk from stress-induced health problems than women. A period of vigorous exercise each day will reduce tension and increase mental clarity and alertness by improving the oxygen supply to the brain.

Saving exercise for the weekends can be dangerous, especially for middle-aged and older men. The only way a body can be kept in good condition is through regular, steady training, at least every other day, throughout the week.

When to take exercise

There are certain times when exercise is especially valuable. For many women the greatest physical test is becoming a mother. Exercises designed to tone the abdomen and back muscles will enable them to go through pregnancy more easily and avoid excessive back pain. There is usually a positive effect on the child's prenatal development too, with a reduced risk of circulatory or cardiac complications for the mother. Exercise tones the muscles before and after the

Before starting to exercise:
● If you are over 30 and thinking about starting a program of vigorous exercise, consult your doctor first. He or she may suggest a medical checkup, possibly including an ECG (electrocardiogram) to make sure that your heart is in good shape
● Do not undertake exercise without consulting your doctor first if you suffer from diabetes, high blood pressure, obesity, or any heart condition or circulatory problem
● Arthritics and anyone else with diseases of the joints should start exercising as part of a planned physiotherapy program. Otherwise the problem may be aggravated
● It is important to choose the right shoes for your sport. Some coaching in technique may be useful, too. The multiple small shocks involved in jogging and many other sports can cause backache and strained leg muscles

birth and enables the new mother to regain her figure as quickly as possible.

Exercise also helps to smooth out the emotional ups and downs of menopause in later years.

It often helps to boost the will power to exercise at the same time every day.

Weight-training equipment can be used to exercise and tone specific muscle groups. Bear in mind that weight-training alone will not improve overall cardiovascular fitness; it needs to be combined with regular aerobic exercise such as walking, jogging, or swimming.

Types of exercise

Type	Effect	Uses
Isotonic (exercises where muscles lengthen and shorten)	Develops muscle strength: muscles shorten, tension remains constant. Stimulates heart, lungs, and circulation	Spot training for lifting weights, rowing, push-ups, etc.
Isometric (exercises with muscles in state of contraction)	Develops muscle strength: muscles operate against a fixed object. Does not shorten muscles, does not place load on heart, blood flow is not increased dramatically	Needs to be combined with running, swimming, or other vigorous exercise to be beneficial overall. Can be practiced at desk or in car to relieve tension in specific muscles or for limited spot training
Callisthenic (gymnastic exercises to achieve bodily health)	Helps build real endurance by encouraging body to take in more oxygen, which is used by muscles; better gauge of fitness than muscular strength	Training for all competitive sports, from athletics to football, where endurance is required. Used in fitness routines: toe touching, push-ups, knee bends. When weather is bad, indoor skipping with a rope and running in place
Yoga (posture and breathing exercises)	Increases flexibility in joints of spine, arms, and legs. Tones muscles, ligaments, and tendons. Improves circulation and relaxation	Good for people who prefer a quiet and more thoughtful method of exercise, affecting all physical, mental, and emotional aspects of life

To create a routine, choose a regular time when you know you will be free. Exercising in the morning shakes off sluggishness, while lunchtime has advantages for dieters; it not only reduces the time available for eating and drinking but it also reduces the appetite. Exercise after work helps to relieve tension and stress.

The main thing is to find the time of day that suits you best, and then stick to it as much as possible.

When not to exercise

There are times when exercise is unwise. During illness the body needs rest to recover, and activity may only aggravate the condition.

Never exercise while suffering from a cold, an acute infection, or the flu. Vigorous activity will simply add to your feeling of exhaustion. Fevers require rest in bed to allow the body to cool down, so never try to exercise when you have one.

Women who suffer from menstrual cramps may prefer not to exercise at this time, but they may find that the pain is alleviated by gentle relaxation exercises.

Tiredness can be due to both fatigue and lethargy. If the body is really exhausted, it needs to recover and build up its reserves. If the problem is lethargy—too little exercise or too much eating and drinking—a brisk but mild activity such as swimming would be the answer.

It is important not to exert yourself too much, however, especially if you are unfit. The first signs of trouble include tightness and pain in the chest, severe breathlessness, dizziness or light-headedness, nausea, or a loss of muscle control. If you suffer one or a combination of these symptoms, you should stop exercising immediately.

Check your pulse rate at the wrist five minutes after exercising. If it is more than 120 beats a minute, you are overdoing it. Ten minutes later it should be down to only 100 beats a minute.

Forms of exercise

The main forms of exercise are isotonics, isometrics, callisthenics, and yoga. They vary in their method and effects, so choose the ones that suit you best. It is helpful to have clear objectives in mind. Is your purpose to use exercise to maintain a basic level of good health? Or do you wish to train for a particular sport?

The most important thing is to choose a form of exercise that you find enjoyable. You will inevitably have to grin and bear it in the beginning, but this will soon pass and you will feel the benefits.

Bicycling with friends is a simple and healthy form of exercise that can be enjoyed throughout much of the year.

Expectorants

Q I have a smoker's cough that bothers me for at least 20 minutes every morning. Would an expectorant help?

A An inhalant expectorant would probably help you first thing in the morning. With a smoker's cough there is usually mild chronic bronchitis. This produces mucus, which builds up overnight and lies in the tubes to the lungs. Once you have coughed this up then you are fine for the day, and the more effective your coughing the better. By using an expectorant for a few minutes in the morning, the mucus will be cleared more quickly. But why not try quitting smoking?

Q Can expectorants be taken when you are having other drug treatment?

A In almost every case, expectorants have little or no interaction with other drugs and are safe to use. Those containing iodine are sometimes an exception. For example, they can interfere with tests on the thyroid gland. If you are at all unsure, consult your doctor about this, especially if you are taking regular medication.

Q My seven-year-old son suffers from a chest cough. Is it safe to give him an expectorant medicine, or is it better to let the mucus dry up on its own?

A Children who suffer from coughs, particularly those with whooping cough where the mucus is exceptionally sticky, do benefit from expectorants. It is very important to give them only on the advice of your doctor, so the correct dose can be prescribed.

Q There are so many cough medicines on the market. How can I tell which is best?

A In general it is best to buy these medicines only on your doctor's advice. If you have a serious cough and feel you need an expectorant, then check that the medicine you buy contains one. This should be printed on the label. If necessary you can ask at the drugstore for information.

Phlegm can be helped up by expectorants, but it is important to get your doctor's advice if coughing persists.

This child is receiving a carefully measured dose of expectorant cough mixture as prescribed by her family doctor.

The purpose of an expectorant preparation is to help you cough up phlegm. Expectorants also make coughing easier and less uncomfortable. They will not cure colds or bronchitis, but they do help prevent pneumonia.

It is normal to produce an amount of a slippery substance called mucus in the membranes that line the lungs and in the other parts of the respiratory tract. These secretions are essential to assist breathing. The mucus traps dirt particles that are then pushed up and out of the lungs and eventually expelled through coughing. Someone with a condition such as chronic bronchitis or a chest infection, however, produces a much greater quantity of mucus. This can be sticky and hard to cough up without help. It is important to make sure the small air passages of the lungs are kept clear, so that it is not difficult to breathe.

How they work

Expectorants work in several ways. Some act by thinning the mucus. Others increase the amount of fluid produced by the respiratory tract, so that their stickier secretions get washed out more easily. One group, known medically as mucolytics, actually break down the chemical bonds holding mucus together so that it is made more fluid and is easier to cough up.

Some doctors consider that these effects only happen to a small degree, although they have been shown scientifically to exist. They believe that the most important effect of an expectorant is the psychological effect.

There are many preparations which have an expectorant effect. Most of the complex modern cough medicines that are combined with an expectorant contain guaiphenesin, which has no known adverse effects. If you are thinking of buying an expectorant medicine from the drugstore, it is a good idea to ask for advice first.

Hot water vapor makes it easier to produce mucus. Inhalant expectorants are substances that are used in conjunction with steam. The best-known are benzoin tincture, and menthol and eucalyptus oil.

An expectorant alone will not cure a bacterial infection. If the cough persists you should consult your doctor as an antibiotic may be needed.

None of the expectorants has a lasting effect, and doses need to be kept up according to the instructions. They usually need to be taken three or four times a day. When the mucus has been brought up then the urge to cough is relieved and the patient is much more comfortable. The expectoration of mucus will have to be kept up, however, until the underlying illness is completely cured.

Eyes and eyesight

A versatile, accurate, and self-repairing moving camera, the eye will provide a person with a lifetime's service and need the minimum of attention. It is also prone to relatively few diseases.

Q I am very nearsighted. Will this condition gradually get worse until I go blind?

A Neither nearsightedness nor farsightedness in themselves lead to blindness. These conditions do not necessarily get worse either, although it may become more and more difficult to see without glasses. Nearsighted people tend to become less nearsighted as they get older, but some farsighted people become even more farsighted over the years.

Q My child has had measles. I have heard it is dangerous to read during or soon after this disease. Is this true?

A No, there is no truth in it at all. Although the disease causes inflammation of the eyes and photophobia (discomfort in strong light) there is no danger to the sight. In general doctors are puzzled as to the reason why this particular old wives' tale should have circulated.

Q My aunt claims that her eyesight has become worse since she started wearing glasses. Why should this happen?

A It is most unlikely that your aunt's eyesight has deteriorated as a result of wearing glasses. What is much more likely is that your aunt had not realized just how bad her eyesight was, so that she now notices the enormous difference when she takes her glasses off.

Q What causes a black eye to happen?

A The tissues surrounding the orbits of the eyes (the cavities in which the eyes are set) are very soft. Any injury to the face or scalp that causes bleeding beneath the skin tends to drain toward the orbits. Disrupted red blood cells in the skin look yellowish at first and then turn black after a while. So all you are seeing in a black eye is a collection of old blood beneath the surface of the skin.

When people want to explain in simple terms how the eye operates, they usually compare it to a brilliantly designed camera. However, to understand fully how the outside world can be viewed inside the tiny chamber of the eye, it is necessary to go back to basics.

Light

Light is essential to the ability to see. One way to think of light is as a transmitting medium. Whether it comes from the sun or from an artificial source, light bounces off objects in countless directions and makes it possible for objects to be seen by the human eye.

Light usually travels in straight lines, but it can be bent if it passes through certain substances, such as the specially shaped glass of a camera lens or the lens made from tissues in a human eye.

The degree of bending can be precisely controlled by the shape in which a lens is made. Light can be bent inward, or concentrated, to form tiny but perfect images of much larger objects. These images are detected by the light-sensitive area at the back of the human eye.

The cornea

When a ray of light strikes the eye, the first thing it encounters is a round, transparent window called the cornea. This is the first of the eye's two lenses. It is fixed in position, is always the same shape, and does a major part of the light bending.

The cornea is surrounded by the white of the eye, a tough substance called the sclera which does not admit any light. The white is covered by a protective membrane, the conjunctiva. This membrane, together with the lacrimal glands behind the upper eyelids, produces a constant film of tears that is essential to the health of the eyes.

The aqueous humor

After it has passed through the cornea, a ray of light enters the outer of two chambers within the eye, properly called the anterior chamber. This chamber is filled with a watery fluid called the aqueous humor, which is constantly drained away and replaced.

The iris

The iris forms the back of this first chamber, with the lens just behind it. It is a round, muscular diaphragm, in other words, a disc with an adjustable hole in the center. In a human eye this hole is called the pupil and its size is altered by two sets of muscles.

Testing the sight of a child below reading age: he looks first at letters displayed at a distance. If he can see them he points to the same letters on the card held in front of him.

Eye Clinic, Dept of Optometry, The City University, London

Q My brother is color-blind but he says he doesn't see in black and white. So what is color blindness?

A There are three types of light-sensitive cells in the retina. Each one specializes in seeing red, green, or blue light. Color blindness results from having too few of one of these types of cell. A color-blind person does not actually see in black and white, but will be unable to distinguish between certain colors, the most common ones being red and green.

Q Should I take vitamins for good eyesight?

A Eyesight is only affected by severe vitamin deficiency, which happens when people are on the verge of starvation. In the days when sailors got scurvy (caused by lack of vitamin C) from being without fresh vegetables for long periods, their eyesight also suffered. In fact, they had night blindness and this improved when they returned to a normal, balanced diet. We now recognize that night blindness can result from severe vitamin A deficiency. Carrots are a rich source of this vitamin, but people with a normal diet cannot, as some believe, improve their night vision by eating large amounts of the vegetable.

Severe vitamin A deficiency can also cause disease of the cornea, the transparent outer window of the eye, ultimately resulting in total blindness. Lack of vitamin B may also cause blindness by interfering with the normal nutrition of the optic nerve. Eyesight is restored to normal if vitamin B is put back in the diet.

Q What do I do about grit in my eye?

A A foreign body in the eye is always worrying because it may scratch and damage the cornea. A simple remedy is to rinse the eye with a warm solution of salt and water, or eye drops, or to blink repeatedly while rolling the eyes. If this fails, then you should go to the doctor. A penetrating injury to the eye, such as happens to people who fail to wear protective glasses at work, is more serious and requires hospital attention.

The iris is pigmented and this gives the eye its color when seen from the outside (in fact the word *iris* is derived from the Greek word meaning "rainbow"). Different eye colors are not due to different pigments, but are the result of varying amounts of one pigment, melanin. Dark colored eyes have a lot of pigment all the way through the iris. Lighter eyes have less melanin concentrated toward the back of the iris, so the color is seen through a layer of aqueous humor and cornea and tends to look blue or green.

The purpose of the iris is to control the amount of light entering the eye, like the aperture of a camera. If too strong a light falls on it, the pupil grows smaller, without our having to make any conscious effort. In dim light, the pupil grows larger.

Emotions such as excitement or fear and the use of certain drugs also make the pupil widen or contract.

The lens
Just behind the iris is the soft, elastic, and transparent lens. Its job is the fine focusing of light rays, and it provides about a third of the eye's focusing power. For this reason, the lens is adjustable. It is held around its outer edges by the ciliary muscle, which can change the shape of the lens to alter the angle at which the light rays passing through it are bent.

The vitreous humor
Behind the lens is the main interior chamber of the eye. This is filled with a substance called the vitreous humor,

Structure of the eye

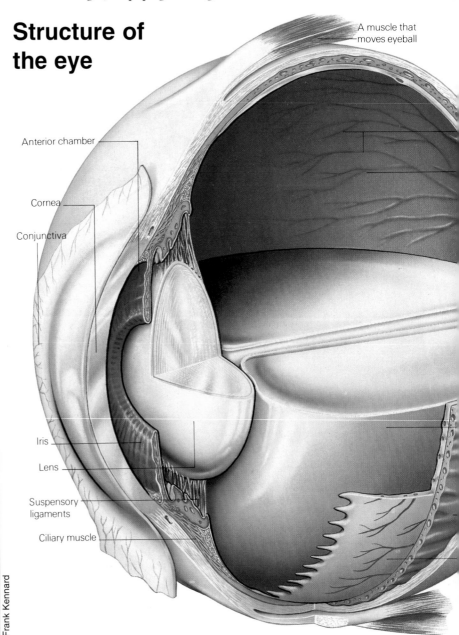

A muscle that moves eyeball

Anterior chamber

Cornea

Conjunctiva

Iris

Lens

Suspensory ligaments

Ciliary muscle

Frank Kennard

which has a jellylike texture. Running through its center is the hyaloid canal, the remains of a channel that carried an artery during the eye's development in the fetus.

The retina

The curved inside of the eye is lined all around the back chamber with a light-sensitive coating, or layer, which is called the retina.

This is made up of two different types of light-sensitive cells. These are called rods and cones because of their shapes. Rods are sensitive to light of low intensity and do not interpret color, which is picked up by the cones. The cones are also responsible for clarity and are most plentiful at the back of the eye in an area called the macula. Here the lens also

focuses its sharpest image, and this is therefore the area where the vision is at its best.

In the area around the macula the retina still registers images with clarity, but out toward its edges is what is called peripheral vision, all that area that we half see. Together this central and peripheral vision make up a complete view of the outside world.

How objects are viewed

The eyes work by rapid scanning; the eyeball moves around with a specially arranged set of muscles attached to it. Looking at someone's face, for example, the eye concentrates on his or her eyes, darting glances from one eye to the other and occasionally down to the mouth.

The optic nerve

All of the information that comes through the eyes—focused by the two lenses, adjusted to a manageable level of intensity by the iris, and then recorded by the light-sensitive surface of the retina—is then sent to an area of the brain called the visual cortex to be processed and understood.

A cable called the optic nerve runs from each eye and transmits information to the brain. All the nerve fibers that lead to the cable are crossed over in a doubling-up system. Each hemisphere, or side, of the brain has its own half of the visual cortex, and each of these has its own separate blood supply. It is thus very rare for a stroke, which nearly always involves a single artery, to cause complete blindness.

Severe damage to one half of the visual cortex will, however, always cause blindness of part of the field of peripheral vision. In most cases stroke damage causes complete loss of the corresponding halves of the visual fields of the two eyes—in other words, the outer half of the field of vision of one eye and the inner half of the field of vision of the other eye. This is called homonymous hemianopia.

Although the loss of visual field is considerable, stroke sufferers do not experience a sense of blackness. They are often unaware that they have any visual loss at all until they discover that they are unable to read properly or find themselves having accidents with objects in the blind part of the field.

Damage to the optic nerve at the point where the nerve fibers cross causes a

different area of visual field loss. In this case, because the crossing fibers come from the inner halves of the two retinas, there is loss of both outer halves of the fields of vision. This is called bitemporal hemianopia. It is usually caused by upward pressure from a tumor of the pituitary gland, which lies immediately under the crossing of the optic nerve fibers.

The blind spot

Where the optic nerve leads away from the back of the eye there is a small area where people are completely blind. We are not actually aware of this, because the eyes overlap their fields of vision and so each eye compensates for the other eye's blind spot. However, it is possible to prove the existence of this area by the simple experiment at the top of the page.

The blind spot is an insensitive area of the retina known as the optic disc and is

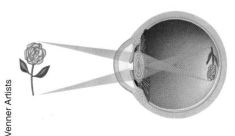

To discover your blind spot, close your right eye and look at the cross (above). While you look, continue to move the page toward your face. There is a point where the dot will vanish—this is your blind spot.

Focusing

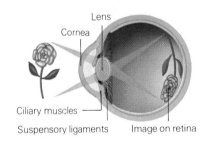

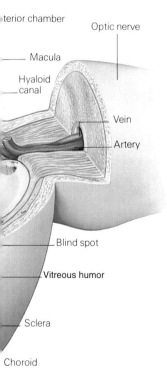

Blood vessels on retina

Anterior chamber

Optic nerve

— Macula

Hyaloid canal

Vein

Artery

— Blind spot

— Vitreous humor

— Sclera

Choroid

— Retina

Venner Artists

Light rays from a near object diverge and the surface of the lens becomes more curved (top) to focus them. From a distant object, light rays are almost parallel and the lens (above) has less focusing to do.

EYES AND EYESIGHT

Six main muscles move the eyeball. Muscle (a) swivels it away from the nose; (b) toward the nose; (c) rotates it upward; (d) downward; (e) moves it down and outward; and (f) moves it upward and outward.

How the eyeball moves

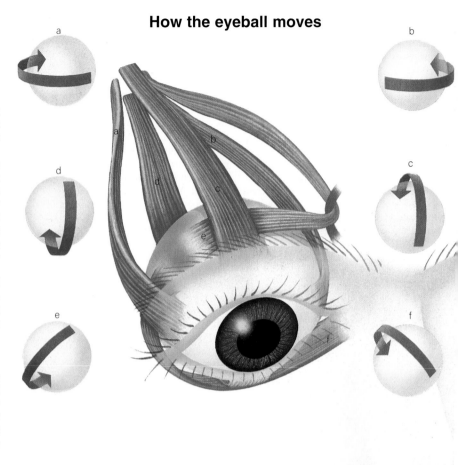

the point at which the million or so optic nerve fibers from the retina emerge from the eyeball through the sclera to form the optic nerve.

Because there are no rods or cones on the optic disc, the part of the image that falls on it is not perceived. We are unaware of our blind spots not only because of the overlap between the two eyes, but also because visual field loss is an absence of perception; we do not see a blank space or a dark patch, we simply do not see anything at all.

The blind spots are also concealed from us because of the constant movements of the eyes. The area of visual field that is covered by the optic disc of each eye is quite small.

The arteries of the eye

A large artery leads into the eye beside the optic nerve. Many smaller blood vessels branch out from this main artery and spread over the retina like tributaries of a river. Their vital job is to supply the nerve cells of the retina with nutrients and drain away waste products.

The presence of this fine network enables a doctor using an ophthalmoscope to examine some of the body's blood vessels without any skin in the way.

The most common cause of nearsight (1) is an eyeball which is too long, so that light rays form an image in front of the retina. It is corrected (2) by a concave lens. In farsight (3), the eyeball is short, so the image cannot be formed within the eye. A convex lens (4) focuses the image on the retina. (The brain turns it the right way around.)

Common problems

Few eye disorders actually end in blindness. Starting at the front of the eye, one of the most common minor problems is conjunctivitis.

This is an inflammation of the conjunctiva, the thin membrane covering the whites of the eyes. It is especially common among babies and young children and is caused by bacteria, viruses, or irritation. Conjunctivitis may also be caused by an allergy such as hay fever. Treatment with antibacterial eye drops or creams usually clears it up quickly.

The cornea is subject to various types of inflammation. Pain in the eyeball, redness, blurred vision, and clouding of the cornea are all typical symptoms. These are often unimportant, but they may also indicate more serious problems, so anyone experiencing them should get immediate medical attention.

Nearsightedness

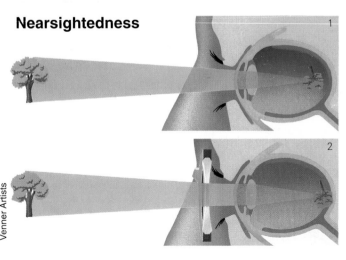

Farsightedness

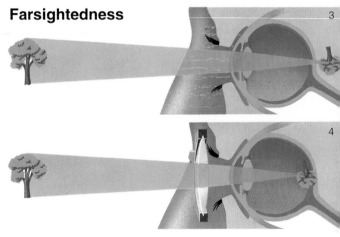

Because the cornea contains no blood vessels, grafting a new one in its place if necessary is usually successful.

Some people have an imperfectly curved cornea, and this throws a distorted image on the retina, causing their vision to be partly blurred. This is called astigmatism, and it can be corrected by glasses or certain types of contact lenses.

Glaucoma

To work properly the eyeball needs to stay the same shape. The normal shape—and hence the relationship of the cornea to the retina—is maintained by the constant secretion of water (aqueous humor) within the eye. This water fills the interior, including the vitreous gel, and passes out by way of a restraining meshwork near the root of the iris.

The balance between the secretion and outflow of fluid normally maintains the pressure in the eye within narrow limits. If the pressure falls, the eyeball will indent and vision will be lost. If the pressure rises too high, the small vessels that supply blood to the retina and optic nerve fibers are constricted and closed off. This causes serious damage to the nerve fibers.

The condition in which pressure rises is called glaucoma and is due to interference with the free outflow of fluid from the globe. This can occur in several ways.

The most common kind of glaucoma, chronic glaucoma, is entirely painless and insidious and it is one of the major causes of blindness in the West. Affected people are often unaware that anything is wrong until a late and irreversible stage of the disease. This is because the optic nerve fibers initially damaged are almost always those concerned with peripheral vision. Serious peripheral visual field loss can occur before any harm is suspected.

For these reasons, everyone should have their eye pressures tested routinely at about the age of 40, and afterward at intervals of a few years. People with a family history of glaucoma should be tested at an earlier age and more often. Raised pressures can easily be brought down, usually by the use of appropriate eye drops. In some cases surgery may be needed to correct glaucoma.

Acute glaucoma, which causes pain, misting of vision, and the perception of colored haloes around lights, is much less

This instrument, called a refracting head, is used to perform eye tests. The patient looks through various lenses at an eye chart on the wall opposite. Different lenses can be selected by turning the knobs on the front until the correct prescription is found. This system has replaced the older method of testing with single lenses in trial frames.

common and is readily detected because of the symptoms. It also requires urgent treatment by an ophthalmologist.

Defects of the lens

The iris rarely gives trouble, but lens problems are common. About half the adult population of most Western countries wear glasses because of defects of the eyeball or of the lens, or the muscle that changes its shape.

If the eyeball is too long from front to back, the lens will be round and fat, giving good close-up vision but poor distant vision. This is nearsightedness, or myopia. If the lens is not thick enough, or the muscle has difficulty in increasing the thickness of the lens, poor near vision but good distant vision results. This is farsightedness, or presbyopia.

Both near- and farsightedness are easy to correct with glasses or contact lenses. A technique has been developed to treat nearsightedness using a laser to flatten the curvature of the cornea .

Cataracts

Cataracts are a clouding of the lens. For the person affected this is like looking through a window that is slowly frosting up. Cataracts are painless and develop slowly and are commonly caused by advancing age or diabetes (an abnormally high level of blood sugar). These days, treatment by removing the lens is effective and safe. Special glasses or contact lenses are worn to restore normal vision.

Diabetes may also affect the retina, because it causes the blood vessels, including those in the back of the eye, to gradually degenerate. If this condition is not treated with insulin, it may eventually lead to blindness.

Squinting

Squinting is an inability to focus both eyes on the same spot at the same time. This is caused by laziness of one of the muscles that moves the eyeball, and it can be corrected by a simple operation or by wearing glasses.

Other visual disorders

Vision can be damaged by hereditary degeneration of the retina, by macular degeneration (which usually affects old people), and by accidental injury to the eye. Certain diseases can lead to serious, permanent vision disorders; multiple sclerosis may inflame the optic nerve, leading to rapid reduction of central vision. The herpes simplex virus may cause a dendritic ulcer if it gets into the eye, which will cause gradual loss of vision and may permanently damage the cornea if left untreated.

Outlook

Near- and farsight may both be common complaints, but at least they are easily corrected. Blindness, of course, is a terrible affliction, but compared with some other serious human ailments, it is quite rare, and becoming more so.

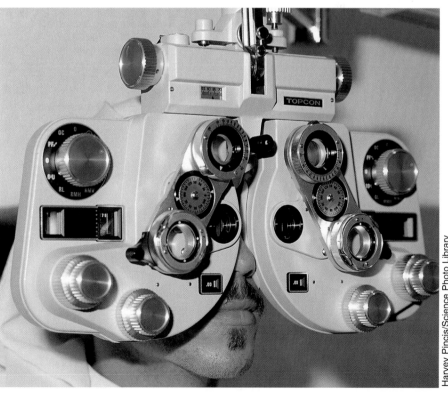

Harvey Pincis/Science Photo Library

Fainting

People faint for a variety of reasons. If you understand why it happens and know what to do, you will be better prepared to help others and avoid fainting yourself.

Q I am three months pregnant and have fainted several times recently. Is this harmful?

A There is no risk that your baby will be harmed by these spells (which are not uncommon in the early months of pregnancy), but you could hurt yourself if the spells make you fall over. If you do feel faint, lie down or sit with your head between your knees. If the fainting spells become more frequent, mention them to a doctor at your next prenatal checkup.

Q My grandmother always used to swear by smelling salts as the best treatment for fainting. Why have they gone out of fashion?

A Smelling salts have gone out of fashion mainly because they have been found to be no more effective in curing fainting than taking a few deep breaths. They consist of a chemical, ammonium carbonate, that gives off strong-smelling gas. Its effect is to make you gasp as you breathe it in. This gasping helps to get more oxygen into the blood, which is then carried to the brain to relieve the lack of oxygen that caused the fainting in the first place.

Q My elderly great-aunt has been prescribed drugs to treat her high blood pressure, and since she started taking them she has fainted several times. What should she do?

A She should go back to her doctor and tell him or her about the problem so that the treatment can be changed if necessary. Sometimes drugs given to treat high blood pressure can work so powerfully that the blood pressure becomes too low. This in turn causes a fainting spell.

Q When someone faints, how can you tell it isn't a coma?

A Doctors make a clear distinction between fainting spells and comas. The main difference is that someone who has fainted will quickly recover consciousness if laid flat, while someone in a true coma will not.

Fainting, known medically as *syncope*, is a sudden loss of consciousness. It is usually preceded by a feeling of weakness, dizziness, and possibly nausea. It is easy to tell when someone is about to faint, because their skin looks white and feels clammy to the touch, and their breathing becomes quick and shallow. As the sufferer faints, he or she falls to the ground, but then generally recovers full consciousness within a couple of minutes.

What happens

The most usual cause of fainting is a reduction in the blood supply to the brain. The blood brings essential oxygen, and the brain cannot work properly without it. Normally the heartbeat, together with the action of the blood, create enough pressure to push the blood up to the brain against the force of gravity. If this system fails for some reason, and the blood pressure falls too low, the body reacts by fainting. This makes the person fall flat. It thus puts the body in a position that allows the blood to travel easily to the brain, so restoring things to normal.

The sequence of events within the body varies. For example, you could faint from the shock of seeing an unpleasant

Fainting can result from standing too long in one position, the experience of this unfortunate soldier on guard duty.

sight, on receiving bad news, or if you experienced intense pain. When such things happen, the brain sends out messages to the vagus nerve, which has branches to the heart, lungs, and stomach. This nerve acts to slow the heart and reduce the strength of its beat, and at the same time widens the blood vessels in the center of the body. As a result, blood becomes dammed in the abdomen and too little reaches the brain.

When fainting is likely

Fainting can occur as a result of standing still for too long. Blood gradually accumulates in the legs, making the heart and blood vessels work too hard to push blood upward. If you have to stand for an extended period, the best way to avoid fainting is to make small movements with your legs and feet, as these help to squeeze the blood upward.

Fainting often occurs when you stand up suddenly after sitting or lying down. The blood vessels do not adjust fast enough to raise the blood pressure, and blood is trapped in the limbs and abdomen and cannot get to the brain as quickly as it should. This adjustment of blood pressure, relative to alterations in the position of the body, is monitored by a small group of nerves in the neck called the carotid sinus. Lack of oxygen in the blood can also cause fainting. This deficit

may be due to anemia, being in a hot stuffy room, or being at high altitude where the air is thin. In this case fainting is not caused by the brain getting insufficient blood, but is because the blood is not bringing enough oxygen with it.

Many people feel faint if they leave home in a rush first thing in the morning without eating breakfast. This faintness may be due to a combination of stress, which lowers the blood pressure, and the lack of nutrients in the blood. Eating a light breakfast may prevent it.

Heart disease is rarely a cause of fainting. In the elderly, however, fainting can be a sign that the blood vessels have become narrowed due to arteriosclerosis, and are not letting enough blood get to the brain.

Fainting in pregnancy

Fainting is not uncommon in early pregnancy. This is because the hormones involved tend to make the muscles in the blood vessel walls more flabby. This dilates the vessels and lowers the blood pressure, causing blood to accumulate in the lower parts of the body. Fainting in the early months of pregnancy may also

be caused by the sudden diversion of blood to the uterus, where it is needed to provide food and oxygen for the developing fetus. This leaves less blood available to be carried to the brain. As pregnancy progresses, however, the volume of blood in the circulation increases and solves the problem naturally.

People prone to fainting

Those who have a very sensitive connection between the vagus nerve and the blood vessels are particularly liable to faint. Such people should always try to avoid situations that tend to cause them to faint.

Fainting episodes are more common in adolescent girls. They are usually due to the emotional effects of growing up, combined with mild anemia due to the onset of menstruation, plus a phase of rapid growth. Teenage girls should be sure to eat a good diet, containing plenty

of protein and iron-rich foods such as liver and spinach. If the fainting persists, it may be caused by a deep-seated psychological problem and medical help should be sought. Epidemics of mass fainting in groups of adolescent girls have been recorded. These tend to be attributed to some kind of mass hysteria.

Tall people often faint more easily than short people when they stand for a long time, simply because their blood has further to travel through the body from the legs to the brain.

Fainting in young children is unusual, but can occur in one rare hereditary condition called dysautonomia.

When someone feels faint, get them to lie down for five minutes or put their head between their knees. Going outside for air is not a good idea; sudden fainting could cause a nasty injury.

Coping with fainting

- If you feel faint lie down or sit with your head between your knees so that the blood can flow to the brain quickly
- If someone else has fainted put him or her in the recovery position and do not allow the person to get up for at least five minutes. You should time this; often a person will insist that he or she is alright and then promptly faint again, with possible injuries
- Loosen any tight clothing around the patient's neck or waist
- Put a handkerchief or sponge, soaked in cold water and wrung out, on the forehead
- When the patient recovers consciousness, give him or her a few sips of cold water to drink
- If you suspect that a bone has been broken or if the fainting was brought on by severe pain, burns, or bleeding, get medical help as soon as possible
- If fainting is accompanied by vomiting and/or diarrhea, it is probably due to an intestinal infection. The patient should go to bed and have fluids only

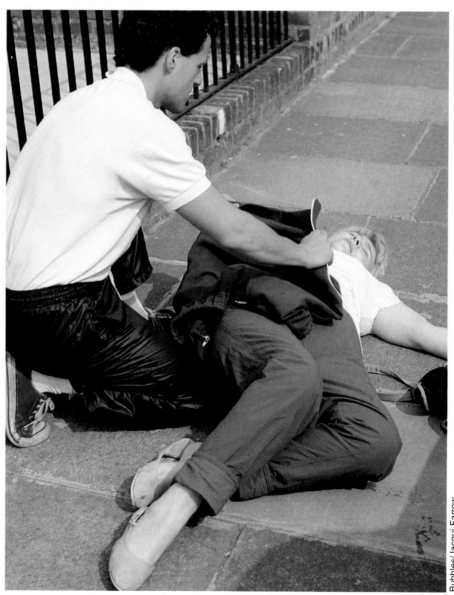

Bubbles/Jacqui Farrow

Faith healing

Q Are faith healers an alternative to doctors?

A No, and few would claim to be. If you are ill, you should always consult your doctor first to get treatment. Some people, according to their beliefs, may find an additional source of strength through faith healing, though many doctors would say that this is purely psychological.

Q Can faith healing or other forms of healing provide a permanent cure?

A Some patients do get better after visiting a healer, but whether this would have happened anyway is impossible to test. Others feel better after a healing session or appear to be cured, only to have their illness or disability return in a few days.

Q Why does healing work sometimes, even if healers have no special powers?

A Even doctors who do not believe in healing recognize the placebo, or dummy drug, effect. Many patients, when given a placebo, will experience genuine relief from pain, just because they believe in it. A healer may affect some people in the same way and because of this, they will feel that they are getting better.

Q Must you believe in healing for it to work?

A Not all healers consider it necessary for patients to share their particular beliefs. However, it is likely that a good healer, just like a good doctor, gives the patient confidence. This may help the patient relax and thus eases pain and tension. Also a sympathetic healer, like a doctor, can often aid recovery by boosting a patient's morale.

Q Is it dangerous to consult a faith healer?

A Faith healing itself can probably do no harm, but it should never be used in place of orthodox treatment, particularly in the case of serious diseases.

Faith healing has its ardent supporters, who believe it can succeed where conventional medicine has failed. Doctors, however, remain skeptical in the absence of scientific proof. What methods do faith healers use?

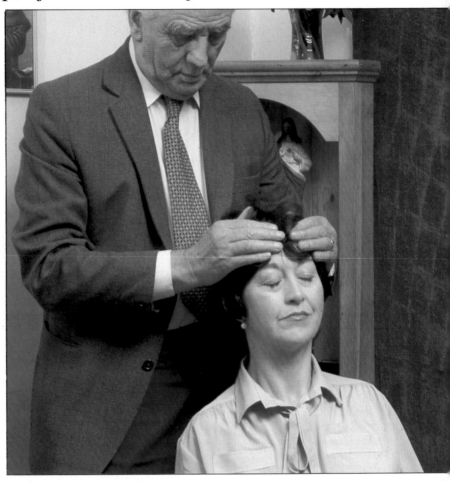

Healers perform laying on of hands by touching the affected area and allowing their healing energy to flow into it.

Faith healers believe they have been chosen to act as channels for healing powers that come from God. These powers can be transmitted to the patient in a variety of ways, ranging from direct physical contact, often called laying on of hands, to distant healing, in which the healer concentrates on a witness, which can refer to a photograph or the name of the sick person, a lock of his or her hair, or even a tiny sample of the patient's blood.

The oldest examples of faith healings in the Western world are the miracles of Jesus, which are described in the *New Testament*. Jesus used many different methods to heal the sick, from touching them to simply commanding them to recover. He is described as possessing a healing force, or virtue, which could be transmitted both to individuals and to large crowds.

Modern faith healers have strong religious convictions, but not all of them insist that the patient must share their beliefs for the cure to be successful. Many nonreligious people have claimed to have been cured by faith healing, while some of the most fervent believers have remained ill in spite of all the efforts of these healers.

Most faith healers also try to persuade patients to seek orthodox medical treatment, in addition to getting help from the healers themselves.

How it works

The most common technique used by faith healers, called laying on of hands, consists of the healer placing his or her hands on the affected area, sometimes accompanied by prayer, to allow the healing energy to flow into the patient ome faith healers, particularly when they are dealing with cancer, use the technique of meditation and also ask the patient to visualize the affected parts being healed.

When such a technique is performed, many patients attest to intense sensations of heat, cold, or tingling—far more than they would experience from ordinary hand contact. Patients also claim to feel immensely relaxed, and this is particularly useful when treating conditions that are psychosomatic in origin.

When faith healing is done in front of a mass audience, laying on of hands is sometimes incorporated into a prayer service led by a healer.

Distant healing

Faith healing can also be done when the patient is not present: this is called distant healing. Sometimes this is combined with the ancient art of dowsing, where a pendulum is held over a patient's witness, and diagnosis and treatment are effected. In distant healing, a prayer for a person's health is said while the healer concentrates on the witness. Some patients attest to feeling better, although whether this occurs because they know that someone is thinking of them, or whether their health would have improved anyway, is not known.

Even if such faith healing methods do not cure patients, they will usually do no physical harm. It is possible, however, that mental harm may result, particularly when a seriously ill person, or what doctors would call a hopeless case, puts their faith in a healer's powers, only to find that nothing can be done to help them.

Other healing methods

Other nonmedical techniques are used by some healers, but the practitioners do not claim religious inspiration. These techniques include spiritual healing, which heals the mind and, as a consequence, heals the body; psychic healing, in which the healer calls on spirit guides to heal the sick; and natural healing, in which, by tapping into the universal healing energy, a cure can be effected. Often these categories overlap, as do the techniques, but laying on of hands is common to nearly all of them. Some observers believe that it is the touching itself that is therapeutic and leads to an improvement in health.

Self-healing is a method of healing that is gaining ground. It is psychoanalytically based and may be used in conjunction with faith healing. Often it is used for a number of complaints that may either be psychosomatic in origin or be aggravated by a sufferer's state of mind, such as depression, insomnia, asthma, high blood pressure, and skin disorders. It is also increasingly being employed by cancer patients. In self-healing the patient repeats phrases that suggest that the body parts are becoming warm and heavy, and this will make them feel deeply relaxed. Such a technique can be practiced on its own to keep the body systems balanced and check any illness that might occur.

Fact or fiction?

Faith healers claim many successes and it must be said that some people do indeed get better after treatment, though why

John Topham Picture Library

Every year thousands of sick and handicapped people visit the Roman Catholic shrine at Lourdes, France, hoping and praying for a cure.

this should be so is a matter of some controversy. Skeptics argue that they would have gotten better anyway. Time produces many cures, and even in serious illnesses such as cancer, cases of spontaneous remission (sudden improvement for no apparent reason) are well documented. That such improvements take place after visits to a healer is, the skeptics insist, purely coincidental.

Healers, on the other hand, say they are able to transmit healing energy to the patient that effects or accelerates a cure. Though this energy has not been identified by science and is not fully understood by the healers themselves, they assert that there are definite indications of its existence.

Controlled tests to demonstrate the power of healing energy are rarely successful, prompting researchers to claim that healers are frauds. Healers counter this by saying that healing energy does not lend itself to scientific examination. They may attribute their lack of success to reasons such as the patients' boredom, poor health, or bereavement. In general, doctors will need more conclusive evidence before they become open to the idea that faith healing works.

Consulting a faith healer
- Find a healer through personal recommendation
- Expect to pay a fee; reputable healers have to earn a living
- Ask for an initial interview, and if you don't feel comfortable with the healer, don't proceed
- Expect to feel relaxed and peaceful after the first session
- Continue the healing treatment for a reasonable length of time; don't expect an instant miracle cure
- Continue with your normal medical treatment

Fatigue

Q Every morning I wake up feeling exhausted, even though I have had a good night's sleep. Why is this?

A This early morning feeling is common and not a sign of illness. You can test this by noting your feelings on the mornings when you have something special to get up for. If you feel better on those mornings, then your fatigue is psychological and an early morning run would do more good than an extra ten minutes asleep.

Q I always feel very tired after a good meal. Why is this?

A Food stimulates the relevant part of the nervous system to make us drowsy and comfortably sluggish and to take blood away from muscles in limbs to aid digestion in the gut. Aerobic exercise after a heavy meal can be dangerous, as swimmers know, so this fatigue is not only natural, it is protective too. If you do have important work to do after lunch, avoid alcohol and eat less than you would want to. You will then remain alert and mentally active and you won't put on as much weight.

Q I am very worried about my father, who always complains of feeling tired and spends most of his spare time lying on the bed. He has become very sloppy in dressing and bathing and doesn't seem to care how he looks. I know he is feeling tense because of the way he is always twiddling his fingers. Tiredness makes him very bad-tempered with my mother and the rest of the family. What should he do?

A It is obvious that your father needs to see his doctor to rule out the possibility of disease being the cause of his fatigue. He seems to be showing the classic symptoms of tension and depression, which in themselves result in fatigue. He would feel better if he spent his spare time outdoors instead of in bed, but you are unlikely to convince him of this. His doctor may suggest professional psychological help as a possible answer.

Everybody knows the natural fatigue that follows strenuous physical or mental exertion. Fatigue is quite normal under these circumstances, but it can also have a psychological basis or be a symptom of illness.

After you have been exercising for a long time you feel exhausted, your limbs ache, and the last thing you want is further exertion. Yet this kind of fatigue is soon replaced by a pleasant glow of health and well-being. Similarly anyone who has ever put in a hard day's work or study knows the mixture of tiredness and satisfaction that you feel at the end of the day. This is simply healthy, natural fatigue.

Fatigue is also normal in early and late pregnancy. The reason in early pregnancy is not fully understood but the increase in hormonal activity must be one factor. Fatigue recurs in late pregnancy, partly because of the weight of the

Fatigue can be caused by the problems of everyday life and may ultimately make it impossible to deal with them.

baby. Fatigue can also arise for psychological reasons, however, and it may be symptom of certain illnesses.

Myths about fatigue

In 80 percent of cases of fatigue without other symptoms the cause is believed to be psychological. This does not mean that there is any question of mental illness. It does mean, however, that the fatigue is the mind and body's response to unhealthy surroundings.

The fatigued person has little or no drive or motivation; it is as if the body's accelerator is missing. Doctors have never traced an isolated cause for this large group of patients, but they believe the overall reason may be a combination of overeating, tobacco, alcohol, lack of exercise, and overwork.

In the past other ailments were thought to cause fatigue; even infected teeth have been blamed. Constipation was also sometimes viewed as a culprit, and it was an accepted medical theory that toxins in the feces were reabsorbed from the bowel to cause illness. This is now known to be incorrect.

Fatigue is not caused by a vitamin deficiency either. A severe lack of vitamins will cause fatigue, but not without other, far more dramatic symptoms. There is little harm in people taking vitamin supplements, but they should not be expected to remove fatigue.

Women with heavy periods often think that they are anemic and that this is the cause of their fatigue. A blood test can rule this cause out.

Causes

Fatigue can be a sign of certain illnesses but it is unlikely to be the only symptom. With undetected diabetes the blood sugar level is high and this seems to make the diabetic fatigued. Similarly poorly controlled diabetes may cause the sufferer to experience fluctuations of blood sugar level and corresponding weariness (see Pancreas).

With severe anemia the blood is thin and it is a considerable effort for the heart and lungs to supply oxygen and deliver it to all parts of the body. The fast heartbeat of severe anemia may be accompanied by a feeling of exhaustion.

Terrible fatigue accompanied by a cough and weight loss are the classic symptoms of tuberculosis.

Addison's disease involves low blood pressure and exhaustion caused by insufficient production of hormones by the adrenal glands. However this is rare.

Myasthenia gravis is an unusual disease where the transmission of the nerve impulse at the nerve muscle junction becomes impaired because of an abnormality in the body's chemistry. The sufferer feels intense fatigue in his or her muscles but characteristically the muscles recover rapidly after rest. As the illness progresses walking involves longer and longer rests between paces. The sufferer's eyelids droop and in very rare cases speech is difficult.

Certain types of mental illness also produce fatigue. With severe anxiety the sufferer is so tense from worry and agitation that any kind of additional mental effort or strain produces exhaustion. The fatigue will only disappear when the tension is reduced (see Anxiety).

The symptoms of severe depression include early morning waking, lack of motivation, weepiness, and guilt, in addition to fatigue. The fatigue has to be treated along with the other facets of the illness and lack of sleep (see Depression).

Most viral infections leave the patient feeling tired. Sometimes they are followed by prolonged fatigue that can last for several months. This effect, called chronic fatigue syndrome (see Chronic fatigue syndrome), often produces difficulty in concentrating and muscular aches and pains after even slight exercise.

Symptoms

Symptoms of fatigue vary and can give a clue as to the cause. Fatigue in the early morning but never late at night is most typical of depression. A person who seems to complain of being tired or

A dance or aerobics class, providing stimulation as well as exercise, could be the answer to fatigue caused by boredom.

Zefa

Q Is simply resting as good a refresher as sleep if you are feeling tired?

A A young person who feels fatigued and bored even though there is no good reason for that fatigue (such as tremendous pressure at work) is best advised to exercise rather than rest. If you are tired from strain and excessive work, however, you would be better off taking a nap. During sleep, dreaming is an important part of refreshment and even a short period of sleep for 30 minutes can be remarkably restorative. In general closing your eyes and daydreaming is almost as good as taking a nap. Going to bed early is a good solution for those who are genuinely exhausted.

Q Why do elderly people seem to sleep so much?

A This effect of aging is nearly always psychological. A busy older person can be as spritely at 90 as at 60. Such energy comes from having hobbies and interests and being able to look forward to various pleasures. Regular exercise of mind and body is essential. With age comes infirmity, and sometimes it is arthritis or poor sight that takes away the zest for living. This is the real problem that makes the older person feel tired, so a regular medical checkup may be helpful. Don't forget that one of the greatest antidepressants is friendship and good company.

Q My sister always looks pale, seems much too thin, and is constantly tired. Could she be anemic?

A Women with heavy periods can become short of iron through losing too much blood, and develop iron deficiency anemia. Far more women, however, simply think they are anemic and offer this as an excuse for tiredness when a deeper cause such as depression may be present. The answer will only come from a medical checkup and possibly a blood test to establish whether your sister has a physical illness. If she is not anemic, then it is very likely that she needs help with some deep problem that is depressing her.

The athlete flops down by the track totally exhausted after a race—but his fatigue is quite normal and healthy.

What you can do to tackle psychological fatigue

- Get a medical checkup
- Try self-analysis to come up with the cause of your fatigue
- Try a change in your lifestyle
- Take up a new sport; perhaps jogging or swimming
- Avoid boredom by reading and taking up a hobby
- Vary your routine
- Try healthier living: less food, less alcohol, less tobacco
- Take positive steps to solve any deep problem which might be worrying you
- Try yoga for relaxation
- Try sleeping less, not more

exhausted all the time is also likely to be suffering from depression.

Fatigue in specific muscles is more likely to have a physical cause, while the feeling of near paralysis that accompanies myasthenia gravis is quite different from any other type of fatigue.

Fatigue at peak activity times (such as on a busy morning at work) could be either physical or psychological in origin, whereas fatigue depending on the room temperature or the weather is likely to be a physical reaction.

Treatment

Where fatigue is one of the symptoms of a major illness, it is treated as part of that illness. Myasthenia gravis can be con-trolled by drugs, and diabetes can be stabilized by balancing insulin with the diet.

The treatment of fatigue which is psychological in origin is more difficult. A medical checkup is a good start, but it is likely that nothing will be found. This is where the sufferer must take over; the cure usually must come from within.

A diet advised by your doctor combined with exercises could help. For others the answer could be taking up a sport. Exercise tones the circulation, provides oxygen for the blood, and should produce a feeling of well-being. Sheer boredom can make people feel lethargic and the solution might be as simple as finding a stimulating new hobby that involves joining a group of likeminded people.

Rest is hardly ever the answer to psychological fatigue. Going to bed earlier might help, but staying in bed in the morning will probably not. Resting during the day is to be avoided; it is far better to have a change of activity.

Sleeping pills should not be taken if possible. Almost all of them leave a hangover in the morning and make it more difficult to get up. Older people are particularly prone to sleeping pill drowsiness and fatigue during the day.

Even an unsolved problem can be the cause of fatigue. This can be treated in a variety of ways, from talking about the matter with a friend to asking your doctor to suggest a counselor. It is not worth endlessly chewing over a problem alone.

Fats

Q Is it true that eating fat makes you fat?

A Yes, fats can make you fat, although it all depends on how much you eat. Weight for weight, fat provides twice as many energy units or calories as proteins or carbohydrates. Fats are often eaten in a pure form (such as butter or margarine) so they can easily add too many calories to your diet and make you overweight.

Q Would I come to any harm if I didn't eat fats?

A A diet with no fat at all would be very boring and difficult to arrange, but it is perfectly possible to survive on a diet containing less than 1 oz (28 g) of fat a week. This amount is necessary to supply essential fatty acids that the body is unable to make itself. Nearly all fats contain these fatty acids but, fish oils such as cod liver oil are particularly good sources.

Q My doctor has told me to eat fewer eggs to cut down on cholesterol. Why is it important to reduce the number of eggs when they do not contain much fat?

A Most of the cholesterol we eat is closely bound to the saturated fats of animal-based foods. Some other foods, notably eggs, are very high in cholesterol although they contain very little fat.

Q Is it healthier to eat meat broiled rather than fried?

A Yes, although it also depends just as much on what meat you eat. It is certainly better to broil fatty meat such as bacon, but there is less fat in fried chicken than in the same weight of broiled bacon.

Q I seem to have a lot of difficulty digesting fats. Is there something wrong?

A It sounds as though there is something wrong with the way your liver is making or releasing bile, a substance essential to fat digestion. Visit your doctor as soon as possible so he or she can investigate the problem.

Fats are foods with a bad reputation; their name has been linked with heart disease, obesity, and other threats to health. So what are fats, what does the body do with them, and are they really necessary?

Alan Becker/Image Bank

In freezing, wintry weather the body needs insulation against the cold. It can get this both from fat and from warm clothing.

Fats are one of the three substances, alongside proteins and carbohydrates, that make up the bulk of the human diet.

Fats are important to us for other reasons, too. They make food more palatable; think of the difference between dry and buttered toast, or salad with and without salad dressing.

They are also the most energy-rich of all foods. For example, 3.5 oz (99 g) of bread supplies about 250 calories. The same weight of butter, which is pure fat, provides 720 calories.

What are fats?
About 90 percent of the fats we eat are known as neutral fats. They are made up of two chemicals, fatty acids and glycerol, which are both formed from carbon, hydrogen, and oxygen. The fatty acids and glycerol form chains called triglycerides.

These fats can be either saturated or unsaturated, depending on the structure of the fatty acids. The more hydrogen atoms a fatty acid has, the more saturated it is. The degree of fatty acid saturation varies widely. Unsaturated fats are described as polyunsaturated if they have at least two hydrogen atoms fewer than the full complement of hydrogen atoms in a saturated fat.

A guide to high-fat foods

Foods containing saturated fats

Food	percentage of fat
Lard	100
Butter	100
Coconut oil	100
Fried bacon	67
Double cream	48
Cheddar cheese	33.5
Broiled steak	32.5
Broiled pork sausage	23
Stewed ground beef	20
Milk (whole)	3.6

Foods containing unsaturated fats

Food	percentage of fat
Olive oil	100
Margarine	100
Peanut butter	48.5
Broiled herring	13
Broiled mackerel	10
Avocado	8
Ice cream (made with vegetable fat)	8

Note: some foods contain a mixture of saturated and unsaturated fats; for example, mayonnaise is 79 percent mixed fats and french fries are around 20 percent, depending on the cooking oil used.

These foods all contain fat, but some is saturated and some unsaturated.

Most saturated fats are solid at room temperature, while unsaturated ones are liquid. One reason is that most saturated fats come from warm-blooded animals, whose fat is just about liquid at their body temperature, which is above the temperature of the surroundings. Unsaturated fats, however, tend to come from fish and plants that are adapted for life at much lower temperatures.

What fat is best?

Saturated fats have gained a bad reputation because of their association with cholesterol. Cholesterol makes up the remaining 10 percent of the fat we eat. It is not a true fat because its structure is different, but it is nearly always found with saturated fat. This means that the more saturated fat you eat, the more cholesterol you will eat at the same time.

The body needs cholesterol for a range of jobs, from making sex hormones to maintaining the tissues of the brain, but it can make all the cholesterol it needs in the liver. The extra cholesterol taken in when saturated fat is eaten seems to interfere with the body's own cholesterol-controlling mechanism, and the bloodstream becomes flooded with it.

The surplus cholesterol, combined with other fats, becomes deposited on the walls of the blood vessels and can lead to arterial and heart disease. This is why doctors recommend changing from eating saturated fats that are high in cholesterol to unsaturated ones low in cholesterol.

How the body uses fats

Fats are part of the wall surrounding every body cell. The body uses fats to insulate it against cold, to store reserve energy, to absorb shock around bones and organs, to insulate nerve cables, to lubricate the skin, and to help transport certain vitamins.

Fats are broken down in the digestive system into fatty acids and glycerol. The fatty acids are then broken down further to release energy for immediate use. Any excess is reconverted to triglycerides and stored in the cells under the skin and around the internal organs.

The glycerol is converted into glycogen, which is either broken down at once to release energy, or stored in the liver until it is needed. Once the liver's glycogen storage system is full, the glycogen is changed into fat and stored in the body cells. If a lot is stored there it makes a person overweight. This is why it is important not to eat more than is actually needed.

Burning up fats

The rate at which the body burns up fats for energy is controlled by hormones from the thyroid, adrenal, and pituitary glands. During intense physical activity or at times of stress, the hormones adrenaline and noradrenaline have a very rapid effect on the rate of fat breakdown in the body. They increase the amount of fatty acids in the blood by as much as 15 times, and push up the level of cholesterol.

If these fatty acids are burned up in exercise it seems to do the body no harm, but if they remain in the body they can, with the cholesterol, contribute to a fatty buildup in the arteries. This is one reason why exercise is a good way of dealing with stress.

Feces

Feces are the remnants of digestion, which are regularly passed out of the body via the anus.

The average amount of feces a person passes each day is 3–7 oz (85–198 g), although this can vary from 1 oz (28 g) on a starvation diet to 13 oz (369 g) on a diet that is rich in vegetables.

Composition and color

Feces are usually composed of about 75 percent fluids and 25 percent solid material. Some of the fluid is mucus, which lubricates the alimentary canal and eases the passage of feces from the body. Of the solids, about a third is bacteria, a third is undigested fats and proteins, and a third is cellulose or roughage, the part of plant foods that cannot be digested (see Excretory systems).

The color of feces is caused by bile pigments called stercobilin and bilirubin, produced by the chemical breakdown of red blood cells. These pigments also help to sterilize and deodorize feces.

Fecal odor is due to bacterial action in the intestine. This produces a variety of nitrogen compounds, and hydrogen sulfide, which gives a typical bad eggs smell.

Dietary effects

What we eat affects both fecal color and odor. Carrots and beetroot produce a vivid orange color, while red wine tends to make feces black. The more protein eaten, the darker and smellier the stools, although vegetables such as cauliflower and brussels sprouts (which contain a lot of sulfur) also produce a strong smell.

The volume of the feces is affected by the diet. People living in less developed countries, who eat a very high-fiber, low-fat diet, produce a much higher volume of feces than those on the average Western diet (up to 6 lb (2.7 kg) a day). Those who regularly produce bulky feces as a result of such a diet are generally free of serious colonic disorders such as cancer and diverticulosis (pouches in the walls of the bowel). In the West dietary differences and other factors lead to a wide range in the number of bowel movements considered normal. This may vary in healthy people from as many as four times a day to as few as twice a week.

Significant changes

Changes in the feces can be signs of a number of health problems. Infections and other disorders of the intestines, for instance, will produce characteristic changes. The most common of these is the watery stools of profuse diarrhea caused by minor infection. Diarrhea results from what doctors call intestinal hurry, often provoked by the irritation of

The color and smell of a baby's feces depend on whether it is breast- or bottle-fed.

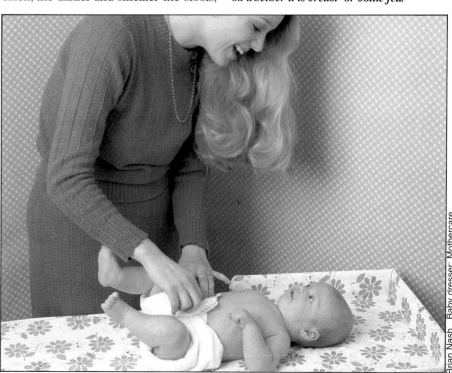

Brian Nash   Baby dresser: Mothercare

the intestine by bacterial toxins and other organic material (see Diarrhea). In the upper intestine, the contents are fluid and a high proportion of the water is normally reabsorbed into the bloodstream from the large intestine in its lower part (the colon). If the intestinal contents are being moved too quickly there will not be time for adequate reabsorption to take place. As a result the feces are still fluid when they reach the lowest part of the intestine (the rectum). Simple diarrhea is seldom serious in adults and is not usually a cause for concern.

Some intestinal infections, however, are more dangerous and these produce characteristic changes in the feces. In bacillary dysentery the feces contain blood, pus, and mucus and may be almost odorless. At first they contain fecal material, but later may consist only of blood and pus. In amebic dysentery the feces characteristically consist of fluid fecal material, mucus, and small amounts of blood. They have a semenlike smell. Cholera feces are watery, voluminous, odorless, and contain numerous white flakes. Doctors commonly describe them as rice-water stools because of this. The flakes are shreds of intestinal lining that have been damaged by the cholera bacterial toxins and thrown off.

Infection is not the only cause of diarrhea. Other causes include overuse of laxatives, eating too many legumes such as beans and peas, or eating indigestible carbohydrates such as lactose, sucrose, mannitol, galactose, or lactulose. Anxiety and irritable bowel syndrome can also produce diarrhea. More seriously, it may be a sign of a hormone-producing tumor.

Loss of color

One of the most striking changes occurring in the feces is the loss of the typical brown color produced by bile. In a healthy person, bile passes from the liver through the bile duct into the intestine. Loss of stool color, so that the feces resemble grayish clay, should be reported to the doctor immediately. It suggests that something may be obstructing the flow of bile from the liver. This may occur in various ways and can be due to gallstones, hepatitis, other liver disorders, or even cancer of the head of the pancreas.

When bile cannot escape into the intestine, it dams up in the blood and will eventually color the skin and the whites of the eyes. This is called jaundice. Bile accumulation will also color the urine.

Blood in the feces

Blood can enter the feces at different stages in the intestine, and will produce different effects according to the point at which it entered.

If bleeding occurs high up in the intestine, perhaps from a stomach or duodenal ulcer, the blood will be digested and chemically changed as it passes down through the intestine to produce a dense black pigment. Tarry black feces will result and this may be an important sign of trouble. Such a change in the feces should be reported to the doctor unless you have been taking iron pills, which can produce a similar change in color.

All other signs of blood in the feces should be reported to the doctor. If blood is released lower in the small intestine, due to telescoping of the bowel, the feces will look like cranberry sauce. If bleeding is occurring in the large intestine, the blood will be less closely mixed with the feces and may be bright red in color.

Bleeding from the rectum or anus usually results in the outside of the feces being smeared with bright red blood. The most common cause of blood on the feces is hemorrhoids, or piles, which are painful clusters of swollen veins in the lower rectum or anus (see Hemorrhoids).

Other changes in consistency

Voluminous feces that float and are hard to flush away may have an abnormally high fat content. Doctors call this steatorrhea. It is characteristic of various intestinal disorders that feature poor fat absorption. Fat malabsorption can also produce a watery diarrhea, because of the irritating effect of the unabsorbed fatty acids on the small intestine and the colon.

The form and consistency of feces may also be important. In constipation, because there has been time for abnormal reabsorption of water, the feces are drier and harder than normal. Sometimes they are pelletlike or near spherical, like bird droppings.

An important change is a sustained ribbonlike appearance of the feces. This can be caused by a cancer of the colon that narrows the inside of the large intestine It should be reported to the doctor at once.

Simple diarrhea is rarely a serious problem for adults, but can be dangerous in small children, who can dehydrate very quickly.

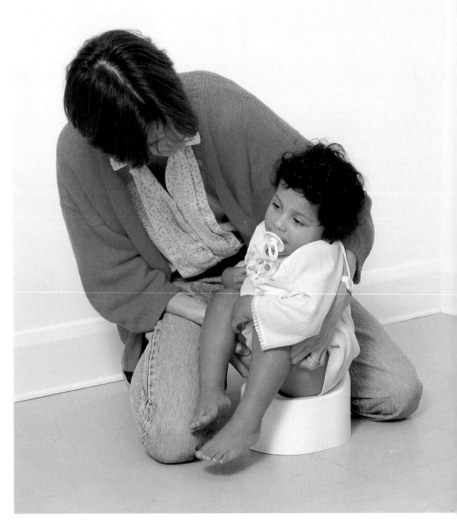

Feet

Q My son's feet turn inward. Does this mean he is pigeon-toed?

A Yes, it can mean this. Pigeon toes are not normally a serious problem, though they can result from either deformities of bones in the foot arch or from weakness in the muscles of the leg that are attached to the foot. In most cases the condition cures itself. Take your son to see your doctor if you are worried.

Q The verrucae on my feet seem to disappear and then come back again after a time. Why does this happen?

A Verrucae are a form of wart on the foot and are caused by a viral infection. All warts are prone to disappear and reappear suddenly, and this unpredictable behavior makes it difficult to assess the effectiveness of any treatment. Generally warts are best left alone, but verrucae should be removed by your doctor.

Q My husband has been told that he will not be able to play soccer for a while because of damage to his Achilles tendon. What is this?

A The Achilles tendon is attached to the heel and is the link between the foot and the powerful calf muscles at the back of the leg. These muscles provide the power for walking and running; when they contract they pull on the tendon and the heel is raised. This tendon is extremely strong, but occasionally gets torn. Surgery is the only means of repair, but a fairly long convalescent period is needed before the tendon can again take the great stress placed on it when it is in action.

Q My friend's feet smell a lot. What can he do about it?

A Feet that spend the day in socks and shoes get hot and sweat a lot. Your friend should wear socks made of wool or cotton and leather shoes, which allow the feet to breathe. Regular washing, foot deodorants, and clean socks each day should also help.

Babies are born with beautiful feet, but these have to stand a lifetime's wear and tear. Commonsense care can help keep them healthy and in good working order.

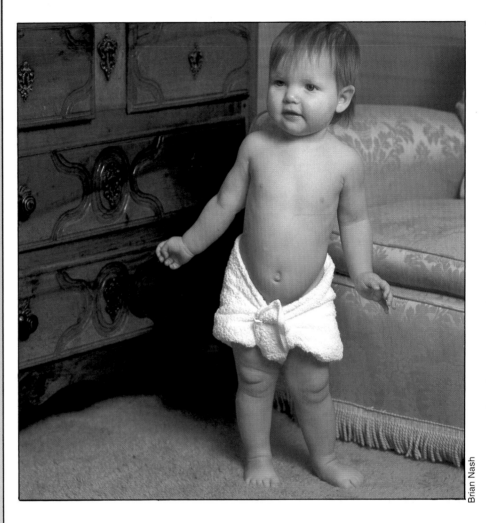

Brian Nash

Healthy feet keep their flexibility and their beauty. It is good for children to go barefoot wherever the ground is safe. When shoes have to be worn, they should always be a good fit.

Each human foot is a mechanical masterpiece that consists of 26 bones, 35 joints, and more than 100 ligaments. In many ways, the formation of the bones, blood vessels, and nerves of the foot resembles the structure of the hand, but the proportions are different; for example, the phalanges, the bones making up the toes, correspond to the phalanges in the fingers of the hand.

It is not very surprising that the hand and the foot have many similarities in structure, because they have both developed over centuries of evolution from limbs that were originally designed for climbing and grasping.

The ability in humans to make controlled movements of the hand was gradually refined, while the foot changed its function as people began to walk on two legs instead of four.

The foot has two important tasks: to support the weight of the body, and to act as a lever to move the body forward when walking or running. However, people who have lost the use of their hands through an accident or disease are able to achieve almost the same dexterity with their feet. Some can even use them for writing or painting.

Walking

The foot is made up of many small parts and joints, so it is flexible and adapted to walking on uneven surfaces. Most of its power is derived from the strong muscles in the leg, with a series of smaller foot muscles to aid them in their task.

The weight of the body is supported on the largest bone in the calcaneum (foot), which forms the heel, and by the heads of the metatarsals, which make up the bones of the foot. The other bones are raised from the ground in the form of an arch, because this is the only way that a segmented structure (like the arch of a bridge) can hold up any weight.

The foot has three arches. To give them their anatomical names, they are the *medial longitudinal arch*, which runs along the inside of the foot; the *lateral longitudinal arch,* which runs along the outside of the foot; and the *transverse arch*, which crosses the foot. If you look at a wet footprint (of someone who is not flat-footed) on the bathroom floor, you will see that it is narrower in the middle, because the inner arch is higher than that on the outside of the foot. All the arches are supported by an elaborate system consisting of ligaments and muscles.

When you stand still, your body weight is supported on the heel and the metatarsals, but when you begin to walk, the load is borne first by the lateral margin (outside edge) of the foot, and then by the heads of the metatarsals (toes). The toes are extended as the heel rises and the contracting muscles shorten the longitudinal arch of the foot.

The body itself is thrown forward by the action of the powerful muscles in the leg (the gastrocnemius and soleus), which pull on the ankle joint using the ankle as a lever, while the flexor muscles of the foot flex the toes for the final thrust forward. The toes are kept extended to prevent them from folding underneath the foot upon the next step. The big toe is the most important of all, but loss of the other toes does not affect your ability to walk.

Why feet ache

Feet may ache after a very long walk, after standing for a long time, or because a person is overweight, ill, or is employed in an occupation, such as waitressing or working in a store, that requires being on the feet all day. Aching feet result when the supporting muscles tire and the ligaments become stretched through supporting the load on the arches. Flat feet are the result of the ligaments having become permanently stretched.

Children's feet

Most babies are born with what appear to be flat feet, and the arch only develops as the tendons, muscles, and ligaments strengthen with use. For this reason it is essential that young children should always wear good-fitting shoes, so that their feet can develop in the right way.

It is not a good idea to give children shoes at too early an age. Let them run around barefoot as long as there is no danger from sharp objects. Once a child has begun to wear shoes, parents should make sure that his or her feet are measured for length and width about every two months. Most reputable shoe stores provide this service and will offer advice.

As soon as shoes become too small, they should be discarded; and the reason that parents should keep an eye on this themselves is that young children are unlikely to complain, even if their shoes are too tight. Cramped shoes are the cause of many deformities, such as bunions, ingrown toenails, and splayed toes, which will be difficult to correct later in adult life.

Preventing foot problems

Adult shoes should be chosen with the same care as children's, despite the dictates of fashion. Unfortunately most foot deformities are acquired as the result of wearing badly fitting shoes; problems can be accentuated by platform soles or stiletto heels, because they tilt the body at an unnatural angle.

The same things that cause feet to ache can also produce calluses and corns, which are hard areas of skin at the pressure points that can irritate the underlying nerves. Although it is tempting to try to treat corns yourself, it is always advisable to consult a chiropodist.

Good foot hygiene is important in preventing infection. Because feet are mostly enclosed in socks and shoes all day, they tend to sweat. Stale sweat not only smells very unpleasant, it also creates a suitable

The mechanics of walking

The flexibility of the human foot is due to its intricate anatomy. Shown here are the many bones, ligaments, and powerful muscles of the foot and leg that go into action with every step that we take.

environment in which infections can easily grow.

To some extent, the chances of contracting skin infections such as athlete's foot can be reduced by a careful choice of footwear. Socks made of cotton or wool absorb sweat better than man-made fibers like nylon, and leather shoes allow the foot to breathe, while plastic ones trap sweat and bacteria.

Foot injuries

Breaking a bone in the foot is a fairly common accident, usually caused by dropping a heavy object on the foot. Fractures of the toes are generally not a problem (excepting the big toe); the fractured toe can be splinted to the sound toe alongside it and can be left to heal like this.

However, fractures of the tarsal bones are serious, because it is difficult to align the broken bones and damage to the joints may occur. Often the victim has to learn to live with a painful foot, but sometimes surgical operations can be undertaken to seal the joint by locking the bones together, providing a joint that is less mobile but painless.

Flat feet

The condition known as flat foot or pes-planovalgus, can happen at any age. As the name suggests, the foot loses the arch on the inside, with the result that the entire sole is in contact with the floor. The bathroom test will show you if your feet are flat; wet footprints made by normal feet are definitely narrower in the middle than those made by flat ones.

Feet have to serve their owner for many thousands of miles during a lifetime; it is no wonder then that the mechanics go wrong sometimes. The inside arch of the foot acts as a spring that helps to distribute a person's weight evenly through the heel and toes. If the feet are flat, it does not necessarily mean that this bracing is absent, merely that it is not shown by the presence of an arch. There are many athletes who have flat feet and perform perfectly well. The only trouble they may suffer from is uneven wear of their shoes.

Perhaps the most common cause of flat feet in adults is due to laxity of the ligaments holding the forefoot bones together. The forefoot splays and the arch drops, and consequently there is often a generalized aching of the foot.

Flat feet in children

Many parents worry about their children's feet. Many babies appear to have flat feet, but the feet contain a large quantity of fatty tissue in the soles, as well as a prominent pad of fat in the front of the heel that fills the arch and gives the flat appearance. By the age of three, when children are walking properly, their feet will no longer have such a flat look. Parents who are concerned about their children's feet should look at the soles of their shoes. If they are markedly worn on the inside, then their feet are probably flat. If parents think that this is affecting their child's walking, it would be worth consulting the doctor.

Treatment

Pain in the feet can happen for various reasons, such as infection of the soft tissues caused by an abscess or boil, abnormality of the bones of the foot, or an acquired deformity such as a bunion, where the anatomical changes can also lead to flat feet. Unfortunately, surgery cannot correct flat feet, but discomfort can be relieved by wearing shoes or sandals with instep inserts for extra support. These can be bought from drugstores and some department stores.

Opinion is divided as to whether remedial exercises can help. They are definitely beneficial when the condition is due to prolonged period of rest in bed.

Choice of footwear

No shoes are really good for the feet, but the best are low-heeled or flat shoes with plenty of room for the toes and good ankle support. A light, flexible sole is also important for easy walking. In suitable climates and inside the house, go barefoot whenever possible.

Caring for your feet

- Wash your feet at least once a day and dry them thoroughly, taking extra care to dry between the toes. Finish with talcum powder
- Change socks or stockings daily. Leave shoes to air between wearings
- Have a weekly pedicure. Soak feet in warm water. Scrub around toes, under feet, and heels with soapy nailbrush. Gently rub away rough skin with pumice stone
- Cut nails straight across, not down into corners. Smooth edges with an emery board. Ease back cuticles with cotton-tipped orange stick, using cuticle remover. Buff nails to finish

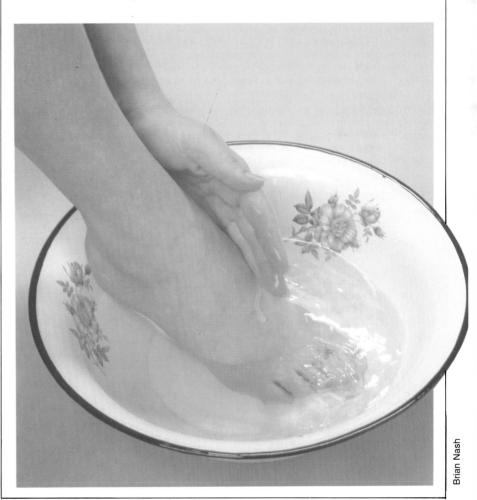

Brian Nash

Q Can flat feet be found in several members of the same family?

A Yes, you can often trace them back through the family tree. There are some races in which up to 35 percent of the population has flat feet; these cases are often symptomfree and, oddly, in the most athletic groups.

Q My son has knock-knees and flat feet. Are the two usually associated?

A Yes they are. What happens is that the knock-knees force the feet to rotate inward, so that the arches of the feet come into contact with the ground. However, this is a condition that often clears up by itself. If your son is unhappy or being teased about this, take him to the doctor for advice.

Q I have recently been sick and have spent a lot of time in bed. Now I am up again and I notice that I have flat feet, which are very painful to walk on. Is the condition permanent?

A This is a temporary condition, due to the muscles in the feet having become flabby and weak with disuse. It will take some time before they regain their ability to support the arch. You should do some exercises to regain the strength in your arches, and the rest of your feet too, but do this gradually, not all at once.

Q My son is badly pigeon-toed. Can this condition cause flat feet?

A No, pigeon toes do not cause flat feet. However, if your son stands the opposite way, with his feet turned outward, Charlie Chaplin-style, then it will. Your doctor will advise you if you need further reassurance.

Q I think I am becoming flat-footed. Will it affect my career as a dancer?

A It depends upon exactly what is causing the problem. Go and speak with your doctor as soon as possible to see if any remedial measures can be taken.

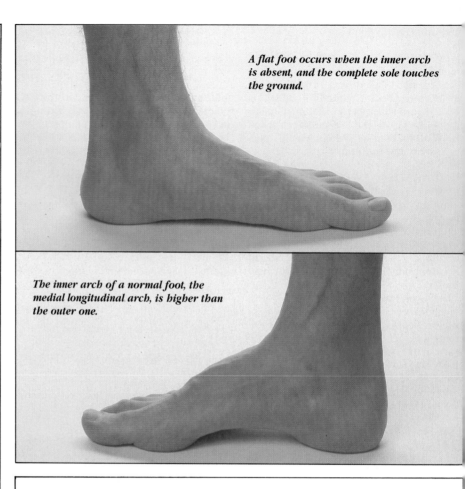

A flat foot occurs when the inner arch is absent, and the complete sole touches the ground.

The inner arch of a normal foot, the medial longitudinal arch, is higher than the outer one.

Foot exercises

The time when exercise can help your feet most is after a period of illness, when your muscles are weak and slack. Even before you are up again, you can practice these exercises regularly in your bedroom. Do them on a hard floor, with bare feet. They will help to retone and strengthen your muscles.

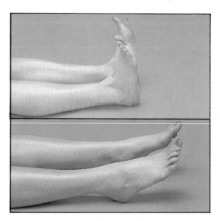

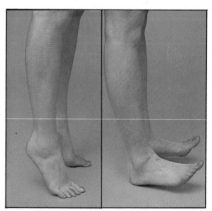

1. Sit on the floor, leaning back very slightly, with your hands supporting your body. Stretch your legs straight out in front of you, keeping them slightly apart. Starting with your feet and toes pointing upward, stretch your feet down toward the floor as far as you can, feeling the stretch in your instep. Relax, then repeat the exercise 10 times.

2. Stand upright with your feet slightly apart. First, stand on tiptoe, stretching upward as high as you can. Hold for a count of five. Now lower your feet to the ground and then stand on your heels and raise your toes. Hold this (if you can) for a count of three. Lower your toes to the ground. Now repeat the whole exercise slowly five times.

Feldenkrais method

Q I work at a keyboard all day and have started to feel intermittent pain in my arms and wrists. Could Feldenkrais help?

A Get medical advice first. This may be the first sign of tenosynovitis, a condition where the tendons become inflamed and painful due to overuse. To help prevent the disease from developing, your doctor may suggest that you take steps to insure your chair is comfortable and you have adequate breaks throughout the day. Rest and anti-inflammatory drugs may be prescribed if you are in great pain. An alternative therapy such as the Feldenkrais method may certainly be helpful in the early stages of the disease or if other therapies have failed. It should help you learn how to avoid putting undue strain on your tendons and muscles.

Q What makes the Feldenkrais method different from other alternative therapies designed to help the body?

A Rather than working on isolated actions of joints or specific conditions, the Feldenkrais practitioner helps the client improve the overall quality of all the body's motions, from breathing and posture to actions such as gait or reaching. Feldenkrais does have something in common with such alternative therapies as the Alexander Technique or holistic massage. However, the emphasis with Feldenkrais tends to be less prescriptive, and more to do with enabling you to explore your body's movements yourself.

Q What requirements do you need to become a Feldenkrais practitioner?

A To practice the Feldenkrais method, a student must have considerable experience developing kinesthetic and tactile skills. Practitioners need to have an enormous repertoire of movements, learned from hundreds of Awareness Through Movement lessons. They learn by experience, involving 160 days of training spread over a period of four years.

The Feldenkrais method uses movement and touch to expand body awareness and explore forgotten ways of sensing, thinking, feeling, and acting to allow for more efficient and comfortable movement.

The Feldenkrais method is named after the Israeli scientist Moshe Feldenkrais (1904–1984). Feldenkrais worked in Paris as a nuclear physicist with the Nobel laureates in chemistry, Fréderic and Irène Joliot-Curie. After injuring his knee in a soccer game, Feldenkrais learned that corrective surgery would provide only a 50 percent chance of improving his condition. If it proved unsuccessful, he would be confined to a wheelchair for life.

Not satisfied, he began to learn about anatomy, kinesiology, and physiology, and combined these with his knowledge of mechanics, physics, electrical engineering, and martial arts. His studies helped him restore most of the function to his injured knee, and marked the start of an investigation into human function, development, and learning that was to last for the rest of his life. It eventually led him to develop the Feldenkrais method.

From the 1970s onward he taught his method throughout the world. He directed the Feldenkrais Institute in Tel Aviv until his death in 1984.

Learning to move
The Feldenkrais method rests on the belief that, unlike other animals who at birth are programmed to move to survive, young humans must learn how to move correctly. While a cat is born with an instinctive knowledge of how to move gracefully, it takes years for people to learn movement well enough to function independently in the world.

Once they have reached a level of proficiency sufficient for walking, jumping, or playing sports, most people stop learning new movements and cease improving their body awareness. Whatever style of movement has been learned up to this point, mostly through trial, error, and imitation, begins to form into a personal set of movement habits. These habits tend to overuse certain muscles and joints while neglecting or ignoring others, thus leading to a limited range of movement and gross inefficiency in the short run.

Personal limitations
As a result of establishing these habits, many people find that they are unable to improve at activities that interest them. They avoid doing anything, such as a sport, that might reveal a lack of coordination and awareness. They may never learn

Learning the Feldenkrais method involves reliving your childhood experience of exploring all sorts of movements.

Q My boyfriend is not happy taking the drugs he has been prescribed to control his panic attacks. Is it safe for him to use Feldenkrais instead?

A Panic attacks—when the heart suddenly beats very quickly and breathing becomes fast and deep—can be very frightening, but they are not usually dangerous. The Feldenkrais method is often useful in teaching sufferers to control anxiety and panic. Provided your boyfriend checks with his doctor, there is no reason why he should not try this rather than his medication.

Q Can the Feldenkrais method help me improve my abilities as an athlete?

A The key to a high level of athletic skill is coordination. You can improve this through increased body awareness, which is what the Feldenkrais method aims to develop. It can help athletes work smarter rather than harder by breaking their worst habits. Through the variety of complex movements involved in Feldenkrais exercises, athletes can also learn details that help improve their performance, for example, how the movement of the left shoulder might affect the action of their right leg in such a way as to create problems with the Achilles tendon or right knee.

Q My mother, who has recently started to experience severe backaches, believes that it's due to old age. Is there anything I can do to stop myself from getting backaches as I get older?

A Lower back pain without any obvious cause such as disease or injury is fairly common in older people. In most cases it has developed through bad habits of posture over the years, whicht put a cumulative strain on the muscles, ligaments, and tendons in your back. Learning a technique such as Feldenkrais that helps you become aware of these bad habits, and break them, can prevent this. However, insure that you check with your doctor if you do have a sudden onset of back pain, as it can be a symptom of disease.

Awareness Through Movement (ATM) lessons are taught in groups, through verbal directions.

the coordination skills that allow them to ski or dance, for example, because it makes them feel uncomfortable.

Feldenkrais said about the limitations that people impose upon themselves: "Through the first years of life, we organize our entire system in a direction which will forever after guide us in that direction. We end up being restricted, we don't do music, we don't do other things. What is more important, we find ourselves capable of only doing those things that we already know."

In the long run these limitations in awareness and coordination give rise to physical difficulties such as recurring pain, repetitive stress injuries, or problems recovering from injuries.

Advanced activities

Human beings have the ability to change and reorganize the way they perform familiar activities in a way that no other animal can. Every person has the capacity to make each walk they take a different kind of walk completely new in style, to make each movement of their body a new experience.

Yet this amazing capacity to learn and change is rarely used. Most of us find one way of doing something and stick to it until finally a knee, back, or other part of the body breaks down. We then assume that our pain and discomfort has been caused by the activity we performed, rather than our particular way of actually performing it.

Body awareness

Through simulating the exploratory style of learning that is so natural to infants, students of the Feldenkrais method learn new patterns of movement, designed to expand body awareness and to enhance the neuromuscular self-image. Eventually these patterns allow you to use more efficient and comfortable movements.

The Feldenkrais method uses two approaches: Awareness Through Movement (ATM) lessons and Functional Integration (FI). ATMs are movement sequences that are taught to groups of people. Lessons generally last from 30–60 minutes. There are hundreds of ATMs to choose from. The mechanisms of breathing, speaking, and all aspects of postural control are explored and improved, while perceptual capacities are increased.

Students engage in precisely structured movement explorations that involve thinking, sensing, moving, and imagining. The lessons are often based on developmental movements, like rolling, crawling, or rising up from a lying to a sitting position; or explorations of joint, muscle, and postural relationships. Lessons begin with comfortable, easy moves that gradually evolve into movements of greater range and complexity. They recapitulate the original childhood experience of learning to organize and control body movements.

An important goal of ATM lessons is to learn how your most basic functions are organized. Students can learn how to

"In a perfectly matured body which has grown without great emotional disturbances, movements tend gradually to conform to the mechanical requirements of the surrounding world. The nervous system has evolved under the influence of these laws and is fitted to them. However, in our society we do, by the promise of great reward or intense punishment, so distort the even development of the system, that many acts become excluded or restricted. The result is that we have to provide special conditions for furthering adult maturation of many arrested functions. The majority of people have to be taught not only the special movements of our repertoire, but also to reform patterns of motions and attitudes that should never have been excluded or neglected."

Moshe Feldenkrais, *Introduction to Higher Judo, 1952*

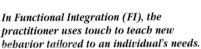

In Functional Integration (FI), the practitioner uses touch to teach new behavior tailored to an individual's needs.

eliminate unnecessary energy expenditure and mobilize their intentions into actions efficiently.

Since learning is a highly individual matter, they are encouraged to learn at their own pace in a noncompetitive manner. This is why the same lesson may often benefit people from different age groups, backgrounds, and abilities.

Functional Integration

For students who want more individual attention, Feldenkrais created a hands-on technique called Functional Integration (FI). FI is usually performed with the student lying on a table designed specifically for the work, but it can also be done with the client sitting or standing. Each FI lesson is tailored for the needs of each individual student.

The practitioner communicates to the student through gentle and noninvasive touch the experience of comfort, pleasure, and ease of movement, while the student learns how to reorganize his or her body and behavior in new and more effective ways. The practitioner's touch is instructive and informative, not corrective. Students are encouraged to explore new, more expanded functional motor patterns that they can then translate into new abilities.

FELDENKRAIS METHOD

Sample Awareness Through Movement Lesson

1. Stand with your legs a comfortable distance apart, as if you were about to walk forward. Shift your weight onto your left leg just enough so that you can easily lift your right heel from the floor by slightly bending your right knee. Then set the right heel down and press it into the floor as you straighten your knee while lifting the ball of your foot and toes off the floor. Rock back and forth lightly and easily from the heel to the ball of your foot like this several times.

Rest standing symmetrically and feel the difference between your two legs.

Awareness advice: During the movement notice how you use your left leg while you rock across the bottom of your right foot. Look forward, preferably out a window. If you have problems with balance, place one hand on the back of a chair for support.

2. Now rock a few times with the weight more toward the outside of your right foot, then across the inside, or arch, of your foot. Then rock the weight across wherever you feel the middle of your foot to be.

3. Stand symmetrically for a moment and notice the difference in the way your two legs bear weight. Walk around and notice the difference in how they move. Does your right leg feel lighter or easier to move? Is your left leg more solid and stable?

Repeat these movements on the other side. Later, before going for a walk or run, spend a couple of minutes repeating this on one or both legs.

Awareness advice: Imagine how useful even this short and simple lesson would be for a runner, both to increase speed and to take stress off an injured leg.

4. Lift the ball of the right foot off the floor at the same time that you lift the heel of the left foot. Now alternate the opposite ball and heel.

Awareness advice: How does your pelvis assist you in this movement? Do your arms move a lot? Try not moving your arms at all and then let them move freely. Observe the difference in the motion of your trunk. Be sure your eyes look forward while doing this.

Note: This lesson can be used as a tune-up for athletes as well as for people who suffer from balance problems.

New choices in movement

The Feldenkrais method offers students new choices in movement by allowing them to experience the differences between great effort and effortlessness, efficiency and inefficiency, as well as the contrast between neutral and pleasurable movements. Unless a student can sense these distinctions, they have no choice over the quality of their movements and are reduced to acting like machines. Once students learn the difference between movements and their unique qualities, they can acquire and put to use alternative ways of performing the same task, and regain a broader range of talents and skills.

Who can benefit

The Feldenkrais method can be used with people who have all types of clinical disorders, from hemiplegia and cerebral palsy to acute or chronic back and other

> "This great ability to form individual nervous paths and muscular patterns makes it possible for faulty functioning to be learned. The earlier the fault occurs, the more ingrained it appears and is. Faulty behavior will appear in the executive motor mechanisms which will seem later, when the nervous system has grown fitted to the undesirable motility, to be inherent in the person and unalterable. It will remain largely so unless the nervous paths producing the undesirable pattern of motility are undone and reshuffled into a better configuration."
>
> Moshe Feldenkrais, *Body and Mature Behavior*

pain problems (see Paraplegia, and Back and backache). It is commonly used by professional athletes, dancers, and musicians who have recurring injuries or stress symptoms, and by coaches and physical education teachers to improve their movement analysis and teaching technique.

Other important areas of application include elderly citizens who have motor limitations, people suffering from breathing disorders, and those suffering from chronic anxiety and psychosomatic disorders. The method has been successful in areas where many other treatments have failed or where there was little hope for improvement.

The Feldenkrais method can be used to help people with back problems who have found little relief from conventional treatment.

Fetal alcohol syndrome

Q I have recently become pregnant and my doctor says I should give up drinking alcohol. Drinking is an important part of my social life; must I really stop altogether?

A Your doctor's advice is the only good advice that can be given. The possible consequences of drinking during pregnancy are so severe that it is not worth taking any risks, especially during the first three or four months.

Also, is it really necessary to drink alcohol at social events? There are many soft drinks to try and fruit juice will do you a lot of good.

Q I'm sure that an occasional alcoholic drink while I am pregnant won't harm my child. Are some kinds of drinks safer than others?

A There are no alcoholic drinks that are better than any other; the point is that any consumption of alcohol is harmful.

As far as an occasional drink goes, there is no firm evidence that one drink will do any harm, in the later stages of pregnancy anyway. But again, the best advice is that drinking anything at any time during pregnancy is definitely not worth the risk.

Q I am pregnant and my husband is a very heavy drinker. Could this cause fetal alcohol syndrome in my child?

A There is nothing to indicate that a father's drinking can damage sperm production in a way that will cause developmental problems in a fetus. If he drinks while you are pregnant, this cannot affect your child's development in the uterus.

Q My friend has a child who suffers from fetal alcohol syndrome. She has been told there is no cure; is this true?

A This depends on what features of the syndrome the child suffers from. The treatment for any aspect of the syndrome will be the same as if it were caused by other reasons. Some aspects can be treated, others cannot.

Only in recent years have doctors become fully aware of the dangers of alcohol in pregnancy. Fetal alcohol syndrome is a particularly serious consequence.

Fetal alcohol syndrome (FAS) is a group of defects in newborn children. The most characteristic aspect of the syndrome is a series of deformities of the head, but there are other serious problems, including retarded growth and development.

Strictly speaking FAS is quite rare and occurs only in the children of mothers who are alcoholic or at least drink steadily and in some quantity throughout pregnancy. It is probable that as many as a third of children of mothers who are alcohol-dependent (or alcoholic) during pregnancy suffer from the syndrome. However, the syndrome has been observed when mothers have drunk as little as two to three glasses of wine, bottles of beer, or their equivalent per day.

Even if a child does not suffer from the full syndrome, alcohol can still affect a child's development in the uterus. Such an affected child may display only a few signs of the syndrome, but these can be serious. Just how much alcohol is needed to have some effect is not exactly known, but it is probable that even small amounts, especially in the first months of pregnancy, can be harmful.

Characteristics

There are many aspects of FAS and they can be present with varying severity. The child's head and brain may be abnormally small, the upper jaw underdeveloped (possibly with a cleft palate), the lower jaw and forehead unusually prominent, and the eyeballs small, with shortened eye slits and folds of skin near the nose. Physical growth is severely retarded, and mental development is badly affected. There may also be joint defects, defects in the development of the spine (such as spina bifida), and in extreme cases, parts of the brain may be missing altogether.

The newborn baby is effectively an alcoholic, suffering from alcohol withdrawal symptoms of irritability, sleeplessness, and poor appetite.

Survival

About one in five babies with FAS dies within days or weeks of being born. Among those that survive, there are varying degrees of mental retardation and physical damage. The retardation and damage are often long-lasting or even, in many cases, permanent.

A woman who drinks heavily during pregnancy, especially during the early months, runs the risk of giving birth to a baby with fetal alcohol syndrome. Babies of alcoholic women may even be born alcoholic themselves.

Bubbles/L.J. Thurston

Fetus

▲

Q I am pregnant and I've got a vaginal yeast infection. Will this damage my fetus?

A No, it will not affect the fetus. In fact, yeast infections are common during pregnancy. Since yeast is harmless, and inserting pessaries or creams into the vagina might start a miscarriage, many doctors prefer to leave it untreated during pregnancy. Although it is uncomfortable, it is nothing to worry about. If you need reassurance, talk to your doctor.

Q Can sexual intercourse during pregnancy damage the fetus?

A No. You can continue to have sexual intercourse for as long as you wish and as long as you are comfortable. Some couples may need to find new positions for intercourse, because any weight on the woman's abdomen is uncomfortable. However, a woman who has miscarried during a previous pregnancy should not have sexual intercourse during the first trimester (the first three months of pregnancy) and intercourse should not take place at all if there is a threat of a miscarriage. Consult your doctor about this if you are at all anxious about miscarrying.

Q I saw a road accident when I was nine weeks pregnant and it upset me very much. Will the experience mark my baby in any way?

A No. It is a myth that a very disturbing or frightening experience could result in a baby with a birthmark or some other disfigurement or abnormality.

Q I love swimming, but a friend has told me that I should stop exercising now that I'm pregnant. Is this true?

A No. You should stay as fit as you can throughout your pregnancy, and as long as you don't overdo it and tire yourself out, exercise such as swimming, tennis, and walking is perfectly safe. But doctors advise pregnant women to avoid horseback riding and diving.

For the pregnant woman, understanding the development of the fetus within her is one of the best ways of insuring that her pregnancy will be a happy time.

A doctor or obstetrician will date the start of a woman's pregnancy from the first day of her last menstrual period, adding on nine calendar months and seven days to arrive at an estimate of the delivery date.

Pregnancy is divided into trimesters (periods of three months in the life of the fetus), but in fact conception will probably take place between the 10th and 14th day of the menstrual cycle, when a woman is most likely to be ovulating and at her most fertile; therefore pregnancy may actually begin during the second week of the first trimester.

At this stage, the pregnancy consists of a single fertilized cell, or egg. For three days after fertilization, this cell moves along the fallopian tube toward the uterus, dividing and redividing to form a small group of cells called the morula.

The fetus in the first trimester:
Weeks 1–14: For about another three days the morula floats in the uterus. It divides and re-divides to form a hollow clump of cells called the blastocyst, which is just visible to the naked eye.

Week 2: The blastocyst embeds itself in the endometrium, the lining of the uterus; this stage is called implantation. Chorionic villi—projections from its covering—burrow into the lining of the uterus, to secure nourishment for the primitive fetus.

The outer lining of the blastocyst, which is called the trophoblast, begins to develop into the placenta, the vital link between the fetus and the mother. Blood cells start to form and the first heart cells are laid down.

Week 3: Hormonal changes in the mother's body cause the endometrium to thicken and the blood from it nourishes the blastocyst.

Week 4: The amniotic sac is by now well developed. The fetus will stay in the sac throughout the pregnancy, comfortably suspended in the amniotic fluid, at a constant temperature and well buffered against any shocks. The heart is already

The fetus at 24 days old.

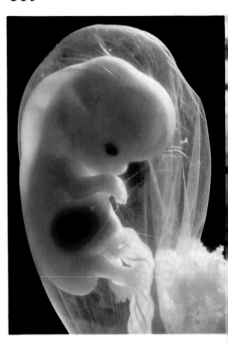

In this nine-week old fetus, all the parts of the body are present, even though they are not all fully formed.

beating, irregularly at first, but soon very steadily and faster than the mother's.

The spine and the beginning of the nervous system are starting to form in the fetus, which is now about ⅕ in (7 mm) in length.

Week 5: The first organs form. The head is growing, enclosing the developing brain, which is linked to a rudimentary spinal cord. The arms and legs show as little buds, and the heart and blood circulatory systems are well established.

The fetus at 28 days old.

.1 in (3 mm)

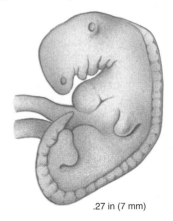

.27 in (7 mm)

Blood vessels from the fetus join with others in the developing placenta to form the umbilical cord. The chorionic villi continue to increase in number and to branch, attaching the fetus firmly to the wall of the uterus.

In the fetus, now about ⅓ in (7.6 mm) long, the digestive system has begun to form, starting with the stomach and parts of the intestines. Although there is as yet no recognizable face, there are little depressions where the eyes and ears will be. The mouth and jaws are also starting to form, and the brain and spine continue to develop.

Week 6: The head continues to develop. The internal parts of the ear and the eyes continue to form (the latter covered with the skin that will become the eyelids). The little holes that later become the nostrils start to develop. The brain and the spinal cord are nearly formed. The development of the digestive and urinary systems continues, although the liver and kidneys are not yet able to function. The arm and leg buds have grown and it is now just possible to see the rudiments of hands and feet. By the end of week 6 the fetus is about ½ in (1.3 cm) long.

Week 7: The placenta—through which the fetus takes nourishment from its mother's circulation and passes back waste products to be excreted—is now well developed. This is an important time for the growth of the eyes and parts of the inner ear, and the heart beats more powerfully. The digestive system continues to form, and many of the internal organs, although still in a very simple state, now exist. The lungs are growing but they are solid at this point. There are small spinal movements and the face continues to form, to the point where it is possible to see the beginnings of the mouth. The arms and legs are growing and have developed hip, knee, shoulder, and elbow joints.

Week 8: The eyes are now almost fully developed, but they are still covered with

Formation of the blastocyst

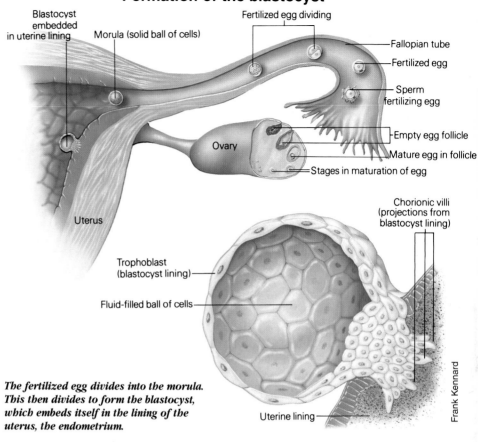

The fertilized egg divides into the morula. This then divides to form the blastocyst, which embeds itself in the lining of the uterus, the endometrium.

Frank Kennard

half-formed eyelid skin. The face continues to form and now has the beginnings of a nose. It is possible to see separate toes and fingers, and the limbs are able to move a little. The head, large in comparison with the rest of the body, leans downward over the chest. The fetus is now approximately 1½ in (3.8 cm) long.

Week 9: The umbilical cord is completely formed and nourishes the fetus's circulatory system with blood. The inner

The fetus at six weeks old.

The fetus at seven weeks old.

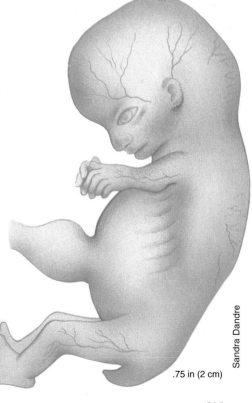

Sandra Dandre

The fetus at five weeks old.

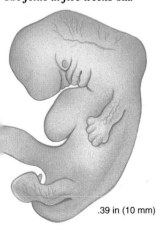

.39 in (10 mm)

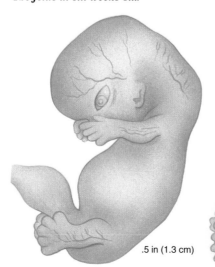

.5 in (1.3 cm)

.75 in (2 cm)

part of the ear is complete; the outer part is starting to form. All the major inner organs of the body continue to develop and the uterus has increased in size. By this point, the fetus is about 1⅞ in (4.8 cm) long.

Week 10: The circulatory system is now pumping blood around the body of the fetus. The reproductive system has begun to form, but only inside the body: the external genitals are not yet visible. The face continues to develop and the arms and legs are now very clearly formed, with tiny webbed fingers and toes. Movement of hands and feet is more vigorous, but still cannot be felt by the mother. By the end of week 10, the fetus measures 2 in (5.3 cm).

Week 11: The face is almost completely formed and the eyelids have developed from the skin covering the eyes. Muscles are starting to form and the development of the external sexual organs has begun. The placenta by now is a separate organ, a soft pad of tissue. The volume of fluid in the amniotic sac continually increases between the 11th and the 40th weeks of pregnancy.

Weeks 12–14: Nearly all the internal organs are now formed, but they cannot yet function independently of the mother. The uterus can now just be felt rising above the pelvic bones, but the mother does not yet show her pregnancy.

The mother in the first trimester
Since this is the three-month period in which the basic formation of the fetus takes place, it is important for the mother to avoid anything which could cause fetal malformation. The doctor should be consulted before any drugs are taken and all

women are advised to give up smoking as soon as they become pregnant.

Before starting a pregnancy, a woman should make sure that she is immune to rubella (German measles) and if she is not, should be vaccinated against it. Contracting it during pregnancy might cause the baby to be born with a number of grave abnormalities.

It is important for the mother to see a doctor at the beginning of the pregnancy for a thorough physical checkup and to arrange for prenatal care. Checking on the progress of the fetus is an important part of this and can range from simply measuring the size of the mother's abdomen to the use of ultrasound.

About a week before the normal menstrual period would start, there may be a little bleeding as new blood vessels are forming to nourish the growing embryo. The doctor should be told of this and of any other symptoms, and he or she will also advise on diet and the extra vitamins and iron that may be needed throughout the pregnancy. Regular blood pressure and urine tests should be made to check that the mother is fit and healthy.

Morning sickness (nausea and vomiting) is common in the first trimester. It is usually of no concern, although very severe morning sickness can lead to dehydration.

The fetus in the second trimester: weeks 14–28
Weeks 14–16: The limbs continue to form, the joints are able to move, finger and toenails develop, and a soft, fine hair, called lanugo, covers the whole fetus.

After week 14 the placenta is fully formed. Growth begins to be rapid: the fetus now weighs about 4⅞ oz (135 g) and is approximately 5 in (12.7 cm) long.

After week 16 or thereabouts, the kidneys begin to produce dilute urine.

Week 20: By now the fetus is able to make vigorous kicking movements, which the mother will be able to feel. The muscles are developing fast and hair has begun to grow on the head. The fetus will now be about 8 in (21 cm) long.

Week 24: The muscles are almost completely formed and the placenta is growing continually: all the necessary nutrients, including oxygen, pass through it from the mother to the fetus, and waste products go back through it into the mother's circulation and she excretes them. The fetus is still not able to exist independently of the mother, although in

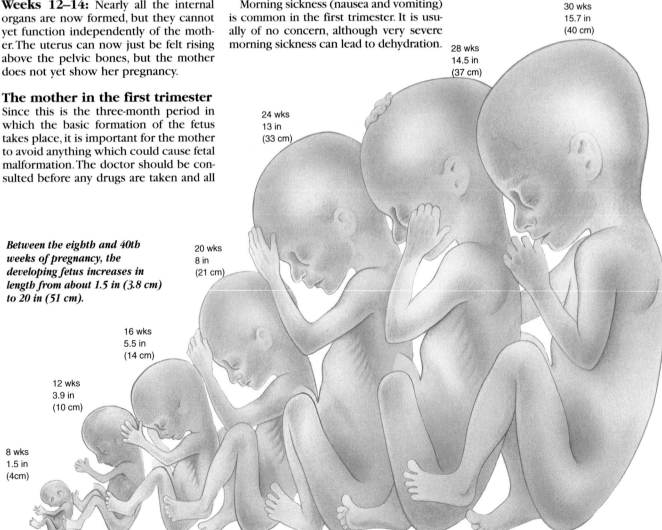

Between the eighth and 40th weeks of pregnancy, the developing fetus increases in length from about 1.5 in (3.8 cm) to 20 in (51 cm).

30 wks
15.7 in
(40 cm)

28 wks
14.5 in
(37 cm)

24 wks
13 in
(33 cm)

20 wks
8 in
(21 cm)

16 wks
5.5 in
(14 cm)

12 wks
3.9 in
(10 cm)

8 wks
1.5 in
(4cm)

very rare instances, babies born prematurely at this point and nursed with expert care have survived. The weight of the fetus is about 20 oz (567 g) and the length about 13 in (33 cm).

Week 28: This is the point at which the fetus is said to become viable, because it would have a 5 percent chance of survival if it were to be born prematurely. It is now approximately 14½ in (37 cm) long and is covered with a grease called vernix to protect it from the fluid in the amniotic sac.

The mother in the second trimester

The mother will feel the fetus moving inside her, particularly just before she falls asleep. Her own blood circulatory system has changed, with a continual increase in the production of blood cells. Many women find that they drink larger quantities of liquid than they usually do in this period, and some may need iron supplements to help in the increased production of blood.

By week 20 the breasts are ready for breast-feeding; some women find that the nipples produce a yellow fluid, called colostrum, but not all pregnant women experience this, and those who do not should not worry that their ability to breast-feed will be affected in any way.

At this stage of the pregnancy, some women have indigestion, heartburn, and constipation, and they need to take these things into account when they are planning their diet. As the pregnancy advances, the increase of weight and pressure on the internal organs can cause hemorrhoids in the rectum and varicose veins in the legs. The hemorrhoids can partly be prevented by avoiding constipation, and the irritation they cause can be relieved by ointment or suppositories, obtained from the doctor. Elastic support stockings or pantihose, put on before getting out of bed in the morning, help to prevent varicose veins.

The fetus in the third trimester: weeks 29–40

The growth of the fetal body has now caught up with that of the head and the fetus has the physical proportions of a baby. It is much thinner, however,

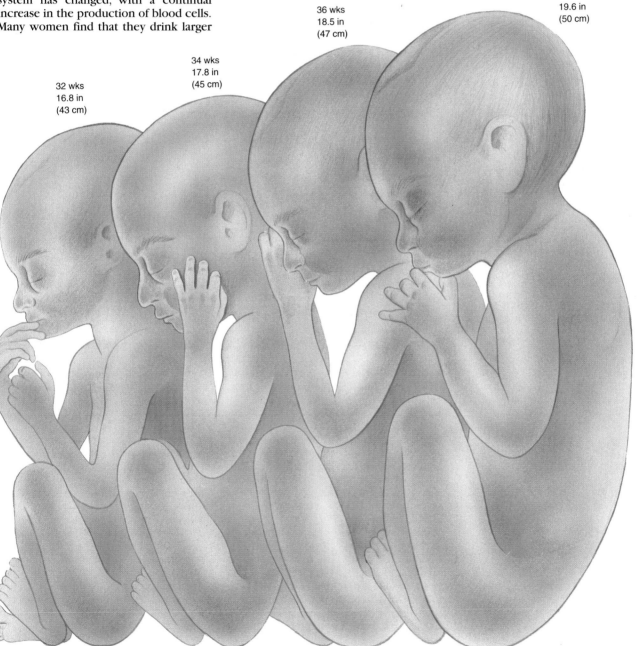

32 wks
16.8 in
(43 cm)

34 wks
17.8 in
(45 cm)

36 wks
18.5 in
(47 cm)

38 wks
19.6 in
(50 cm)

Sandra Dandre

Q My sister had a baby with spina bifida. Does this mean that I will, too?

A There is some evidence that spina bifida (a serious spinal abnormality) occurs more in some families than others. Many clinics and hospitals now run prenatal screening services and you should ask your doctor about this.

Q Do I need to take vitamin pills during pregnancy?

A If you are keeping to a good diet, you may not need to, but many women find that the demands of pregnancy mean that they do need extra vitamins. Most doctors recommend vitamin supplements as a precaution.

Q Is it dangerous to drive a car during pregnancy?

A No, as long as you are sure that you haven't lost the power of concentration: some women find that they do in the later months of pregnancy. By the seventh or eighth month, wearing a seat belt may be uncomfortable and you should ask someone else to drive.

Q Can I find out the sex of my baby through amniocentesis or another type of test?

A In amniocentesis, a fine needle is passed through the woman's abdomen to draw off a sample of amniotic fluid. A chorionic villus biopsy samples cells surrounding the embryo. Both techniques are used to test for fetal abnormalities and they can detect the sex of the fetus. Later in pregnancy, an ultrasound scan might reveal the sex, depending on the baby's position. High-frequency sound waves produce a picture of the baby in the uterus. The technique is routinely used to check the health and size of the fetus and to diagnose twins.

Q Should I stop smoking while I'm pregnant?

A Yes, most definitely. If you smoke, your baby may have a low birth weight and be more vulnerable to illness.

Carnegie Institution of Washington. Dept. of Embryology, Davis Division

The development of the hands

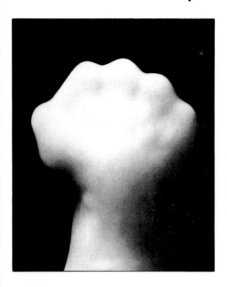

By the sixth week of pregnancy, the arm buds are growing and the fetus has rudimentary hands.

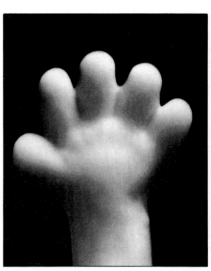

In the seventh week, the structure of the hand begins to form: the finger ridges are clearly visible.

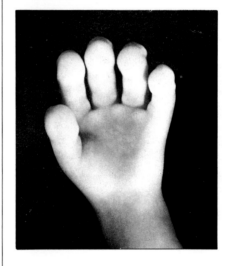

In the eighth week, the fingers and thumb, with their broad pads, are separate from one another.

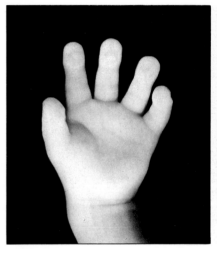

By the 13th week, the pads are smaller, the nail beds have begun to develop, and the hands curl.

because the subcutaneous (under the skin) fat has not yet developed. The amount of vernix has increased. The length of the baby at 34 weeks is about 17½ in (44.4 cm), and a baby that is born prematurely at this stage has a 15 percent chance of survival.

Week 36: By this point, the chance of survival is increased to 90 percent, because the lungs are fully formed. In many cases, the baby has turned to rest head downward in the uterus, but in women who have already had a child, this may not happen until later. The testicles of the male baby have come down into the scrotal sac, and the vernix has increased. The baby's weight goes up by about 1 oz (28 g) per day.

Some babies are born with the fine lanugo hair still on the arms, legs, or shoulders, but it usually disappears in the final weeks of pregnancy.

Birth will take place at about the 40th week, although some women go into labor later or earlier than this.

When the baby is born, there will still be patches of vernix on the body but not on the eyes and mouth. The child will be about 20 in (51 cm) long and have an average weight of about 7¾ lb (3.5 kg).

The development of the feet

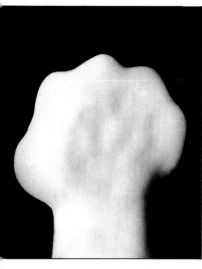

...y the seventh week, little clefts have ...ormed at the ends of the leg buds, which ...ill separate into toes.

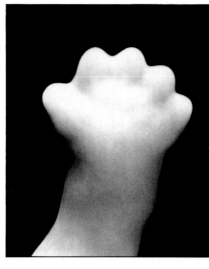

Very early in the eighth week of pregnancy, the toe ridges develop in the feet. The rudimentary toes are webbed.

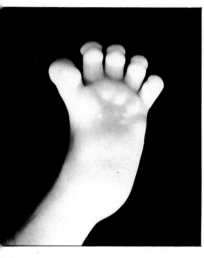

...y the ninth week, the pads of the toes are ...sible, and so is the beginning of the heel. ...e legs are lengthening.

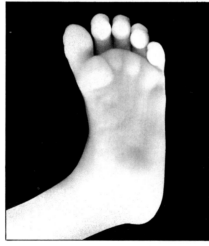

By the 13th week, the toes, like the fingers, are separate from one another and their pads are smaller.

The mother in the third trimester

By now, the uterus has expanded a great deal and many women find that it is difficult to walk without leaning back a little, which can cause backache. There will be occasional, painless contractions of the uterus, which are normal and help with circulation through the placenta.

Lying on the stomach will become uncomfortable. However, once the baby's head has engaged—descended into the pelvis—many women feel a great deal more comfortable, because the pressure on the stomach and diaphragm is substantially reduced.

Some time around the 40th week, labor will begin. The mother's pelvic bones have already become more separated in readiness for the delivery of the baby. Powerful contractions, rupture of the amniotic sac, or the loss of the mucus plug in the cervix—the neck of the uterus—are among the first signs that the baby is about to be born. The cervix starts to dilate and the baby begins the journey to the outside world.

At birth, the average baby weighs about 7¾ lb (3.5 kg), but the size of a newborn baby is determined by many factors, including the parents' size and how well it was nourished during the pregnancy.

The hair on the newborn baby's head varies in length from hardly visible to about 1½ in (3.8 cm), the nails reach to the ends of the fingers and toes, or even a little beyond them, and the eyes are almost always blue in color, or have a bluish tinge, because the eye coloring is not yet fully formed.

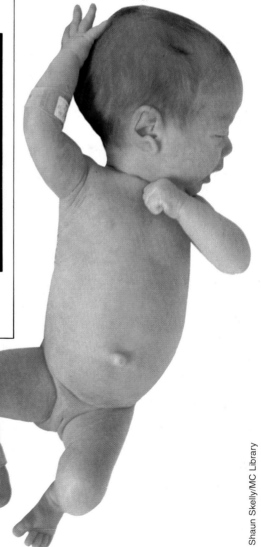

At birth, an average baby will measure 20 in (51 cm) in length, and weigh about 7¾ lb (3.5 kg).

Fevers

Q Is it important to bundle up and stay warm when you have a temperature?

A You should not allow yourself to get too cold. On the other hand, there is no need to pile blankets on the bed or heat the room to oven temperature. Rest, get as comfortable as you can, and your body will do what is needed.

Q When I have a temperature, I shiver one minute and sweat the next. Why is this?

A In a fever, the temperature not only goes up, it swings up and down much more than usual. When it is on its way up, people may get shivering chills, which may be so intense as to cause uncontrollable shaking attacks, called rigors. As soon as the temperature starts to fall again, there is a lot of sweating.

Q Is it possible for a fever to keep returning?

A Yes. The most outstanding example is the fever that accompanies malaria, a disease transmitted by mosquitoes, which can continue years after people have left the tropics. Fevers may keep recurring with other chronic infections. Often, of course, people have no sooner recovered from one virus than they pick up a new infection from a different virus.

Q Does a fever leave any lasting damage?

A No. Any damage after a feverish illness results from the disease itself, rather than from the amount of fever. However, all feverish illnesses, even slight ones, make people feel a little weak for at least a day or two and often longer.

Q I've been told that you shouldn't take strenuous exercise when you've got a temperature. Is it really harmful?

A This is sensible advice. When your body starts to feel hot and your temperature begins to rise, the infection is becoming established. The infection is likely to become more widespread if you exercise strenuously at this point.

A fever is not an illness: it is a raised body temperature and is usually a sign of some form of infection. Plenty of fluids and rest in bed will aid recovery.

Everyone has had a temperature at some point and usually the cause is obvious—it may coincide with a cold, a cough, or a sore throat. Most fevers are due to infections by bacteria or by a virus, but they can occur as a result of any sort of inflammation anywhere in the body.

Changes in body temperature

The body temperature is generally kept within fairly close limits by the hypothalamus, the brain region concerned with the control of many of the body's automatic functions. If the body temperature rises too much, the body sweats to lose heat. If the temperature goes down too low, heat is made in the body by activity of the muscles, which burn glucose fuel and so create heat. This minor increase in muscular activity is not usually noticeable, but if someone becomes very cold, the activity increases greatly and they start to shiver.

Normal body temperature

The normal body temperature—98.6°F (37°C)—is only an average value: it is not uncommon for healthy people to have temperatures anywhere between 96° and 99°F (35.6°–37.2°C). In healthy people, body temperature goes up through the day, starting at about 4:00 A.M. and reaching a peak about 6:00 P.M., and the variation may be as much as 2–3°F (1–1.7°C). The tendency of people with raised temperatures to sweat at night is nothing more than an exaggeration of normal heat loss during the day.

High temperatures

Very high temperatures can be fatal. A temperature over 106°F (41.1°C) can cause a convulsion in an adult, and permanent brain damage may occur if the temperature rises to 108°F (42.2°C). However, temperatures as high as this are extremely rare. In most cases, a high temperature can be brought down simply by sponging the patient's body all over with tepid water and by taking a medication such as acetaminophen.

To lower the temperature in a feverish child, sponge the whole body with tepid water. The child should be given plenty of fluids to drink.

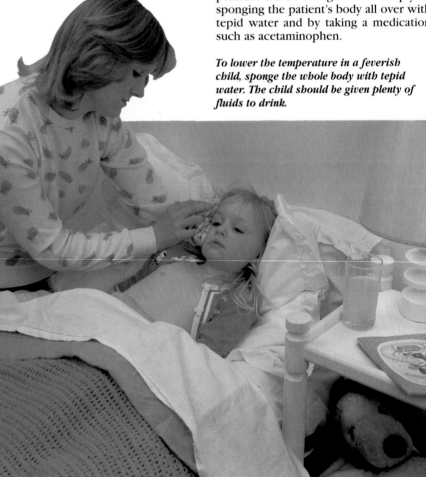

The exact reason why people develop a raised temperature with infections and other causes of inflammation is not well understood. The white blood cells, which are an essential part of the body's defense system, produce a substance called pyrogen. This acts upon the hypothalamus, causing the body temperature to rise. Some drugs such as acetaminophen or aspirin can bring about a reduction in high temperatures by blocking messages sent out by the hypothalamus.

Causes of fevers

The most common causes of fevers are, of course, viral infections such as influenza, which are usually associated with colds or sore throats. There is no specific treatment for viruses: the only thing to do is to rest until the fever passes.

Almost all other fevers in temperate parts of the world are brought about by bacteria, which cause infections of the respiratory passages, the urinary tract, or the intestines and bowels. Bacteria also

Strip thermometers are easy to use but can sometimes be inaccurate. They are held against the child's forehead.

In case of fever . . .

- Take the patient's temperature, but don't become a slave to the thermometer! The patient's general condition is a better guide than his or her exact temperature
- Rest. Don't go to work or school. Drink plenty of fluids: they are much more important than food, especially for very young children, who may be in great danger from dehydration
- Keep children with a mild fever indoors and occupied. There is no need to insist that they go to bed
- Keep bedclothes warm but light
- Use acetaminophen to bring the fever down. This is particularly important when a child has a very high temperature, to avoid the risk of convulsions
- If a feverish child has a convulsion, do not leave him or her alone at all. Call the doctor once the convulsion is over
- Do not take a child who has been in contact with an infection and has developed a temperature to the doctor's office: it is likely to spread infection. Call the doctor and ask for advice

---

cause more serious infections, such as tuberculosis and typhoid fever, and collections of pus—abscesses—that are accompanied by fever. Bacterial infections can be treated with antibiotics.

In the tropics, there are many feverish diseases caused by parasites slightly larger than bacteria, called protozoa; a common example is malaria. Finally, there are rare fevers that may result from unusual forms of tumors or from drugs.

Children with fevers

A child can produce quite a high temperature with a very minor infection, and so temperature alone is not a particularly good guide to a child's health. A much better one is whether he or she seems generally ill. Symptoms such as loss of appetite, vomiting, and lethargic behavior are much more important signs than the degree of a fever.

The most common viral infections that cause fevers in children are usually accompanied by a cold, cough, or sore throat. However, children are also likely to catch childhood illnesses that cause fevers, such as measles, rubella, mumps, chicken pox, and whooping cough.

Spreading illnesses

The belief that it is a good thing for children to catch these illnesses and get them over with is probably sensible in some cases; mumps is certainly more unpleasant in adults than in children. Measles and whooping cough, however, are very unpleasant at any age: both can be fatal in babies and very young children. As the risks of vaccination are less than the risks involved in having these illnesses, vaccination is recommended.

Children with fevers do not necessarily have to be kept in bed. They are often happier taking things easy in the company of their family, instead of being lonely and bored in their bedrooms.

It is not necessary to force feverish children to eat solid food, but it is important for them to drink as much as possible; the danger of dehydration is particularly great in babies and small children.

Convulsions

Children tend to develop convulsions with very high temperatures, e.g. above 103°F (39.4°C). This happens mainly between the ages of one and three and rarely after the age of five.

A feverish child can be given acetaminophen to bring the temperature down and avoid the risk of a convulsion. Aspirin should never be given to children with viral infections because of the possibility of developing Reye's syndrome, a dangerous condition involving liver inflammation and brain damage.

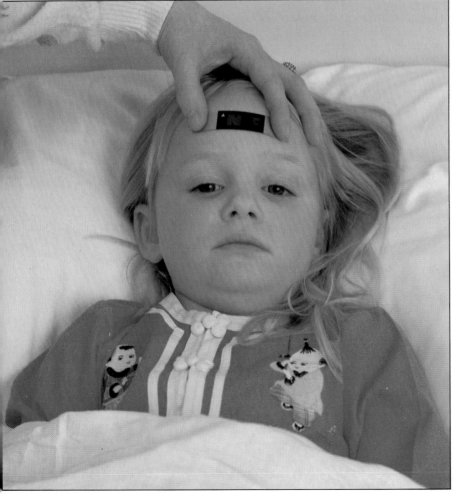

Fibroids

Q **Is there any difference between a fibroid and a polyp?**

A Both fibroids and polyps are benign tumors in the reproductive organs. Fibroids appear on the uterus; polyps can either appear inside the uterus or along the cervical canal. Both may cause excessive bleeding during periods or bleeding midcycle; in a few cases fibroids may prevent conception. If difficulties arise, the fibroids or polyps can be removed using surgical techniques.

Q **I have recently had a fibroid removed. How long will I have to wait before I try for another baby?**

A It is probably sensible to wait until your scars have healed and you have had two normal periods. This should be a minimum time of eight weeks.

Q **I have a bloodstained discharge between periods. Since it may be due to fibroids, do I need to see a doctor?**

A Yes. There are many other reasons for such a discharge and it may be necessary to have a D&C (dilatation and curettage, where the lining of the uterus is scraped). If a polyp rather than a fibroid is found it can be removed during the D&C. Alternatively other surgery may be necessary.

Q **I have some small fibroids that give me heavy periods. Since I am nearing menopause, is it necessary to have a hysterectomy?**

A It is important to be certain that the heavy periods are only due to fibroids; your doctor may arrange diagnostic tests to confirm this. If fibroids are the cause, hormone pills can sometimes control the heavy periods. If the pills do not work, then you will have to decide how inconvenient the periods are and whether you can wait for menopause, or whether you would be happier with a hysterectomy to remove the uterus. Fibroids often disappear after menopause.

One in five women under 40 (and many more above this age) has fibroids, the most common tumor of the female reproductive organs.

Fibroids are solid, white-colored tumors composed of muscle and fibrous tissue that grow in the uterus. They can vary greatly in size, from as small as a pea to as large as a football.

Causes
Fibroids are the most common tumor of the uterus and are found in 20 to 30 percent of all women over 30 years old. They are more prevalent in women who have reached middle age.

The growth of fibroids in women who already have these tumors may be stimulated by the hormone estrogen, which is at a higher level in pregnant women and women on the Pill. After menopause, when the level of estrogen falls, the fibroids may shrink or disappear.

Symptoms
Fibroids can cause excessive menstrual bleeding or a bloodstained vaginal discharge, especially if they hang into the uterus cavity by a fine stalk. Women with very large fibroids may experience some discomfort from the pressure on the bowel or bladder.

In rare cases, fibroids may interfere with getting pregnant if they block the tubes. If a woman is already pregnant, the blood supply to the fibroid may be blocked up, in which case the fibroid will degenerate and cause some pain.

Dangers
There is a very tiny risk that a large fibroid can change into a cancerous tumor called a sarcoma. However, this is a rare occurrence.

Treatment
Fibroids that cause no problems should be left alone. If difficulties occur, especially in women who wish to have more children, then the fibroids can be surgically removed from the uterus, which is left intact (this is called a myomectomy). In older women who do not wish to have further children, a hysterectomy (removal of the uterus) can be performed.

Outlook
In a tiny proportion of women who have had a myomectomy, the fibroids may recur within a few years.

Fibroids in the uterus

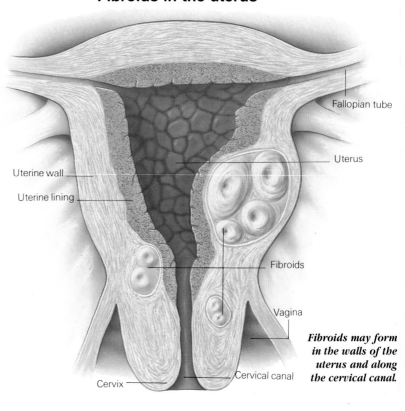

Uterine wall

Uterine lining

Fallopian tube

Uterus

Fibroids

Vagina

Cervix

Cervical canal

Fibroids may form in the walls of the uterus and along the cervical canal.

Frank Kennard

Fibrositis

Q I strained my thigh muscle while playing hockey. The doctor says I have fibrositis now. How has this happened?

A The strain that affected the muscle has obviously resulted in a degree of inflammation within the muscle that can correctly be termed fibrositis. More accurately, it might be called fibromyositis—myositis implying that the inflammation of the fibrous tissue is in the muscle. In time the injury should heal and the inflammation should die down.

Q My grandfather complains all the time that he has fibrositis. Why should this be?

A Old people nearly all have a degree of arthritis in one or several joints, and in particular, the neck and back. This is likely to be the cause of the fibrositis. To make matters even more confusing, many old people with aches in the soft tissue of the body could have other conditions that they accept as fibrositis, but which really need a different treatment. The elderly should be encouraged to visit their doctor and not put up with the pain, which can often be relieved.

Q When I went to my doctor with a backache, he took blood samples. When he got the results, he told me I had fibrositis. Is there a blood test for this disease?

A No. Your doctor was probably testing for other conditions, such as rheumatoid arthritis or polymyositis (an inflammation of the muscles). When these tests proved to be normal, your doctor felt more comfortable giving you the diagnosis of fibrositis.

Q I have a muscular complaint which has been diagnosed as fibrositis. How can I relieve the intense pain?

A Your doctor can prescribe painkilling drugs and muscle relaxant drugs. You can also massage the area gently, apply local heat from an infrared lamp or even a hot water bottle, and rest the affected area.

The term fibrositis is used to refer to secondary symptoms set up in the muscles and the joints by certain specific diseases. Although the condition is painful, there are now various forms of relief.

Fibrositis is a somewhat vague term that is used by some doctors to cover any ache in the soft tissue of the body. In turn, many patients tell their doctor that they have fibrositis when they simply mean that they feel pain in a muscle.

Most doctors, however, use the word fibrositis to describe a group of conditions where there is pain and tenderness in the soft tissue, usually in the muscle or around the joints, which occurs as a secondary symptom of another, more specific disease.

Causes
There are three principal causes that account for nearly all cases of fibrositis. The first of these is arthritis. Not only

Areas prone to fibrositis

The red areas show the typical sites where fibrositis can attack with sharp pain.

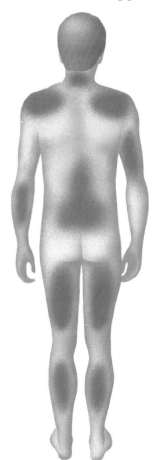

Venner Artists

does arthritis deform joints, and therefore place differing stresses on surrounding muscles and ligaments, but it often causes chronically inflamed bone to protrude into the muscles close to the affected joint. It is the combination of these two effects that causes muscle aches, spasms, and tenderness.

This is why many patients with arthritis complain not only of pain in the affected joint, but also of pain in the surrounding muscle tissue, which they correctly call fibrositis.

Second, the disks between the vertebrae of the spine are a frequent cause of trouble, especially if a disk is out of position, as in a slipped disk. When an abnormally placed disk presses on a nerve in the spinal cord, or intrudes into the surrounding muscle, this can frequently cause pain and spasm in the affected area of the back.

Third, where a muscle has suffered damage or a ligament is stretched and strained, the pain in the area is referred to as fibrositis.

Whatever the condition that is causing fibrositis, it is frequently made worse by cold and damp weather.

Symptoms and treatment
The sudden onset of pain in a muscle of the neck, back, arm, thigh, or calf is typical of fibrositis. The sufferer complains of pain when moving and tenderness when the affected place is touched.

The doctor will be able to detect areas of muscular spasm, often with tightly knotted muscles in constant contraction. Having identified the fibrositis, the doctor will want to find and treat the underlying cause. Fibrositis that is caused by arthritis will improve with an antiarthritic treatment, and that caused by disk conditions may improve with manipulation, performed either by a doctor or by an osteopath or physiotherapist.

Anti-inflammatory and painkilling drugs can help considerably, especially if an attack of fibrositis is treated promptly. In severe cases, where pain is unbearable, an injection of a local anesthetic such as procaine may be given. However, the relief may only be temporary.

In most cases, massage by a physiotherapist can relieve the muscle spasm. Resting the affected part and applying heat can also bring relief.

Fistula

A fistula sometimes forms in the body as a result of infection or may be present from birth. The condition is less common nowadays and surgery can correct it.

Q I had my appendix removed about two months ago and still have a slight discharge from the scar. Is this due to a fistula?

A A slight discharge following an operation for appendicitis is more often due to infection in the skin, or perhaps around one of the stitches, than to a fistula. However, it is important to clear up every discharge as quickly as possible, so tell your doctor about this.

Q My husband has been told that he has a fistula. Can it close up of its own accord?

A Even when the cause of the fistula has been removed, it is unusual for it to close by itself and heal. This is because the fistula develops a skinlike lining. Usually, the treatment is to remove the whole fistula surgically. The healing process may take several weeks. The exception to this is when an artificial fistula is made using a plastic tube. When this is removed the tissues should heal normally, without forming a further connecting tract or fistula.

Q My mother has recently had a colostomy. Is this a sort of fistula?

A No, it is not strictly speaking a fistula. It is an operation that is done to bring the end of the large intestine out onto the front wall of the abdomen. It is usually performed because the lower part of the bowel has been removed and the rectum no longer works properly.

Q My friend has a fistula as a result of Crohn's disease. How has this happened?

A Although its basic cause is not known, Crohn's disease produces a chronic inflammation in the wall of the bowel that can result in diarrhea, loss of weight, and abdominal pain. Fistulae can form between two adjacent parts of the bowel, between the bowel and the bladder, or between the bowel and the skin. Anti-inflammatory drugs like steroids (cortisone and related drugs) are effective forms of treatment, but surgery is sometimes necessary.

A common type of internal fistula

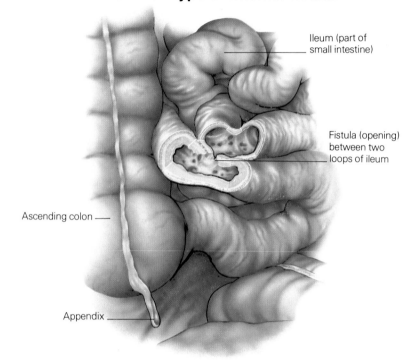

Ileum (part of small intestine)

Fistula (opening) between two loops of ileum

Ascending colon

Appendix

Frank Kennard

The word *fistula* is Latin for "pipe" and this is an appropriate description. In medical terms, it means an abnormal communicating channel, either between the inside and outside of the body or between two different internal structures. A fistula can run between one of the body's hollow organs (like the intestines) and the skin, or it can form a connection between two different organs, e.g. the intestines and bladder.

Confusingly, a discharging channel which opens onto the skin, but which ends in an abscess cavity, is also described medically as a *sinus*. Sinuses and fistulae may be lined by epithelium of a type that lines the structures they connect, or they may be lined by inflamed scar tissue. In either case, it makes the fistula slow to heal.

Despite the fact that fistulae are less common than they once were, they still occur as a result of infection. Sometimes this happens after a surgical operation, when a fistula may open up through the operation scar. Fistulae also sometimes occur as a result of a rare bone infection called osteomyelitis. Because bone does not have much of a blood supply, this type of infection can be difficult to clear up. Antibiotics cannot easily penetrate the bone and kill the organism responsible. If

an area of osteomyelitis goes on to develop into an abscess (collection of abscess; see Abscess), then it may form a fistula that leads to the outside of the body. Infection can also play a part in the formation of fistulae around the anus. Treatment is by surgery.

Present from birth

Perhaps the most serious congenital condition is a connection between the windpipe and the gullet, called a tracheo-esophageal fistula. This stops a baby from feeding properly, since milk goes into the lungs whenever the child tries to drink. There are several variations of this condition, which must be diagnosed in the first few days of the child's life and then dealt with by surgery. Fistulae in the circulation may also be present from birth, but rarely cause trouble.

Created surgically

Fistulae can also be created artificially. Surgeons do this for many reasons, one of the most common of which is when an abscess is drained. The surgeon often leaves a little piece of corrugated rubber or plastic in the base of the abscess, and stitches the skin around this, so that any further pus that forms can drain away.

Flatulence

Q I am three months pregnant and have developed awful flatulence. Why is this and what should I do about it?

A In the early months of pregnancy, flatulence is often caused by swallowing air. This is a particular problem in women who suffer from morning sickness or nausea at other times of the day; they gulp in air in an attempt to relieve the unpleasant sensations. In addition, the hormones of pregnancy are said to diminish movements of the intestine, causing constipation and so increasing the amount of gases in the intestine. To help get rid of the problem, try taking a very mild laxative, for example one containing magnesium hydroxide. You should also avoid foods such as onions, cauliflower, brussels sprouts, cabbage, and baked beans, which lead to the production of extra gas in the intestine. Also try to avoid swallowing air.

Q Although I eat a healthy, high-fiber diet I often get embarrassing rumblings in my stomach. What causes this?

A These rumblings are due to flatulence. A high-fiber diet can cause flatulence, but a little gas is a small price to pay for good health.

Q Since I started weaning my baby from breast milk to solid food, he has passed a lot of very smelly gas. Is this normal?

A Yes, as long as the gas is not associated with diarrhea or constipation, this is quite normal. It means your baby's intestine is adjusting to solid foods.

Q Sodium bicarbonate is our family remedy for gas attacks. Is it really helpful?

A No. Sodium bicarbonate (an antacid, like Maalox) simply releases carbon dioxide into the stomach. After a while, the gas is belched up, giving people the mistaken idea that the sodium bicarbonate may have done them some good.

The discomfort and embarrassment of flatulence, the presence of excessive gas in the intestine, is usually relieved by attention to diet and eating habits.

The word flatulence comes from *flatus*, the technical name for gas. Gas may be ingested with foods and drinks, delivered into the intestine from the bloodstream, or formed by intestinal bacteria. Between 12–17½ pt (5.6–8 l) of gas enter or are formed in the intestine each day.

How it occurs

In the small intestine, between five–15 percent of the air that is swallowed—mostly oxygen—is absorbed into the blood, while a considerable amount of carbon dioxide is released from the blood into the intestine.

The oxygen and carbon dioxide move on to the large intestine. Here their volume is increased by gases produced as a result of the decomposition of undigested food by bacteria, including carbon dioxide, methane, hydrogen, oxygen, and hydrogen sulfide. A considerable proportion of these gases is absorbed back into the blood through the large intestine wall, so that from the total 17½ pt (8 l), only ¾ pt (0.35 l) of gas is actually expelled during defecation.

On average, the gas mixture leaving the anus contains 59 percent nitrogen, 21 percent hydrogen, nine percent carbon dioxide, seven percent methane, and four percent oxygen. The actual smell of this mixture depends very much on what people eat. Foods containing a lot of sulfur, particularly eggs, meat, and vegetables such as cabbage and cauliflower, lead to the production of hydrogen sulfide, which smells like rotten eggs!

Excess gas can be formed by eating too much protein, fat, or high-fiber foods such as beans. Stress is also a common cause of flatulence, because it leads either to air swallowing or to intestinal hurry. The habit of air swallowing can be hard to break: the best long-term solution is to learn to relax and not to rush meals.

Constipation is a very common cause of flatulence; because the contents of the intestine are dammed up, they trap gas and create discomfort.

A change to a high-fiber diet may temporarily cause a lot of pungent flatus to be passed, but that is a much better solution than taking laxatives, which can make the problem worse by rushing food and gases through the intestine too quickly.

Flatulence as a symptom

At the stomach end of the intestine, excess gas can be a symptom of inflammation, ulcers of the stomach or duodenum, or faulty action of the muscles in the esophagus or at the stomach's entry or exit.

However, there are likely to be other symptoms, including pain, and they need the prompt attention of a doctor.

Foods that are likely to cause flatulence.

Brian Nash

Fleas

Q When my little sister woke up one morning recently she had five or six tiny insect bites on her stomach. Could this be the work of fleas?

A Yes. Even if you don't have a household pet and you clean your house regularly, these could be flea bites. If your sister had been playing with a cat or dog, a flea might have jumped onto her and then settled down to biting.

People tend to notice flea bites at night because the warmth of the bed increases the blood flow in the skin, which results in more itchiness than usual.

The other possible culprits could have been mosquitoes. The bites would not, as some people think, have been caused by house mites, which are microscopically tiny creatures that collect in bedding. Mites don't bite, but they can cause asthma.

Q How often should I treat my dog and cat to be sure they don't have fleas?

A The frequency of treatment depends on the activities of the animal. For a suburban dog, the interval should be about every three months. If a dog is a working farm dog or has access to farmland, treatment is usually needed every six weeks. Cats need regular treatments every six weeks, because they tend to wander.

Q How can I tell if my dog has fleas?

A Your dog will be irritable and will scratch or nibble the bitten areas frequently. You may be able to see the bites on your dog's skin, or you may actually see a flea in the fur. If you see one, there are probably others.

Q Is it true that cat fleas cannot live on humans for any length of time and must return to the host?

A No. Although a cat flea prefers the blood of a cat, it will not automatically return to the cat it came from. Humans living in the same house are therefore likely to be infested.

Fleas are no longer serious pests, but they are an unhygienic nuisance. Household pets such as dogs and cats are the most likely carriers of fleas.

Fleas are tiny, bloodsucking insects that live by biting through the skin of animals, including humans. Their small size and ability to hop several feet makes them difficult to catch.

There is a flea that specializes in living off human blood—*Pulex irritans*, or the human flea—but it is only one of a number that may bother us.

Dangers

As a result of improved standards of hygiene, pest control, and widespread immunization against disease, fleas are no longer a really serious threat to health. In the past, they were notorious for spreading bubonic plague (the Black Death) from rats to humans. Today, they still occasionally transmit a form of typhus to humans which, however, rarely endangers life (unlike proper typhus, which is highly infectious and fatal if not treated).

The cat flea (inset) is, as its name suggests, most likely to feed on cats, but it can also infest dogs and humans. Regular spraying with a formula from your vet will keep your cat flea-free.

Tony Stone Associates

London Scientific Fotos

London Scientific Fotos

However, fleas can transmit bacteria that cause unpleasant skin infections.

How fleas operate

To obtain its food, the adult flea punctures the skin of its host. In the process, it injects saliva containing a mild anticlotting agent, which prevents the host's blood from hardening in the normal way when exposed to air. It is the saliva that causes the irritating, but mild, allergic response that makes the bite itch.

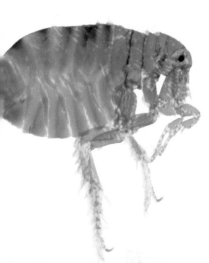

London Scientific Fotos

The human flea, Pulex irritans, prefers a human as its host, but it is only one of several that may pester us. Here it is shown magnified 30 times.

The true dog flea (inset) rarely bites people. However, the majority of fleas found on dogs are actually cat fleas.

Because flea saliva cannot hold off the blood's tendency to clot for long, the first hole becomes blocked and the flea moves on to start a second. So the crop of bites that appears on your skin after a few minutes is usually the result of only one flea attacking you.

Treatment

The allergic response is felt as irritation and swelling. Treatment consists of cleaning the site and reducing the irritation by applying calamine lotion or taking an antihistamine tablet. If possible, scratching should be avoided; it damages the skin and slows down the healing process.

In search of fleas

Most flea bites are not caused by the human flea, but by one that belongs on another animal. This is most likely to be the household dog or cat, but fleas also live on other animals including mice, rats, cattle, pigs, and hens.

The cat flea is the least fussy of them all, equally content to feast on a dog or a human. In fact, 60 percent of fleas found on dogs are cat fleas. A true dog flea rarely bites humans.

How to deal with fleas on your household pets

- If your dog is carrying fleas, they will most likely be breeding in its sleeping quarters. If the bedding is burnable, burn it; if boilable, boil it; and if neither, scald it with boiling water. Spray the dog with insecticide and get it a flea collar
- If a cat is the culprit, find its lair—the place, often outside, where it regularly goes to nap. If possible, destroy the lair or treat it with a suitable insecticide. Treat cat bedding as for dogs' and spray the cat
- Spray household pets every few weeks
- Vacuum all floors regularly
- Immersing your dog in water so the fleas are forced off is not a foolproof method, as many people believe. The fleas will simply use their considerable jumping ability to escape, then lie in wait to jump back on. The only certain banishment for fleas is spraying the animal with a suitable insecticide

CLARKSTON